Cracking the

AP®

SPANISH
LANGUAGE & CULTURE
EXAM WITH AUDIO CD

2014 Edition

By Mary Leech
Updated by Michael Giammarino

PrincetonReview.com

Random House, Inc. New York

The Princeton Review, Inc.
111 Speen Street, Suite 550
Framingham, MA 01701
E-mail: editorialsupport@review.com

ISBN: 978-0-8041-2428-7
ISSN: 2330-8451

Editor: Meave Shelton
Production Editor: Seamus Mullarkey
Production Artist: Maurice Kessler

Printed in the United States of America on partially recycled paper.

10 9 8 7 6 5 4 3 2 1

2014 Edition

Editorial

Rob Franek, Senior VP, Publisher
Mary Beth Garrick, Director of Production
Selena Coppock, Senior Editor
Calvin Cato, Editor
Kristen O'Toole, Editor
Meave Shelton, Editor
Alyssa Wolff, Editorial Assistant

Random House Publishing Team

Tom Russell, Publisher
Nicole Benhabib, Publishing Director
Ellen L. Reed, Production Manager
Alison Stoltzfus, Managing Editor
Erika Pepe, Associate Production Manager
Kristin Lindner, Production Supervisor
Andrea Lau, Designer

ACKNOWLEDGMENTS

I would like to thank Lesly Atlas, Marika Alzadon, Evelin Sanchez-O'Hara, Allegra Viner, Patricia Dublin, Katie O'Neill, Jennifer Arias, Omar Amador, John Moscatiello, and Dan Edmonds for their tireless efforts producing this book. I would also like to thank Daniel Wallance and Chad Singer for their expert technical support. I feel indebted to Josette Amsellem, James P. Godfrey, and William Moore for their guidance and friendship, which greatly enhanced my initiation into the field of teaching. I would like to thank my colleague Margaret Callery, and also Amy Brown and Nelly Rosario, for their expert review of the Spanish portions of the manuscript.

I would also like to thank my parents for encouraging and facilitating my advanced studies of Spanish. Last, but certainly not least, I would like to thank my husband, David, for his continued love and support.

– Mary Leech

The Princeton Review would like to thank Michael Giammarino for his dedication and hard work updating this edition.

CONTENTS

AUDIO TRACK LIST

...So Much More Online!

More Information, More Resources

- Academic tutoring options for all subjects and test types, including AP, SAT, and ACT.

- Free SAT and ACT practice tests

- Detailed profiles of hundreds of colleges

- Dozens of Top 10 ranking lists including Quality of Professors, Worst Campus Food, Most Beautiful Campus, Party Schools, Diverse Student Population, and tons more

- Helpful information and articles about the college admissions process, applications, financial aid, scholarships, and more

- Learn more about The Princeton Review's guide books to college— *The Best 378 Colleges, The Complete Book of Colleges, Paying for College Without Going Broke*

- Research study-abroad programs by country, and exciting summer programs and internships

To Access the Online Content for This Book

You can opt to stream or download the accompanying audio CD tracks directly from our website. Here's how:

- Go to PrincetonReview.com/cracking

- You'll see a welcome page where you should register your book using the ISBN. You can find the ISBN on the back cover of this book, printed just above the barcode. Type in this ISBN and create a username and password so that next time you can log into PrincetonReview.com easily.

- Click on the "My Prep" tab of your account once you're logged in. Next to the title of this book you'll see a link that says "Launch Online Content."

- Click on this link, and you're good to go!

princetonreview.com/cracking

INTRODUCTION

WHAT IS THE PRINCETON REVIEW?

The Princeton Review is an international test-preparation company with branches in all major U.S. cities and several cities abroad. In 1981, John Katzman started teaching an SAT course in his parents' living room. Within five years, The Princeton Review had become the largest SAT coaching program in the country.

The Princeton Review's phenomenal success in improving students' scores on standardized tests is the result of a simple, innovative, and radically effective approach: Study the test, not what the test *claims* to test. This approach has led to the development of techniques for taking standardized tests based on the principles the test writers use to write the tests.

The Princeton Review has found that its methods work not only for cracking the SAT, but also for any standardized test. We've successfully applied our system to the GMAT, GRE, LSAT, and MCAT, to name just a few. Although the AP Spanish Language and Culture Exam is different than the exams mentioned above, a standardized test is a standardized test.

WHY DO YOU NEED THIS BOOK?

Of course, it is important to know Spanish in order to do well on the AP Spanish Language and Culture Exam, but it is also important to be a shrewd test taker. In this book, you'll find strategies for smart test taking. We offer suggestions to help you scrutinize and maximize your performance on test day. In addition, we will give you some background on the Advanced Placement (AP) program, and provide you with practice tests so that you can perfect your test-taking skills before test day.

ABOUT THE ADVANCED
PLACEMENT PROGRAM

WHAT IS THE ADVANCED PLACEMENT PROGRAM?

The Advanced Placement program is administered by the College Board, which is the same organization that coordinates college admissions exams. The College Board consists of college educators, administrators, and admissions officers in addition to high school educators, guidance counselors, and administrators. Advanced Placement courses are offered in high schools across the United States in thirty-two disciplines.

As you may know, the Advanced Placement courses offered in high schools are generally the most demanding and therefore the most prestigious courses available. They are considered college-level high school courses.

Students enrolled in AP courses are expected, although not obligated, to take the corresponding AP exam offered in May. Exams are graded on a scale of 1 to 5 with 5 being the highest grade. Depending on the college, the student may earn hours of college credit for a grade of 3 or better. It is important to note that a student does not have to enroll in the AP course offered to take the AP exam in May. This is particularly important information for native speakers of any language. Most native speakers with strong written skills will earn a 5 on the AP Spanish Language and Culture exam with little or no advance preparation. In fact, most strong language students or native speakers have nothing but the price of the exam to lose. In fact, the process of taking the test is considered by many educators to be a valuable learning experience.

WHY ENROLL IN AP COURSES? WHY TAKE THE AP EXAMS?

As the name implies, Advanced Placement courses are more demanding than regular high school courses. AP classes require more outside reading and much more writing in the form of weekly essays, textual analyses, tests, and, in some cases, research papers. In addition to the increased workload, students in AP courses will most likely encounter harder grading standards and possibly a lower grade. So, why take AP courses?

- **Admissions officers look favorably upon transcripts that include AP courses.**

  The student with college aspirations will find that the AP program provides several advantages. For one, some admissions officers consider an AP grade equivalent to one grade higher in the regular course. Thus a B in an AP course would be equivalent to an A in a regular course.

- **AP courses demonstrate that you are committed to a rigorous level of study.**

  A second advantage to AP courses is that they provide a good introduction to college-level courses. In other words, AP courses prepare students best by emphasizing the skills most needed in college, such as extensive outside reading and frequent essay writing. In many cases, students accustomed to AP courses make a very smooth transition to college-level study because these courses teach students to think. Simply stated, students in AP courses are likely to learn more in any educational environment.

- **AP courses can save you time and money.**

  AP courses culminate with the AP exam. If you earn a grade of 3 or higher, you may be awarded college credit. Considering the cost of college credit hours, AP courses may save a considerable amount of money for successful AP exam takers. In some colleges, a student who receives high enough grades on three or more AP exams may be admitted as a sophomore. There is virtually nothing to lose by taking the AP Spanish Language and Culture Exam, except the cost of the exam.

WHAT IS THE AP SPANISH LANGUAGE AND CULTURE EXAM?

The AP Spanish Language and Culture Exam is intended to test the four basic language skills: reading, writing, listening, and speaking. The exam is made up of two main sections that test these skills. Part I is the multiple-choice section, which is divided into listening and reading portions. Part II of the exam is the free-response section, which includes both written and spoken responses.

Detailed information about the exam will follow in the coming chapters.

HOW TO GET STARTED

If you are interested in taking an AP exam, you should speak to your school guidance counselor. The guidance counselor should direct you to the school's AP coordinator. The AP coordinator is responsible for registering students for the exam, collecting exam fees, and ordering and administering exams. If, for any reason, you are not able to take the AP exam at your own school, arrangements may be made for you to take the test at another school. You may inquire about schools offering the test by calling the College Board's AP Services office at 609-771-7300, or write by March 1 to PO Box 6671, Princeton, New Jersey, 08541-6671.

The fee for each exam is $89. Generally, the school keeps a small amount of that fee for administrative costs. The school may, upon request, refund part or all of this amount to students with financial need. The College Board also offers a fee reduction to students with financial need. If, for some reason, a student needs to take the test at a time different from the scheduled date, an additional fee may be assessed. All fees are to be paid to the school AP coordinator. The College Board will not accept direct payments from students.

RECOMMENDED TIMETABLE FOR STUDENTS

The AP Spanish Language and Culture Exam is generally taken during junior or senior year, although native Spanish speakers could probably take it earlier if necessary.

JANUARY: You should meet with your Spanish teacher to discuss the exam. If you choose to take the exam, you should speak to the appointed AP coordinator to register and submit the fees. If you have any special needs (which we discuss in greater detail later), you should make arrangements at this time. If, for any reason, your school does not offer the AP exam, you should contact the College Board and request the nearest location of a school offering the exam.

MARCH: If you have not expressed your interest in taking the exam, do so ASAP!

Early to mid MAY*: The AP Spanish Language and Culture Exam is offered in the morning session.

JUNE: Exams are graded by more than 3,000 college and high school faculty consultants. If you wish to send your scores to colleges other than those listed on the exam registration form, or if you wish to cancel the reporting of the scores, you may submit your request to ETS until June 15.

JULY: Exam grades are sent to students' designated colleges, home high schools, and home addresses.

*Check the most up-to-date exam schedule at http://professionals.collegeboard.com/testing/ap/about/dates/next-year

ON EXAM DAY

You will want to bring the following items:

- two No. 2 pencils for the multiple-choice section (make sure you have an eraser)
- a pencil sharpener
- a black or blue pen for the essay questions
- a watch
- photo identification
- your school code

You may NOT bring the following items:

- dictionaries, books, notes, scratch paper
- electronic translators or laptop computers
- cameras or radios
- cell phones or MP3 players

Special Circumstances

Students with special needs, such as disabilities, who require particular testing conditions should have either a signed letter from the appropriate professional (psychologist, doctor, learning specialist, and so on) or a current Individualized Education Program (IEP) on file at the school. The IEP should describe the disability and confirm the need for different testing conditions. Students with valid disabilities have a variety of options. Vision-impaired students, for example, may take large-type or Braille tests, or they may use a reader.

It is very important that students with special needs document their disabilities so that score reports accurately reflect the testing situation as a "Certified Disability." Without the proper documentation, the score report will indicate "Nonstandard Administration," which would be the designation given to students without disabilities who took the exam untimed. Clearly, an untimed exam suggests an unfair advantage if there is no documented disability and reflects poorly on a student's score report. Thus, students with disabilities should contact the AP coordinator as soon as possible (no later than April 1) to stipulate testing conditions. Documentation should be prepared and ready well before the exam date.

Exam-Day Errors

Although they are not very common, errors do occasionally occur on exam day. Occasionally, the College Board writes a lousy question. Once in a blue moon ETS misprints a test question, misprints a page of the exam, or even leaves it blank! It is important to remember that these errors are very infrequent. If, during the test, you believe that one or more of the questions on the test is invalid or unfair, you should contact the College Board as soon as possible after the test. Provide the test title, the question number, and a description of what you think was wrong with the question. Such errors are very unlikely to occur on the AP Spanish Language and Culture Exam. They generally occur on math or science exams.

It is more likely that an error may occur in the administering of the actual exam, for instance, if the directions are poorly stated. You should have no difficulty with poorly read instructions on exam day because this book will review instructions and the format of the AP exams in great detail. More troublesome, however, is a proctor who times the exam incorrectly. If you find that you've been given too little time to complete the exam, you should contact the school's administration immediately. If you wait too long, you may be forced to retake the exam, or even worse, get stuck with the score you received on the mistimed exam.

That covers what happens when the College Board, ETS, or your proctor messes up. What about when *you* mess up? If you think (or know) that you blew the exam, you have until June 15 to contact the College Board and cancel your score. You should also contact the College Board by June 15 if you wish to change the list of colleges receiving score reports. In most cases, unless you feel you have earned a score of 1 or lower, scores should not be canceled.

The following is a list of things that you should avoid doing at all costs on exam day. Any one of them could get you thrown out of the test (leading to your scores being canceled), or question the validity of your performance on the exam.

- Leafing through the exam booklet before the exam begins

- Working on the wrong section of the exam

- Trying to get answers from or give answers to another student during the exam

- Continuing to work on the exam after you have been instructed to stop

- Tearing a page out of the exam booklet or trying to sneak the exam out of the testing location

- Using notes, textbooks, dictionaries, electronic translators, and so on during the exam

FINALLY...

Much of the information covered in this chapter also appears in a free College Board publication called *Bulletin for AP Students and Parents*. You should be able to get a copy of it from your college counselor. If not, write for your copy to

AP Services
PO Box 6671
Princeton, New Jersey
08541-6671

The College Board website is another good source of information. Please check out **http://apcentral.collegeboard.com**

2

GOOD TEST-TAKING
STRATEGIES

Very few students stop to think about how to improve their test-taking skills. Most assume that if they study very hard, they will test well; if they don't study, they will do poorly. Most students continue to believe this even after experience teaches them otherwise. Have you ever studied really hard for an exam, then blown it on test day? Or, maybe you aced an exam you barely studied for. If the latter is true, you were probably employing good test-taking strategies without even realizing it.

Make no mistake; studying thoroughly will enhance your performance on the exam. However, in addition to that, this section targets the best test-taking techniques that will help you perform better on the AP Spanish Language and Culture Exam—and on other exams as well.

TEST ANXIETY

Everyone experiences some kind of nervousness or anxiety before and during an important exam. Some students are able to channel that energy and use it to help them enhance their performance. A little anxiety can actually help students focus more clearly and work more effectively on an exam. However, that is not always the case. In high-stress situations, some students find they are unable to recall any of the information they so painstakingly studied. These students may become increasingly nervous and make poor decisions on the remaining portions of the exam. If you find that you stress out during exams, here are a few preemptive actions you can take.

- **Take a reality check.** Assess your strengths and weaknesses before entering the testing room. If you have in fact studied thoroughly, you should feel satisfied that you've done your best to prepare for the exam. Also, keep in mind that not all students taking the exam will be as prepared as you are, so you already have an advantage. If you didn't study enough, you probably won't ace the test.

- **Don't forget to breathe!** Deep breathing works for almost everybody. Take a few seconds, close your eyes, and take a few slow deep breaths, concentrating on nothing but inhaling and exhaling. This is a basic form of meditation and should help you clear your mind of stress and facilitate good concentration. Learning to relax is the key to a successful performance in almost any situation, especially during standardized tests.

- **Be prepared.** Those Boy Scouts couldn't be more right about this one. The best way to avoid excessive anxiety on test day is to study the subject material and the test itself. By reading this book, you are taking a major step toward a stress-free AP Spanish Language and Culture Exam. Also, make sure you know where the test is, when it starts, what type of questions are going to be asked, and how long the test will take. Of course, you should have with you all the materials you'll need during the exam (see page 5). You don't want to be worrying about any of this on the day of the test.

- **Be realistic about your final score.** Given your background, preparation, and interest level, you should aim to do your own personal best. For native speakers with good written skills, the exam should be an easy 5, although you will need to be prepared and focus well on the exam. For excellent nonnative speakers, the exam should be challenging, but manageable.

PACING

A large part of scoring well on an exam is working at a consistent pace. The worst mistake made by test takers is that they spend too long on a single question. Rather than skipping a question they can't answer, they panic and stall. Students lose all sense of time when they are trying to answer a question that puzzles them. You want to be sure to get to every question you *do* know something about.

It is very important for you to pace yourself, and to pay close attention to the number of multiple-choice questions per section and the total time allotted for that section. Try not to skip too many of the easy questions, and don't spend an inordinate amount of time pondering the difficult ones. If you draw a complete blank on a few questions, it may be appropriate to skip them and come back to them later. Often, after returning to a question later, you are able to think more clearly and answer the previously puzzling question more easily. Such minor victories often provide a significant boost in morale and help to refuel your energy. However, if you are still unable to answer a couple of difficult questions, you should just skip them.

One important note: If you decide to skip any of the questions and return to them later, you must be certain that you also skip the corresponding oval on the answer sheet. This may seem obvious, but, nonetheless, it can be a costly mistake that would throw off the rest of your answers on the test, resulting in a disastrous score. Make a note next to any skipped questions in your test booklet, not on your answer sheet.

PROCESS OF ELIMINATION (POE)

The usefulness of the Process of Elimination is one of the gifts of multiple-choice questions. The idea is simple: Knowing which answer is right is the same as knowing which answers are wrong, so if you can do either, you can pick up a point. If you can eliminate answers that you know are wrong, you will eventually stumble upon the right answer because it will be the only one left. POE may vary a bit for different types of questions, but the general idea is always the same.

THE WEEKS BEFORE THE EXAM

There are a few things you should start doing some time after January 1 (but certainly before May 1). One of them is to read this book. Here are some others.

- **Review previous exams.** You can purchase the official 2010 AP Spanish Language Released Exam through the College Board's website. You can also study past multiple-choice and free-response questions at http://apcentral.collegeboard.com/apc/public/courses/teachers_corner/221848.html. Be sure to take into account the changes in format for 2014!

- **Practice!** You may also try making your own outline of Spanish grammar and verb forms. For the listening portion of the exam, you may want to listen to language recordings and check your own comprehension. Listening to Spanish radio stations and television programs may also increase listening comprehension.

- **Commit a little time each night to test preparation.** Spend time each night reviewing the grammar topics, verb forms, and vocabulary lists. In addition, you should practice speaking about various thematic topics, such as your favorite pastimes, class schedule, and so on. You should also practice reading comprehension passages and questions. A regular short period of study time each night is preferable to cramming the week prior to the exam. By late March, you should ideally spend about 45 minutes four times per week reviewing this book, primary texts, class notes, outlines, and any other class materials.

You may also consider forming study groups in which each member is responsible for a specific portion of the material, as you can benefit from explaining your understanding of the material verbally in Spanish.

THE FINAL WEEK BEFORE THE EXAM

- **Maintain your usual routine**. You may have more than one AP exam to take during the month of May. Get plenty of rest the week before and during the week of the exams, but try not to change your sleeping patterns too drastically. You should also avoid drastic changes in diet or exercise.

- **Do a general subject review.** You should focus less on details and more on general issues. For this exam, you should do a general grammar review, looking over your own outlines. You should practice speaking and writing about various academic and conversational topics, such as your daily routine, your favorite foods, as well as prominent social issues, such as equal rights for women, or the increasing threat of pollution in the environment.

- **Know all the directions for the exam**. Familiarize yourself with the instructions to each portion of the exam by reading them in this book. You should clearly understand all instructions before test day.

THE DAY OF THE EXAM

- **Start the day with a reasonable, but not huge, breakfast.** You'll need energy for the exam. Beware of drinking too much liquid, such as coffee or tea, because it may cause frequent trips to the restroom.

- **Wear comfortable clothing.** Dressing in light layers is a good idea. You don't want to feel too hot or too cold while trying to concentrate on an important exam.

- **Take a snack.** A piece of fruit or a candy bar during the break can give you a much-needed energy boost.

FINALLY

The fewer surprises encountered on test day, the better the chances of your success. If you are holding this book right now, congratulations—you're already ahead of the game.

SUMMARY

- Begin preparing for your exam a few months in advance. Study for at least 45 minutes three to four times per week. Review questions from past exams (keeping in mind that the format of the test is changing in 2014).

- Practice your speaking skills, study vocabulary and grammar, and ask your teacher to review the essays you have written.

- Get plenty of rest, and maintain a regular routine during the week before the exams.

- On test day, you should dress comfortably, eat sensibly, and take the proper materials to the testing site.

- Maintain a consistent pace throughout the exam and avoid spending too much time on any one question.

- Beat test anxiety. Prepare for the test so that there will be few surprises on test day. Don't forget to breathe.

PART ◆ **I**

How to Crack the System

OVERVIEW

The AP Spanish Language and Culture Exam consists of the following two sections:

- **Section I** is the multiple-choice section, which tests *listening* and *reading* skills.
- **Section II** is the free-response section, which tests *writing*, *listening*, and *speaking* skills.

The College Board provides a breakdown of the types of questions covered on the exam. This breakdown will *not* appear in your test booklet: It comes from the preparatory material the College Board publishes. The chart below summarizes exactly what you need to know for the exam.

Section	Number of Questions	Percent of Final Score	Time
Section I: Multiple Choice			**Approx. 95 minutes**
Interpretive Communication: Print Texts	30 questions	50%	Approx. 40 minutes
Interpretive Communication: Print and Audio Texts (combined)	35 questions		Approx. 55 minutes
Interpretive Communication: Audio Texts			
Section II: Free Response			**Approx. 85 minutes**
Interpersonal Writing: Email Reply	1 prompt	12.5%	15 minutes
Presentational Writing: Persuasive Essay	1 prompt	12.5%	Approx. 55 minutes
Interpersonal Speaking: Conversation	5 prompts	12.5%	20 seconds for each response
Presentational Speaking: Cultural Comparison	1 prompt	12.5%	2 minutes to respond

The exam is approximately 3 hours long and has two parts—multiple choice and free response. Each section of the exam is worth 50 percent of the final exam grade.

Section I: Multiple Choice—65 questions; 1 hour and 35 minutes (50% of grade)

Print Texts (Reading)—30 questions; 40 minutes

- Reading comprehension questions based on several passages, including prose fiction, journalistic articles, or essays. Some of the written texts may include a visual component or a web page. Questions will ask you to identify the main points and significant details and make inferences and predictions from the written texts. Some questions may require making cultural inferences or inserting an additional sentence in the appropriate place in the reading passage.

Listening—35 questions; 55 minutes

- Short dialogues and narratives. These questions are spoken on the master recording but not printed in the exam book, while the answer choices are printed but not spoken.

- Longer dialogues and narratives that may include interviews, cultural communications, broadcasts, or other spoken materials. In addition, print material will be added as well; students will answer questions on both sources. These are like the previous years' Presentational Speaking prompts, but now multiple-choice questions are added instead. These questions are not spoken on the master recording; they are printed in the test booklet.

You are encouraged to take notes during this part of the exam and are given writing space for that purpose. Your notes will not affect your scores. Total scores on the multiple-choice section are based on the number of questions answered correctly. Points are not deducted for incorrect answers, and no points are awarded for unanswered questions.

Section II: Free Response—4 tasks; 1 hour and 25 minutes (50% of grade)

Writing

- Simulated interpersonal writing task such as writing an email message or a letter (15 minutes; 12.5% of final exam grade)

- Answer a written essay prompt based on provided documents and a related audio source. (15 minutes to review materials plus 40 minutes to write; 12.5% of final exam grade)

Speaking

- Respond to 5–6 questions as part of a simulated conversation (20 seconds per response; 12.5% of final exam grade)

- Make a 2-minute presentation on a given topic. You will be provided with a document and recording you can use to prepare the presentation. (12.5% of final exam grade)

Let's take a closer look at the question types on the Writing portion of the exam:

- **Interpersonal Writing:** As the name suggests, you'll be asked to write in a formal style and format; for example, the assignment may involve writing an email or an email reply to a job or scholarship offer. You'll have only 15 minutes for this section, so you shouldn't plan to write more than a couple of paragraphs.

- **Presentational Writing:** This persuasive essay requires you to synthesize information from a variety of print and audio sources, and present the different viewpoints and indicate your own viewpoint and defend it thoroughly. You'll be given an essay prompt and several minutes to read and listen to the materials before you start writing.

Here's what you can expect to find on the Speaking portion:

- **Interpersonal Speaking:** This section requires you to verbally respond to a series of recorded cues. Your responses will be guided by an outline of a short conversation, which will be provided. You will be assigned one side of the conversation, and the recording will supply the other. Your responses will be recorded.

- **Presentational Speaking:** You will be given a prompt, as well as a question in which you reflect upon your own personal experiences relating to a given topic.

A NOTE ON DIRECTIONS

All directions in the examination booklet will be printed in English and in Spanish. You won't really need to spend much time reading directions on test day because you are using this book and will be very familiar with the test directions already. Nevertheless, choose the language you are more comfortable with and skim only that set of the directions. Don't waste time reading both sets of directions, or worse yet, comparing the translations for accuracy. Use that time to jot down notes and organize your responses if possible.

3

THE MULTIPLE-CHOICE SECTION: INTERPRETIVE COMMUNICATION (LISTENING AND READING)

THE BASICS

The multiple-choice section (Section I) of the AP Spanish Language and Culture Exam tests two major skills: listening and reading. The listening portion of the exam tests your understanding of spoken Spanish. The reading portion of the exam tests your knowledge of Spanish vocabulary, as well as structure and comprehension of written passages.

Both the listening and reading portions will also assess your ability to interpret and synthesize information. The reading portion of the exam will feature print texts, charts, and other authentic materials from the Spanish-speaking world. The multiple-choice questions will ask you to demonstrate comprehension, interdisciplinary relationships, key messages, and the authors' points of view. The listening portions will include two sections—one that is just straight listening passages, and a new part which will contain a combination of printed reading passages with a listening component. You will have to answer questions based on both sources.

Here again, for your reference, is the table showing the breakdown of the multiple-choice section.

Section	Number of Questions	Percent of Final Score	Time
Section I: Multiple Choice			**Approx. 95 minutes**
Interpretive Communication: Print Texts	30 questions	50%	Approx. 40 minutes
Interpretive Communication: Print and Audio Texts (combined)	35 questions		Approx. 55 minutes
Interpretive Communication: Audio Texts			

The following exercises will give you a pretty good indication of the types of multiple-choice questions you'll see on the actual test.

LISTENING

The listening portion of the exam is accompanied by a recording. In the sample passages and questions that follow, the information that is printed in *italics* is heard only by the student, and *does not* appear printed in the examination booklet. You can listen to these sections on the audio CD included with this book as well as online, once you register your book at PrincetonReview.com (step-by-step instructions on how to do this are on page ix). General directions for the dialogues and narratives appear at the beginning of each new set of exercises, printed in the test booklet in both English and Spanish.

In the listening portion, you will encounter four different types of spoken exercises. These include dialogues, short narratives, and then slightly longer narratives, each approximately five minutes in length. For these five-minute narrative exercises, the questions are heard on the master recording, but do not appear printed in the examination booklets; conversely, the answer choices are not spoken on the master recording, but appear printed in the test booklets. A fourth variation of spoken exercise is the interpretive communication section which combines both print and audio texts.

DIALOGUES

You will hear a series of dialogues on various subjects and be asked to choose the correct answer for three to five questions per dialogue.

Remember: Information printed in this text in italics is heard, not read. You can listen to these sections on the audio CD or online.

Sample Dialogue

Here are the general directions for the dialogues that you will see printed in your test booklet on test day.

Directions: You will now listen to a series of dialogues. After each one, you will be asked some questions about what you have just heard. Select the best answer to each question from among the four choices printed in your test booklet and fill in the corresponding oval on the answer sheet.

Remember: Information printed here in italics is heard, not read.

AUDIO CD: Track 1

Anita: *Buenos días, Doña Clara, ¿cómo le va?*

Doña Clara: *Pues aquí, fregando el suelo, con los niños pasando continuamente por esta cocina. Siempre me dejan los pies marcados en el suelo.*

Anita: *Perdone, siento que la interrumpa, pero ¿está Elena en casa?*

Doña Clara: *No, no es nada. Sí, Elenita está con su abuela. Están hablando de la boda de su hermana.*

Anita: *¿Dónde están? ¿Están en el salón?*

Doña Clara: *No, están en el jardín.*

1. *¿Dónde tiene lugar esta conversación?*
    (A) En el salón
    (B) En el jardín
    (C) En la cocina
    (D) En la casa de Anita

2. *¿Qué está haciendo Doña Clara?*
    (A) Limpiando
    (B) Interrumpiendo
    (C) Pasando
    (D) Cantando

3. *¿Qué está haciendo Elena?*
    (A) Hablando con su hermana
    (B) Paseando con los niños
    (C) Hablando con su abuela
    (D) Casándose

Here's How to Crack It

In these dialogues, a considerable bit of information is communicated. Remember: You will *hear* these dialogues and the accompanying questions only once; you will not see them in printed form. You will have about twelve seconds to choose the correct answers and blacken the corresponding ovals on your answer sheet. It is important to listen carefully and choose the most obvious answer. Do your best to follow along with the conversations, and do not fall behind answering the numbered questions after the dialogues.

Listening comprehension is what is being tested here, and most answers will not be conceptually difficult. Don't bother trying to write down any notes at this point; simply listen attentively. You will need to remember the context of the conversation to answer the questions accurately.

Answers and Explanations for the Sample Dialogue

Translation

Anita: Good morning, Doña Clara. How are you?

Doña Clara: Well, I'm here, scrubbing the floor, with the children continually passing through this kitchen. They always leave footprints marked on the floor for me!

Anita: Excuse me, I'm sorry to interrupt, but is Elena home?

Doña Clara: No, it's no bother. Yes, Elenita is with her grandmother. They are talking about her sister's wedding.

Anita: Where are they? In the living room?

Doña Clara: No, they are in the garden.

1. Where does this conversation take place?
   (A) In the living room
   (B) In the garden
   (C) In the kitchen
   (D) In Anita's house

The conversation takes place in the kitchen where Doña Clara is cleaning the floor. We know that she is in the kitchen because Doña Clara complains about the children constantly running through *esta cocina*, or "this kitchen." Anita comes into the kitchen and interrupts Doña Clara in her work.

2. What is Doña Clara doing?
   (A) Cleaning
   (B) Interrupting
   (C) Passing through
   (D) Singing

As suggested above, Doña Clara is cleaning. *Fregando* literally means "scrubbing" or "mopping." Thus, of the choices, (A) is the obvious answer.

3. What is Elena doing?

(A) Talking with her sister

(B) Walking around with the children

(C) Talking with her grandmother

(D) Getting married

Elena, as it turns out, is not present in the dialogue. Her friend Anita comes calling on her. Doña Clara tells Anita that Elenita, her affectionate name for Elena, is talking with her grandmother.

SHORT NARRATIVES

You will also hear a series of two to three short narratives on various topics. You will be asked three to five oral questions on what you have just heard. You must choose among the four answers printed in your test booklet and blacken the corresponding oval on your answer sheet.

Sample Short Narrative

Here are the general directions for the short narratives that you will see printed in your test booklet on test day.

> **Directions:** You will now listen to a series of short narratives. After each one, you will be asked some questions about what you have just heard. Select the best answer to each question from among the four choices printed in your test booklet and fill in the corresponding oval on the answer sheet.

Remember: Information printed here in italics is heard, not read.

AUDIO CD: Track 2

El mercado hispano en Estados Unidos

El mercado hispano en Estados Unidos es una fuente de oportunidad para muchas compañías grandes. El mercado hispano en EE.UU. es un mercado que está creciendo más día a día. Hay hispanohablantes en casi todas las ciudades grandes del país, sobre todo en Nueva York, Los Angeles, Chicago, Dallas, San Antonio y San Francisco, por mencionar sólo algunas. Todas las grandes compañías han visto el valor del consumidor hispano en el mercado actual. Muchas compañías grandes como los productores de refrescos, los restaurantes de servicio rápido y los productores de zapatillas deportivas gastan mucho dinero en publicidad dirigida al consumidor hispano. El típico consumidor hispano es muy tradicional, le gusta la familia. También le gustan los valores tradicionales. Es un consumidor fiel a las marcas que considera de buena calidad. El consumidor hispano identifica fácilmente las marcas que le gustan. No le importa gastar más dinero en un producto si es un producto de buena calidad.

El mercado hispano seguirá creciendo. Las compañías que ignoran la importancia del mercado hispano lo hacen a su propio riesgo. El consumidor hispano es una fuerza potente en el mercado del futuro.

4. *¿Qué tienen en común las ciudades de Nueva York, Los Angeles, Chicago, Dallas, San Antonio y San Francisco?*

(A) Tienen una gran población de personas que hablan español.

(B) Los nombres son de origen hispano.

(C) Son ciudades crecientes.

(D) Son ciudades con grandes compañías.

5. *¿Qué están haciendo con respecto al mercado hispano las compañías grandes como los productores de refrescos y zapatillas deportivas?*

   (A) Están comprando más productos.

   (B) Están creciendo más y más.

   (C) Están comprando publicidad para el mercado hispano.

   (D) Están comprando productos hechos por hispanos.

6. *¿Cómo es el típico consumidor hispano?*

   (A) Joven

   (B) Mayor

   (C) Liberal

   (D) Conservador

7. *¿Con cuáles marcas se identifica el consumidor hispano?*

   (A) Marcas hispanas

   (B) Marcas de buena calidad

   (C) Marcas de mala calidad

   (D) Marcas que cuestan menos

Here's How to Crack It

Again, in this portion of the exam it is important to follow along with the narrative, as the oral questions that follow it will be based on the context of the narrative. Try not to fall behind, and don't get stressed out if you hear a few words you don't understand. Try to understand the main ideas and, most important, try to keep pace with the narrative. You shouldn't try to take notes at this point, but listen very attentively. Also listen carefully to the oral questions. In most cases, they are fairly straightforward. If they aren't, remember to try to weed out the wrong answers using POE (Process of Elimination).

Answers and Explanations for the Sample Short Narrative

Translation

The Hispanic Market in the United States

The U.S. Hispanic market is a source of opportunity for many large companies. The U.S. Hispanic market is a market that is growing daily. There are Spanish speakers in almost all of the major U.S. cities, especially in New York, Los Angeles, Chicago, Dallas, San Antonio, and San Francisco, just to name a few. All of the large companies have seen the value of the Hispanic consumer in today's marketplace. Many of these companies, such as beverage producers, quick-service restaurants, and sport-shoe producers, spend a lot of money on advertising directed at the Hispanic consumer. The typical Hispanic consumer is very traditional; he likes the family. He also likes traditional values. The Hispanic consumer is also one who is loyal to the brand names that he considers of good quality. He identifies very easily with the brands that he likes. It doesn't matter to him to spend more money on a product if it is of better quality. The Hispanic market will continue to grow. The companies that ignore the importance of the Hispanic market do so at their own risk. The Hispanic consumer is a strong force in the marketplace of the future.

4. What do the cities New York, Los Angeles, Chicago, San Antonio, and San Francisco have in common?

   (A) They have a large population of Spanish speakers.

   (B) Their names are of Hispanic origin.

   (C) They are growing cities.

   (D) They are cities with large companies.

Answer choices (B), (C), and (D) may or may not be true, but they have nothing to do with the short narrative. Therefore, the correct answer is (A); each of those cities has a large Spanish-speaking population.

5. What are the large companies, such as the beverage producers and the sport-shoe producers, doing with respect to the Hispanic market?

   (A) They are buying more products.

   (B) They are growing more and more.

   (C) They are buying advertising for the Hispanic market.

   (D) They are buying products made by Hispanics.

The word for advertising is *publicidad.* The large companies are, in fact, buying advertising directed at the Hispanic market. Notice that incorrect answer choices (A) and (D) also include the verb *comprando* to see if you can be easily fooled; don't fall into this trap.

6. What is the typical Hispanic consumer like?

   (A) Young

   (B) Old

   (C) Liberal

   (D) Conservative

The typical Hispanic consumer is *tradicional,* which is closest to *conservador.* If this isn't immediately apparent, you may use POE to rule out the other answer choices. The age range (*joven* or *mayor*) of the typical Hispanic consumer is impossible to identify without detailed demographic information, which is not discussed in the short narrative. *Liberal* doesn't really make any sense, so it is an obvious wrong answer.

7. With which brand names does the Hispanic consumer identify?

   (A) Hispanic brand names

   (B) Good-quality brand names

   (C) Bad-quality brand names

   (D) Economical brand names

Hispanic consumers identify with good-quality brands. In fact, we are told that they do not mind paying more for an item if it is of better quality. Therefore, you should use POE to rule out answer choices (C) and (D). Nothing in the narrative indicates that the Hispanic market identifies with only Hispanic brand names, so you can say *adiós* to (A) as well.

FIVE-MINUTE NARRATIVES

In addition to the dialogues and short narratives, you will hear two oral pieces of about five minutes in length each. These five-minute narratives may be interviews, cultural communications, broadcasts, or anything else deemed appropriate for oral communication. In this portion of the exam, you will be allowed and, in fact, encouraged to take notes. Your notes will not be graded. Remember: Everything printed in italics will be spoken on the master recording but *not* printed in your test booklet.

> **Note:** Unlike the dialogues and short narratives, you will *not* be permitted to see the printed questions while listening to the recording during these five-minute narratives.

Sample Five-Minute Narrative

Here are the general directions for the five-minute narratives that you will see printed in your test booklet on test day.

Directions: You will now listen to a selection of about five minutes in duration. You should take notes in the blank space provided. You will not be graded on these notes. At the end of the selection, you will read a number of questions about what you have heard. Based on the information provided in the selection, select the BEST answer for each question from among the four choices printed in your test booklet and fill in the corresponding oval on the answer sheet.

Remember: Information printed here in italics is heard, not read.

> AUDIO CD: Track 3

Interview with Luz Hurtado, Fashion Editor of the magazine *Mujer Moderna*.

(Ahora, vamos a escuchar una entrevista con una persona muy informada en el mundo de la moda, Srta. Luz Hurtado, editora de la revista Mujer Moderna.*)*

MAN: *Luz, para empezar, ¿puedes describirnos a la lectora típica de la revista* Mujer Moderna? *Es decir, ¿a quién va dirigida la revista?*

WOMAN: *Nuestra revista va dirigida a la mujer de hoy, principalmente entre los veinte y treinta y cinco años. Muchas de nuestras lectoras trabajan, pero otras se dedican a la familia y el hogar. Casi todas tienen en común un interés apasionado en la moda. No son necesariamente mujeres que trabajan en la industria de la moda, pero muchas mujeres de la industria también leen nuestra revista. Digamos que nuestra revista lleva el mundo interior de la moda a la mujer contemporánea.*

MAN: *¿Cómo se diferencia* Mujer Moderna *de las otras revistas de moda?*

WOMAN: *Es una pregunta muy importante. Cuando me ofrecieron el puesto de editora de esta revista, me pregunté, '¿quiero de verdad trabajar en otra revista de moda?' Yo había trabajado en el pasado como reportera en otras revistas de moda, y no me interesaba la idea de trabajar en otra revista igual a las demás. Pero* Mujer Moderna *es distinta porque se dirige a la mujer que vive en el mundo real de hoy. No se trata de una revista de muñecas en un mundo protegido, o un mundo de fantasía. Nuestras lectoras viven en el mundo real, trabajan en el mundo real y se ocupan de la familia en el mundo real. No nos dedicamos exclusivamente a la moda, sino al papel de la moda dentro del complicado mundo moderno.*

MAN: *He leído que la revista* Mujer Moderna *está muy metida en varias causas sociales, sobre todo los niños que nacen con el virus del SIDA. ¿Puedes explicarnos la relación entre la moda y esta causa social tan importante?*

WOMAN: *Aunque quizás sea un poco fuera de lo corriente en el mundo de la moda, yo creo que es sumamente importante que ayudemos a los menos afortunados. ¿Hay víctima más inocente que un pobre niño que nace contaminado con el virus del SIDA?* Mujer Moderna *procura cultivar una relación con causas sociales para demostrar a nuestras lectoras que es la responsabilidad de cada una de nosotras contribuir a mejorar la sociedad. Además, hubo otros que crearon relaciones entre la moda y la causa social; por ejemplo, recordemos la figura de la Princesa Diana.*

MAN: *Es cierto, Diana fue símbolo de la moda y la causa social. Era una persona muy admirable, ¿no crees?*

WOMAN: *Claro que fue admirable. Era una persona buenísima. La figura pública era solamente una parte de la persona de Diana. La conocí en varias ocasiones y me impresionaron muchísimo su sinceridad y su interés genuino en la gente que sufre.*

MAN: *Cambiando un poco de tema, ¿tiene valor tu revista para el hombre moderno?*

WOMAN: *Yo creo que hay mucho valor para el hombre moderno que se interese en causas sociales que nos afectan a todos. Claro que también tendrá interés para el hombre que quiere enterarse de la última moda de sus amigas, su novia, su esposa, su madre, su hermana, etcétera. En fin, es una revista dirigida principalmente a la gente interesada en la moda femenina, basándose en una filosofía filantrópica. Por eso, puede interesarle también a muchos hombres. Sin embargo, también tenemos una sección de deportes muy buena. (Ella ríe.)*

MAN: *¿Qué relación hay, si es que hay, entre la moda y el deporte?*

WOMAN: *Claro que hay relación entre ambos. La moda puede ser considerada como una actitud hacia la vida. Se puede ver la moda en cada cosa que hacemos. O las hacemos con o sin estilo. Todo depende de la mentalidad y el nivel de interés del individuo. En los deportes, por ejemplo, hay un mundo de moda que ha evolucionado precisamente alrededor del deporte. El tenis y el golf son dos ejemplos muy claros. Tienen una moda muy concreta que permite expresar el estilo individualista también. Por ejemplo, los tenistas americanos Andre Agassi y las hermanas Williams muestran su individualidad con la ropa poco tradicional que llevan y la forma en el diseño de sus peinados. Gusten o no los estilos que llevan, hay que admirar su estilo individualista.*

MAN: *Claro, los tres son muy originales. Pero dinos, Luz, ¿cómo empezaste en el mundo de la moda?*

WOMAN: *Siempre, desde pequeña me ha interesado la moda de los hombres y las mujeres. Mi padre trabajaba con el cuerpo diplomático español, y nosotros pasamos mucho tiempo en el extranjero. Vivimos en Milán, en París, en Singapur y en Nueva York. Quizás por los cambios que observé entre los estilos de las culturas variadas, me incliné al mundo de la moda. También, sentí desde muy pequeña una responsabilidad por los desafortunados. Mi madre siempre se dedicaba a las causas sociales. Aprendí mucho de ella.*

MAN: *Bueno, Srta. Luz Hurtado, ya se nos acabó el tiempo. Muchas gracias por estar aquí con nosotros.*

(Ha terminado esta selección. No se leerán las preguntas en voz alta, pues las tienes impresas en tu libreta de examen. Ahora pasa a las preguntas. Te quedan cuatro minutos para elegir las respuestas correctas. FIN DE LA GRABACIÓN)

8. *¿A quién va dirigida la revista* Mujer Moderna?

   (A) Las mujeres del mundo interior de moda.

   (B) Las mujeres que trabajan.

   (C) La mujer que se ocupa de la familia y la casa.

   (D) La mujer contemporánea del mundo actual.

9. *¿Cómo se distingue* Mujer Moderna *de las otras revistas de moda?*

   (A) Es una revista de muñecas.

   (B) Es una revista de fantasía.

   (C) Se dedica a cómo la moda forma parte de la vida en el mundo actual.

   (D) Se dedica exclusivamente al mundo interior de la moda.

10. *¿Por qué está metida la revista* Mujer Moderna *en la causa social de los niños que nacen con el virus del SIDA?*

    (A) Quiere dar ejemplo de responsabilidad hacia los desafortunados.

    (B) Quiere ser más contemporánea.

    (C) Era la causa de la Princesa Diana.

    (D) Es la moda ayudar a los menesterosos.

11. *¿Qué hay de interés para el hombre moderno en* Mujer Moderna?

    (A) Puede aprender de la moda para hombres.

    (B) Puede aprender de la moda para su madre, hermana, novia o esposa.

    (C) Puede aprender sobre la Princesa Diana.

    (D) Puede aprender sobre sí mismo.

12. *¿Qué relación hay entre la moda y el deporte, según la entrevista?*

    (A) Muchos deportes tienen una moda desarrollada alrededor de ellos.

    (B) Muchos deportistas son modelos.

    (C) Todos los deportistas tienen mucho estilo.

    (D) La moda y el deporte son sinónimos.

Answers and Explanations for the Sample Five-Minute Narrative

Translation

Now we are going to listen to an interview with someone very informed in the world of fashion, Ms. Luz Hurtado, editor of the magazine *Modern Woman*.

> MAN: Luz, to begin, can you describe for us the typical reader of *Modern Woman*? In other words, who is your target audience?

> WOMAN: Our magazine is directed at the woman of today, primarily between the ages of twenty and thirty-five years of age. Many of our readers work, but others devote themselves to the care of family and the home.

Almost all of them have in common a deep interest in fashion. They are not necessarily those who work in the fashion industry, although many women in the fashion world do read our magazine. Let's say that our magazine brings the insider world of fashion to the contemporary woman.

MAN: How is *Modern Woman* different from other fashion magazines?

WOMAN: That is a very important question. When they offered me the job of editor at this magazine, I asked myself, "Do I really want to work for another fashion magazine?" I had worked in the past as a reporter for other fashion magazines, and I was no longer interested in working for another magazine like all of the others. But *Modern Woman* is different because it is directed at the woman who lives in the real world of today. It is not about silly dolls in a protected world or fantasy world. Our readers live in the real world, they work in the real world, and they care for their families in the real world. We don't devote ourselves exclusively to fashion but rather to the role of fashion in the complicated modern world.

MAN: I have read that *Modern Woman* is very involved in various social causes, above all, children who are born with the AIDS virus. Can you explain to us the relationship between fashion and this very important social cause?

WOMAN: Although it may be a bit out of the ordinary in the world of fashion, I think it is extremely important that we help those who are less fortunate. Is there a more innocent victim than a poor child who has been born contaminated with the AIDS virus? *Modern Woman* tries to foster a relationship with social causes to show our readers that it is the responsibility of each and every one of us to contribute to the improvement of society. Furthermore, there have been others who have cultivated a relationship between fashion and social causes; for example, let's remember the image of Princess Diana.

MAN: That's true. Princess Diana was a symbol of fashion and of dedication to social causes. She was a very admirable person, don't you think so?

WOMAN: Of course she was admirable. She was a very good person. The public figure was only a part of Diana. I met her on various occasions and was impressed by her sincerity and her genuine concern for those who suffer.

MAN: Changing the topic a bit if I may, is your magazine valuable for the modern man?

WOMAN: I think that there is a lot of value for the modern man who is interested in social causes that affect us all. Of course, it will also be interesting to the man who wants to find out about the latest fashion trends of his female friends, his girlfriend, his wife, his mother, or his sister. In short, it is a magazine directed primarily at those interested in feminine fashion, based on a philanthropic philosophy. For that reason, it can also be interesting to many men. However, we also have a very good sports section. (She laughs.)

MAN: What relationship is there, if any, between fashion and sports?

WOMAN: Of course there is a relationship between them. Fashion could be considered an attitude toward life. Fashion can be seen in everything that we do. We either do them with style or without style. It all depends on the mentality and the level of interest of the individual. For example, there is an entire fashion that has evolved precisely around sports. Tennis and golf are two very clear examples. They have a very determined fashion requirement that allows for individual styles as well. For example, the American tennis players Andre Agassi and the Williams sisters show their individuality with the unique clothing that they wear and their hairstyles. Whether or not we care for the styles they wear, we must admire their individualistic styles.

MAN: Of course, all three are very original. But tell us Luz, how did you get started in the world of fashion?

WOMAN: Always, ever since I was young, men's and women's fashions have interested me. My father worked in the Spanish Diplomatic Service, so we spent a lot of time abroad. We lived in Milan, Paris, Singapore, and New York. Perhaps because of the differences I observed between the styles of clothing of the various cultures, I leaned toward the field of fashion. I have also, since I was young, always felt a sense of responsibility for the less fortunate. My mother always dedicated herself to social causes. I learned a great deal from her.

MAN: Well, Ms. Luz Hurtado, we've run out of time. Thank you very much for being here with us.

The short narrative has finished. The questions will not be read out loud because you have them printed in your test booklet. Now you may go on to the questions. You have four minutes to choose the correct answers. End of recording.

Here's How to Crack It

As with the short narratives, it is imperative that you keep up with the pace of the five-minute narrative. Don't worry if there are words that you don't understand. Try to comprehend the major ideas being discussed. Use the space provided to take notes, which should help you maintain focus on the narrative. You may write your notes in any language that you choose, although it may be easier to jot things down in Spanish and later translate your notes into English if necessary. Make sure not to draw from your own opinions or ideas that may not have been voiced in the five-minute narrative. For example, in question 11, you may feel that there is nothing pertinent for the modern man in *Modern Woman*, but that is not what is discussed in the interview. Luz Hurtado tried to identify reasons for the modern man to read her magazine, and that is the basis we have for answering the question. Always remember to use POE to eliminate any ridiculous or obviously wrong answers. The test writers know that it is difficult to retain everything you hear in the five-minute narrative, and they are certain to throw in a few easily eliminated answers to get you on the right track.

8. Who is the target audience of *Modern Woman*?

   (A) Women from the inside world of fashion.

   (B) Women who work.

   (C) Women who care for their homes and families.

   (D) The contemporary women of the real world.

The correct answer is (D). The target audience of the magazine *Modern Woman* is the contemporary woman of today. Luz Hurtado says that the magazine is directed at those women who work and those who stay home and take care of the family. It tries to appeal to as many groups as possible. Use POE to eliminate answer choices (A), (B), and (C).

9. How is the magazine *Modern Woman* different from other fashion magazines?

   (A) It is a magazine about dolls.

   (B) It is a fantasy magazine.

   (C) It is devoted to the role of fashion in the real world today.

   (D) It is devoted exclusively to the inside world of fashion.

Modern Woman is different from other magazines because, according to the interview, it tries to explore the relationship between fashion and life in the modern world of today. It is not a magazine about dolls (A), nor of fantasy (B), nor an insider fashion magazine (D). Answer choices (C) and (D) may seem close, but the word *exclusivamente* in choice (D) should clue you in to the correct answer, choice (C), since you already know that the magazine tries to encompass a wide audience.

10. Why is *Modern Woman* involved with children that are born with the AIDS virus?

   (A) To provide an example of responsibility to the needy.

   (B) To be more contemporary.

   (C) It was Princess Diana's cause.

   (D) It is fashionable to help the needy.

Even if you didn't know that SIDA means AIDS in Spanish, you should be able to identify the one reasonable response among these four choices. If you use POE, you would quickly eliminate (C) and (D): The magazine would not be involved with a social cause just because Princess Diana had been involved without talking in greater detail about her. To say that it is fashionable to help those in need is just plain silly. Choice (B) is more reasonable, but once you compare it with (A), you'll find the correct answer.

11. What is of interest to the modern man in *Modern Woman*?

   (A) He can learn about men's fashions.

   (B) He can learn of the fashion trends affecting his mother, sister, girlfriend, or wife.

   (C) He can learn about Princess Diana.

   (D) He can learn about himself.

Choice (B) is the correct answer. According to the interview, the modern man can learn about the fashion interests of his sister, female friends, mother, girlfriend, or wife by reading *Modern Woman*. Rule out (A) since men's fashion is never discussed in the interview except for a mention of Andre Agassi's individuality on the tennis court. Choices (C) and (D) simply refer to topics mentioned in the interview but not thoroughly discussed.

12. What relationship exists between fashion and sports, according to the interview?

   (A) Many sports have a fashion developed around them.

   (B) Many sports figures are models.

   (C) All sports figures have a lot of style.

   (D) Fashion and sports are synonymous.

According to what is said in the interview, the relationship between sports and fashion is that many sports figures, such as those in golf and tennis, develop their own styles within the sport. Choice (D) is completely wrong; fashion and sports are not synonymous. Choices (B) and (C) may be true but are not discussed in the interview. POE cancels these out right away.

READING

The reading portion of the exam is designed to test your reading comprehension skills as well as your knowledge of Spanish grammar and vocabulary. In this section, you are asked to read short passages and answer the questions that follow. There are approximately three to five passages in this section.

As we mentioned earlier, when you begin the multiple-choice portion of any standardized test, it is up to you to find the easier questions to do first. Reading comprehension passages are no exception. You should skim through the reading comprehension passages to determine the order in which you will work. Leave the most difficult one for last, and start with an easier passage. This is important; if you run out of time, it is better to be working on the passage that is most difficult and where you would potentially miss the most questions anyway.

THE BIG PICTURE (HOW TO READ)

For the reading comprehension passages, you should read through the entire passage once for the general meaning. Next, you should scan the questions that follow the reading, and then go back through the reading and find the answers. Most of the questions will follow very logically from the order of the actual reading. In the first reading, try to identify the main topic of the passage, and get the general idea of the content. If you understand what the overall passage is about, and you can identify the main point in each paragraph, you've read the passage properly. Don't worry about facts or details (such as names, dates, places, or titles). Focus on the whole passage. Don't dwell on a few words that you do not understand or read a sentence over and over again if you don't understand it. Focus on general ideas and main ideas from each paragraph; this way you will know where to find the answers to the questions that do focus on the details.

TYPES OF PASSAGES

The main types of passages include authentic samples that discuss current events, cultural topics, and social, economic, and political issues. Passages can now include web pages or other multimedia materials. Subject matter has nothing to do with the difficulty of a passage. You may feel that if a certain passage is about a topic familiar to you, it will contain vocabulary that you understand. Don't assume anything. Read a few sentences to make sure.

QUESTION ORDER

The questions for each passage are best done in the order in which they appear (although you want to follow the golden rule of skipping any question that looks really difficult). This is because the order of questions usually follows the progression of the passage—early questions come from the beginning of the passage, and subsequent questions come from the middle and end of the passage. Something that you read in the early part of the passage can sometimes help on a later question.

As with the paragraph completion exercises we discussed earlier, there may be a tendency to feel as if you're not done until you've answered every question for each passage. However, if you've done all the questions that you understand and can easily find the answers to, then move on to the next passage and see if you can find some easy questions there.

ANSWERING QUESTIONS

Most questions will ask you about the main idea or the overall content of the passage, as well as inferences and conclusions that can be made from the content presented. These are the two types of questions: general and specific.

General Questions

After finishing the first reading, you should scan the set of questions and look for those that may be of a general nature. If you looked for the main idea and structure of the reading the first time through, then you will be able to answer these general questions quite easily. Some sample general questions include the following:

¿Quién narra este pasaje?
Who is narrating the passage?

¿De qué se trata este pasaje?
What is this passage about?

¿Cuál es el propósito del artículo?
What is the purpose of the article?

¿Cuál de las siguientes afirmaciones resume mejor el artículo?
Which of the following statements best summarizes the article?

¿Cuáles es una conclusión lógica que se puede hacer del contenido?
What is a logical conclusion based on the content?

Specific Questions

Some of the reading comprehension questions ask you to refer back to the passage to look for details. This is why it is crucial to get a sense of the structure of the passage during the first reading. If you don't, you may waste a good deal of time looking for the specific point in the passage that answers the question. The approach to these questions is as follows:

- Read the question.
- Locate the source of the question by examining key words from the question.
- Carefully read the section in the passage that answers the question.
- Go to the answers and select the choice that best matches the information you read in the passage.

DON'T FORGET THE PROCESS OF ELIMINATION (POE)

One of the biggest problems students have with the reading comprehension section is that they don't like or understand any of the answer choices for some questions. Sometimes the correct answer to a reading comprehension question is so obvious that it will practically leap off the page. Other times, however, it may not be quite so simple. But with POE, even the most difficult questions can be conquered.

Sample Reading Comprehension Passage

Directions: Read the following passage carefully for comprehension. The passage is followed by a number of incomplete statements. Select the completion or answer that is best according to the passage and fill in the corresponding oval on the answer sheet.

Introducción

El siguiente artículo apareció en 1996 en el periódico *La Jornada de Lima*.

LIMA, PERÚ: "No hubo ningún otro remedio" explicó el presidente peruano Alberto Fujimori al hablar con Eduardo Taboada, corresponsal extranjero de la
Línea emisora Univisión, durante una entrevista realizada
5 en la capital peruana. Fujimori habló pocos minutos después del ataque militar contra el grupo terrorista Tupac Amaru, que se había apoderado de la embajada japonesa hacía 4 meses. El grupo, integrado por 22 guerrilleros y sus cuatro líderes, secuestró a 72 rehenes,
10 la mayoría de ellos diplomáticos extranjeros, quienes habían sido cautivos dentro del recinto japonés por 130 días.

Los soldados peruanos iniciaron el ataque a las tres de la tarde, según el periodista Taboada, quien presenció
15 el evento tan inesperado. A pesar de que el ataque empleara muchas estrategias, apenas duró cuarenta minutos. Un grupo de soldados se dirigió por la parte delantera de la embajada y otro grupo se abalanzó a la parte posterior. Utilizaron armas con láser y rifles que
20 hasta pudieron ubicar a los terroristas adentro, gracias a la ayuda de una computadora especial. Ninguno de los terroristas salió con vida de la residencia, de acuerdo con los informes del noticiero Univisión de Miami. La emisora nacional de Perú, NotiUno, interrumpió su pro-
25 gramación para transmitir en vivo escenas de la crisis. Pocos detalles fueron divulgados por la censura de la prensa para proteger a los rehenes.

Fujimori proclamó orgullosamente que habían acabado de una vez con el terrorismo y nunca negociaría con
30 terroristas, lo cual sigue siendo la política oficial del Perú. Sin embargo, Fujimori se vio obligado a iniciar conversaciones con los rebeldes fuertemente armados después de que varios gobiernos extranjeros, cuyos ciudadanos se encontraban dentro de la embajada, presion-
35 aron para evitar un ataque militar. Fujimori sí dialogó con los rebeldes, pero al mismo tiempo iba planeando clandestinamente un asalto militar.

Mucha gente de la comunidad mundial opinó que las acciones del gobierno peruano eran innecesarias. Un

sacerdote conocido en el Perú, el Padre Xavier Venan-
40 cio, reiterando la opinión de la iglesia peruana, pensó que la situación podría haberse resuelto a través de una manera pacífica. El presidente Fujimori reafirmó que no había otra manera de resolver la crisis, ya que "se nos acababa el tiempo y nuestro compromiso principal
45 fue garantizar la seguridad y bienestar de los rehenes. Esperar más no nos convenía". El presidente japonés Hashimoto dijo pocos minutos después de la exitosa liberación de los rehenes que "no debe haber nadie que pueda criticar al presidente". La prensa peruana
50 confirmó esto, a través de unas encuestas realizadas en todo el territorio nacional en las cuales el noventa por ciento (90%) de la población peruana estuvo a favor de la acción militar de Fujimori. Con esta nueva derrota de otro grupo subversivo, Fujimori ya marca su segunda
55 victoria militar contra el terrorismo. En 1992, Fujimori arrasó con el grupo terrorista más temido del país, El Sendero Luminoso, tras el arresto de su enigmático líder, Abimael Guzmán. Sendero Luminoso fue el grupo terrorista de mayor involucramiento y hegemonía al
60 nivel nacional, habiendo aterrorizado el país por más de 25 años; un periodo sumamente violento que ocasionó la muerte de más de 35.000 peruanos. En su auge el grupo se apoderó de casi el 40% del territorio peruano. Ese grupo maoísta inspiró a su vez a otros grupos tales
65 como Tupac Amaru que se desafiaran del gobierno peruano a través del conflicto armado. Con estos gloriosos éxitos, el gobierno peruano pretende restaurar, según Fujimori, "el progreso, la paz, y la prosperidad" en la nación andina.
70

Por ahora reinará la estabilidad en el Perú, pero como nos ha narrado la historia, la tranquilidad es un deleite que se saborea por unos cortos momentos, y sabremos cuándo surgirá otro movimiento subversivo que busque desalojar la tan deseada paz que tanto anhela el pueblo
75 peruano.

La Jornada de Lima, 1996

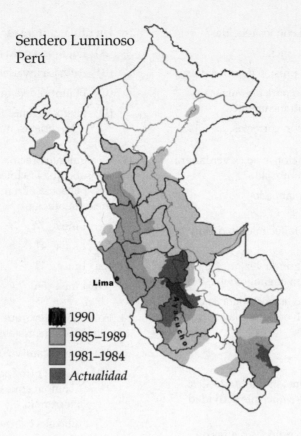

Sendero Luminoso
Perú

Lima

Ayacucho

1990
1985–1989
1981–1984
Actualidad

Víctimas de Ataques Terroristas en el Perú

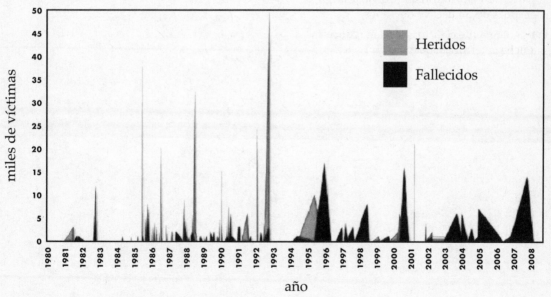

Heridos

Fallecidos

miles de víctimas

año

Fuente: RAND Database of Worldwide Terrorism Incidents
(http://www.rand.org/nsrd/projects/terrirosim-incidents.html)

15. ¿Por qué Fujimori negoció con los rebeldes?

    (A) Porque era su política oficial.

    (B) Porque había sentido presión de otros países.

    (C) Porque le daba tiempo para organizar un ataque militar simultáneamente.

    (D) Todas las respuestas son correctas.

16. ¿Cuál de las siguientes oraciones no es verdadera sobre el asalto militar a la embajada?

    (A) El ataque había sido planeado detalladamente.

    (B) El ataque ocasionó el fallecimiento de muchos terroristas.

    (C) El ataque marcó la segunda vez que Fujimori había derrotado a un enemigo del Estado.

    (D) Si se hubiera utilizado la tecnología, la crisis habría podido resolverse de una forma más eficaz y pacífica.

17. Podemos inferir que

    (A) después de la intervención militar de 1996, no se irrumpió más semejante actividad terrorista

    (B) el gobierno peruano siguió las pautas de Fujimori y continuó su política de no negociar con los rebeldes

    (C) al partir de 1996, terrorismo volvió a surgir después de un declive de 5 años

    (D) la tecnología fue el factor clave en reducir la amenaza terrorista después de 1996

18. Un titular apropiado para este artículo sería

    (A) Fujimori en un jaque mate con los terroristas

    (B) Salvajes invaden embajada, perecen muchos

    (C) Fujimori deja que los terroristas lo pisoteen

    (D) Negociaciones logran defraudar a los terroristas, militares triunfan

19. La siguiente oración se puede añadir al texto: "Se sabe que la violencia no resuelve nada, y a su vez, perpetúa aún más violencia". ¿Dónde serviría mejor la oración?

    (A) Línea 37

    (B) Línea 41

    (C) Línea 43

    (D) Línea 56

20. Podemos inferir que 1992 fue un año de mucha actividad terrorista en el Perú ya que

    (A) quedó cautivo el líder del grupo subversivo

    (B) existían otros actos violentos por otros grupos como respuesta de la captura del líder terrorista

    (C) hubo elecciones presidenciales en el Perú ese año

    (D) los terroristas aumentaron el territorio bajo su control

Answers and Explanations for the Sample Reading Comprehension Passage

Translation

The following article appeared in 1996 in the newspaper *La Jornada de Lima*.

LIMA, PERU: "There was no other solution," explained the Peruvian president Alberto Fujimori while speaking with Eduardo Taboada, foreign correspondent for the broadcast station Univisión, during an interview taking place in the Peruvian capital. Fujimori spoke several minutes after the military attack against the terrorist group Tupac Amaru, who had taken control of the Japanese embassy four months earlier. The group, comprised of 22 guerillas and their four leaders, had kidnapped 72 hostages—the majority of whom were foreign diplomats—and who were held captive inside the Japanese residence for 130 days.

The Peruvian soldiers began the attack at 3 P.M., according to the journalist Taboada, who witnessed the unexpected event. Yesterday's attack lasted only 40 minutes in spite of the fact that it involved many strategies. One group of soldiers rushed through the front part of the embassy, while the other group went to the back. They utilized weapons with lasers and rifles that were even able to locate the terrorists inside, thanks to the use of a special computer. None of the terrorists left the residence alive, according to reports from the news station Univisión in Miami. The national broadcast station of Peru, Notiuno, interrupted its programming to transmit live scenes of the crisis. Few details were divulged by the press in order to protect the hostages.

Fujimori proudly proclaimed that he had eliminated terrorism once and for all, and would never negotiate with terrorists, which continues to be the official policy of Peru. However, Fujimori was obliged to begin conversations with the heavily armed rebels, after various foreign governments, whose citizens were inside the embassy, pressured him to avoid a military assault. Fujimori did indeed speak with the rebels, but at the same time was secretly planning a military attack.

Many people of the global community felt that the actions of the Peruvian government were unnecessary. A well-known priest in Peru, Father Xavier Venancio, reiterating the opinion of the Peruvian church, felt that the situation could have been resolved through peaceful means. President Fujimori reaffirmed that there wasn't any other way to resolve the crisis, given that "time was running out for us, and our main goal was to guarantee the safety and well-being of the hostages. To wait any longer wouldn't have been beneficial. The Japanese president Hashimoto said a few minutes after the successful liberation of the hostages that "no one should be criticizing the president." The Peruvian press confirmed this, through interviews carried out throughout the nation in which ninety percent (90%) of Peruvians were in favor of Fujimori's military action. With this recent defeat of yet another subversive group, Fujimori marks his second victory against terrorism. In 1992, Fujimori obliterated the most feared terrorist group in the country, The Shining Path, with the arrest of its enigmatic leader, Abimael Guzman. The Shining Path was the most active and dangerous terrorist group in the nation, having terrorized the country for more than 25 years; an extremely violent period that saw the deaths of more than 35,000 Peruvians. At its peak, the group controlled almost 40% of the country. This Maoist group inspired other groups like Tupac Amaru to challenge the Peruvian government through armed conflict. With these glorious successes, the Peruvian government intends to restore, according to Fujimori, "progress, peace, and prosperity" to the Andean nation.

For now, all is calm in Peru, but as history has shown us, peace is a delicacy that can be savored for only a few short moments, and who knows when other subversive group will appear and attempt to destroy the much desired peace the Peruvian people hope for.

Here's How to Crack It

15. Why did Fujimori negotiate with the rebels?

    (A) Because it was his official policy.

    (B) Because he received pressure from other countries.

    (C) Because it gave him time to organize a military
        attack at the same time.

    (D) All of these answers are correct.

Choice (B) is the correct answer because the article states that he began to dialogue with the rebels because the foreign governments wanted him to avoid a military attack. While choice (C) may be correct, the article doesn't state that Fujimori used the negotiations to "buy time." Choice (A) is incorrect, because Fujimori is quoted as saying he would never negotiate with terrorists. As a result, choice (D) is also incorrect.

16. Which of the following phrases is not correct
    concerning the military assault on the embassy?

    (A) The attack was planned with great detail.

    (B) The attack caused the death of many terrorists.

    (C) The attack marks the second time that Fujimori
        defeats an enemy of the state.

    **(D) If technology had been used, the crisis could have
        been solved in a more efficient and peaceful manner.**

This type of question is sometimes included to trip up the fast reader. Be sure to focus on the qualifying word "no" in the question. Thus, this question is looking for a false statement. The article states that the attack employed many strategies, which would suggest that Answer (A) is a true statement. Likewise, Answer (B) is also true, as the article stated that there were 26 terrorists and that none escaped. Answer (C) is a true statement as the article at the end discusses Fujimori's past successes. Answer (D) is a false statement, as technology (lasers and computers) was indeed used to end the crisis quickly. Thus, (D) is the correct answer.

17. We can infer that

    (A) after the military intervention of 1996, there wasn't any
        more similar terrorist activity

    (B) the Peruvian government followed Fujimori's lead and
        continued it policy of not negotiating with rebels

    **(C) after 1996, terrorism resurged after a decline over 5
        years**

    (D) technology was a key factor in reducing the terrorist
        threat after 1996

Choice (C) is the correct answer, as the graph shows that terrorism declined for five years after 1996, but then had a sharp increase in 2001. This is a direct contradiction of choice (A). Choices (B) and (D) may be true, but there isn't any data to support those inferences.

18. An appropriate title for this article would be

   (A) Fujimori in a checkmate with the terrorists

   (B) Savages invade embassy, many perish

   (C) Fujimori lets terrorists step all over him

   **(D) Negotiations manage to mislead terrorists,
       military triumphs**

The best answer is (D), as it captures the overall main idea of the article. While choice (A) does show that Fujimori has the upper hand, it doesn't give the detail of choice (D). Choice (B) refers to savages, which would not be used to describe the military in this article. Choice (C) is also incorrect, as it clearly is the opposite of the outcome of the standoff between the president and the terrorists.

19. The following sentence can be added to the text:
   **"It is known that violence doesn't resolve anything,
   and in turn, perpetuates even more violence."** Where
   would this fit best?

   (A) Line 37

   (B) Line 41

   (C) Line 43

   (D) Line 56

The correct answer is (C), as it would be a logical quote by the nonviolent priest mentioned in the article. In this position it advances the flow and meaning of the paragraph. Choice (A), line 37, does reinforce the idea of a nonviolent solution, but as our inserted sentence is an opinion, it wouldn't fit here since the following sentence is about planning a military intervention. Choice (D) is incorrect, as the previous sentence in the article speaks of the nation's overwhelming approval of the attack. While choice (B) could also accommodate the sentence, a clearly better fit would be choice (C) given the preceding and subsequent sentences. These types of questions are testing your ability to accommodate sentences in a paragraph where they would have the best flow and impact; be sure to read the surrounding sentences to get a better idea of where to put them.

20. We can infer that 1992 was a year of much terrorist activity in Peru since

   (A) the leader of a subversive group was captured

   (B) there were other violent acts by other groups as a
       response to the capture of the terrorist leader

   (C) there were elections in Peru that year

   **(D) the terrorists increased the territory under their
       control**

Choice (D) is the correct answer as shown by the map. There are no references to choice (C) anywhere so it can be eliminated. Choices (A) and (B) are too similar for one of them to be the right answer. And the graph does not show which groups are responsible for the terrorist acts so it isn't possible to determine. In addition, the terrorist leader was captured in December, so the year had already ended, another reason by choice (B) is incorrect.

READING COMPREHENSION SUMMARY

- Choose the order in which you want to do the passages. Read a couple of sentences to see if the writing style is easy to follow and the vocabulary is manageable. If so, go for it. If not, look ahead for something easier.

- Read the passage for topic and structure only. Don't read for detail, and don't try to memorize the whole thing. The first read is for you to get a sense of the general idea and the overall structure—that's all.

- Go straight to the general questions. Ideally, you should be able to answer any general questions without looking back to the passage. However, very few passages have specific questions, so don't expect to find too many.

- Now, do the specific questions in order. For these, you're going to let the key words in the question tell you where to look in the passage. Then, read the area that the question comes from slowly and carefully. Find an answer choice that basically says the same thing. Answer choices are often paraphrases from the passage.

- Avoid specific answers on general questions, and on specific questions avoid answers that are reasonable but are not present in the passage.

- Don't be afraid to leave blanks if there are questions that stump you. You're done with a passage whenever you've answered all the questions that you can answer. Instead of wasting time trying to answer the last remaining question on a passage after all other techniques have failed to indicate the correct answer, go on to the next passage.

- Don't pick an answer choice just because you recall hearing the word in the passage. Frequently that is a trick; correct answers will often use synonyms rather than the word originally used in the passage.

4

THE FREE-RESPONSE SECTION: WRITING AND SPEAKING

THE BASICS

WHAT IS THE FREE-RESPONSE SECTION?

The free-response section (Section II) of the AP Spanish Language and Culture Exam also tests two important skills: writing and speaking. The Writing portion consists of two samples of writing: Interpersonal and Presentational. The Speaking portion consists of Interpersonal Speaking in the form of a simulated conversation, as well as a Presentational Speaking sample in which an integration of reading and listening skills will yield an oral presentation. On the speaking part, you will be paced and prompted by a master recording for a total of 20 minutes.

Here is the free-response portion of that handy chart we showed you in the beginning of Part I:

Section	Number of Questions	Percent of Final Score	Time
Section II: Free Response			Approx. 85 minutes
Interpersonal Writing: Email Reply	1 prompt	12.5%	15 minutes
Presentational Writing: Persuasive Essay	1 prompt	12.5%	Approx. 55 minutes
Interpersonal Speaking: Conversation	5 prompts	12.5%	20 seconds for each response
Presentational Speaking: Cultural Comparison	1 prompt	12.5%	2 minutes to respond

WRITING

The Writing portion of the free-response section consists of two compositions. The first part is a formal writing task. You will have 15 minutes to read a prompt and reply with your response. Some samples of this could be an e-mail, a postcard, a letter to a friend, or a journal, diary, or blog entry. The second part examines your ability to write formally. Here, you will have 10 minutes to read a few printed sources and listen to an audio prompt. After this, you will have about 5 minutes to formulate your ideas and plan your response. Then, you will have 40 minutes to write your essay for a total time allotment of 55 minutes.

INTERPERSONAL WRITING

Let's take a look at a sample question for the interpersonal writing section. Typically, a response prompt will be an email from a professional offering you a study opportunity, a scholarship, a job, or an internship. It might also be a response to your request for a letter of recommendation. When presented with these situations, try to immerse yourself in the situation. Maybe you have never worked or traveled overseas before. It doesn't matter—you can make up things! Graders are looking to see how convincing you are in your writing piece, that's all.

The key to this limited-time assignment is to read the prompt quickly; to touch upon all the points required, expanding upon them as much as possible; and to do so in a grammatically correct and stylistically advanced manner. Spend less than 5 minutes reading the prompt and planning your answer, and begin writing your answer directly after having done so.

As you write, be sure to vary your vocabulary and your grammar. Graders don't want to see you use "bueno" and "malo" throughout your writing, and they definitely don't want to see you use only the present tense. Think about your speaking pattern in English. You don't speak only in present tense. You use a variety of tenses. Try to use some idiomatic expressions as well to show that you are familiar with the intricacies of the language. Remember to use original ways to open and close your letter. Use appropriate structural indicators and transitional words like *por lo tanto*, *sin embargo*, *en primer lugar*, *para concluir*, *finalmente*, and *adicionalmente*. Also, because this writing sample is so short, do not repeat yourself. Some final tips would be to avoid Anglicism and never, under any circumstance, use English in your writing. If you don't know the word for something, find a way to describe it.

This section is also testing your ability to write a formal letter using correct register, possessive pronouns, appropriate vocabulary, and correct openings and closings. Remember, a basic and grammatically correct essay will score no more than a 3. An essay with dynamism, upper-level structures, and depth will score much higher.

Scoring Guidelines

Writing samples are graded on their degree of task completion, topic development, and use of language. As AP graders are grading large numbers of compositions, make sure yours stands out with creative and memorable vocabulary and content. Scores are awarded on a 1 to 5 scale, just like the overall scores of the AP are given. Here are the rubrics for receiving scores from 5 to 1.

Five: Demonstrates Excellence

For a response to merit a 5, students must fully address and complete the task, and respond completely or almost completely to all the parts/prompts of the writing task. Responses should be thorough, well-organized, and culturally and socially appropriate. Vocabulary and grammar are rich, high level, and virtually error-free. There should be demonstrated command of orthography, sentence structure, paragraphing, and punctuation.

Four: Demonstrates Command

Responses appropriately address and complete the task; it responds fully or almost fully to the parts/prompts of the writing task. Responses are well-developed and generally well-organized, and are generally culturally and socially appropriate. There is use of complex vocabulary and grammar, but there are a few errors. Vocabulary, pronunciation, and overall fluency are very good. Orthography, sentence structure, paragraphing and punctuation are generally correct.

Three: Demonstrates Competence

To achieve this score, students must address the task and adequately answer most parts/prompts of the writing task. Answers are adequately relevant, organized, and generally socially and culturally appropriate. Grammatically, the student shows mastery of simple structures, but struggles with more complex forms. There is good vocabulary, but some English influence may be detected. There may be errors in spelling and structure.

Two: Suggests Lack of Competence

Responses in this category only partially complete or address the task. Some responses to certain parts of the writing prompt may be irrelevant or inappropriate. Parts of the response may have some irrelevancies; answers may lack organization and social and cultural appropriateness. Responses show limited control of the simple grammatical and vocabulary structures: limited breadth of vocabulary, frequent English influence, and frequent grammatical and structural errors.

One: Lack of Competence

Student does not complete the task and does not respond appropriately to most parts of the prompt. Most responses are irrelevant, disorganized, and are not socially and culturally appropriate. There are frequent grammar and vocabulary errors, frequent English influence, and poor comprehension which make understandability difficult.

Zero

Answer is in a language other than Spanish, blank or nearly blank, completely off topic, or simply a restatement of the question.

Sample Question

Directions: For the following question, you will write a letter. You will have 15 minutes to read the question and write your answer.

Instrucciones: Para la siguiente pregunta, escribirás una carta. Tendrás 15 minutos para leer la pregunta y escribir tu respuesta.

La siguiente correo electrónico le llegó de parte de la Señorita Ciara Duran de la Universidad Interamericana de Puerto Rico, Es una invitación para asistir a un Congreso juvenil durante el verano.

UNIVERSIDAD INTERAMERICANA
SAN JUAN, PUERTO RICO
OFICINA DE PROGRAMAS ESPECIALES

Estimado/a candidato/a:

Muchas gracias por haber expresado su interés en participar en nuestro Congreso Interamericano Juvenil que tendrá lugar el 14 de junio hasta el 5 de julio de este año en La Universidad Interamericana en San Juan, Puerto Rico. Me es muy grato ofrecerle un puesto como delegado representante este año.

Cada verano, nuestra universidad acoge a estudiantes visitantes de varios rincones del mundo hispanohablante, lo cual nos aporta una perspectiva verdaderamente internacional ante los problemas que confrontan al joven de hoy. Como ya sabe, nuestra meta es alentar diálogo entre los jóvenes para definir cuáles son los problemas más contundentes que abarcan al joven. Y es de esperar que después de un intercambio de ideas, consigamos un mayor enfoque de cómo resolver la problemática regional que afecta a tantos jóvenes hoy en día.

Nosotros contamos con el esfuerzo y dedicación de los delegados voluntarios, ya que brindan una energía y espíritu servicial perspectiva única a las situaciones contundentes que confronta a nuestros países

Para proveerle una experiencia de lo más agradable, además de confirmar su asistencia al Congreso, sería necesario que nos clarificara alguna información preliminar:

- Por favor díganos cuáles son algunos de los problemas actuales que confrontan a los jóvenes para que se incluyan en la agenda del Congreso. ¿Por qué le son importantes estos problemas?

- Durante su estadía aquí, puede optar por su alojamiento en un hotel o con una familia puertorriqueña ¿Cuál sería su preferencia, y por qué?

- En el tiempo libre, habrá excursiones y oportunidades para intercambiar con la gente de Puerto Rico. ¿Qué actividades le interesarían a usted, y por qué?

Le pedimos que nos mande esta información de inmediato, ya que se aproxima la fecha límite para inscribirse en el programa.

Le saluda cordialmente,

Ciara Duran
Directora de Programas Estudiantes
Universidad Interamericana

Here's How to Crack It

Quickly brainstorm the vocabulary necessary for the task (*intercambiar, lograr, meta, en cuanto a, en cambio, por otra parte*, etc). Also, as it is a formal communication, have some of your generic lines in your back pocket that can be used for the opening and ending parts, for example: *Me dirijo a Usted* (I am writing to you); *Si fuera posible* (If it were possible); *Le doy las gracias de antemano por haberme atendido* (I thank you in advance for your attention). And of course, don't forget all that great grammar: subjunctive, indirect object pronouns, transitional words, variety of tenses, and idiomatic expressions. Try to have several in each category prepared beforehand so you can refer to them and use them quickly. It's almost like having your clothes picked out the night before school; it makes things a lot easier when you are under pressure. Also, don't forget the inverted exclamation points and question marks. Don't overdo commas and semicolons; Spanish uses them much more sparingly than English.

Student Response and Translation

Estimada Señorita Duran:

Me dirijo a usted con el propósito de informarle sobre mi deseo de participar en el Congreso. Siempre he soñado con participar en un evento así de importante, y espero con ganas la oportunidad de intercambiar ideas con diferentes jóvenes del mundo hispano. Ojalá podamos lograr nuestra meta de definir y lidiar con los problemas que afectan a los jóvenes de hoy. Con el esfuerzo y el positivismo, ¡todo es posible!

Usted me preguntó sobre mis ideas acerca de los temas más contundentes que afectan a los jóvenes del mundo hispanohablante. Yo diría que entre estos problemas se encuentran el desempleo, la falta de alfabetismo en las zonas rurales, y el daño al medioambiente. Son problemas muy globales en el sentido que afectan a toda la sociedad, y creo que si podemos progresar en la lucha contra sus efectos, podemos desarrollar un mundo mejor para futuras generaciones. Estos problemas me son importantes ya que estoy al punto de emprender mi carrera universitaria, y la crisis global de muchas maneras me limita las oportunidades profesionales. En cuanto al alfabetismo, gracias a la tecnología, vivimos en un mundo donde nadie tiene que aislarse. La educación ayuda no solo a que la gente pueda participar en la sociedad, sino también les da una voz para votar y ayudar a los demás, así creando el sentido de igualdad entre todos los ciudadanos. Y finalmente, vivimos en un mundo comprometido por la industrialización, la deforestación, y explotación de los recursos naturales. Los ríos y lagos se ven cada día más contaminados, y el agua es tal vital a nuestra vida de tantas maneras. Espero poder informarles a mis compañeros la importancia de considerar estos problemas, pero al mismo tiempo, tengo muchas ganas de escuchar sus ideas también.

En cuanto al alojamiento, me gusta experimentar toda la cultura nativa, así que me encantaría vivir con una familia puertorriqueña. Es la mejor forma de entender y apreciar las perspectivas de otras culturas—ver el mundo a través de sus ojos!

Sé que Puerto Rico cuenta con muchos lugares turísticos. Si fuera posible, seria excelente visitar las zonas agrícolas de café y piñas para ver cómo se cosechan estos productos. También sé que la zona colonial de San Juan es muy histórica y pintoresca; y como soy fanática de la historia, tengo que visitar esa parte de la capital. Y claro está, ¡pasar un rato en sus lindas playas no vendría mal tampoco!

Nuevamente, le doy las gracias por esta oportunidad y espero mayor información sobre el evento. Si necesita más información de mi parte, sírvase de comunicarse conmigo a su conveniencia.

Un saludo cordial,

Victoria Hirsch

Translation

Dear Ms. Duran:

I am writing to you to inform you of my desire to participate in the Congress. I have always dreamed about participating in an event of this importance, and I am looking forward to the opportunity to share ideas with different young people from the Hispanic world. I hope we can reach our goal of defining and dealing with the problems that affect the young people of today. With effort and positive thinking, anything is possible!

You asked me about my ideas about the most pressing issues facing the youth of the Spanish speaking world. I would say that among these problems we find unemployment, the lack of literacy in rural areas, and damage to the environment. These are worldwide problems in the sense that they affect all levels of society and I think that if we can progress in fighting their effects, we can create a better world for future generations. These problems are important to me because I am at beginning of my university career and the global crisis in many ways has limited my professional opportunities. In terms of illiteracy, thanks to technology, we live in a world where no one has to be isolated. Education not only helps people participate in society, but also it gives them a voice to vote and help others, thus creating a sense of equality among all citizens. And finally, the world we live in is one compromised by industrialization, deforestation, and the exploitation of natural resources. The rivers and lakes are becoming more contaminated each day, and water is vital to our lives in so many ways. I hope to have the chance to inform my colleagues about the importance of considering these problems, but at the same time I am interested in hearing their ideas as well.

In terms of lodging, I enjoy experiencing everything about the native culture, so I would love to live with a Puerto Rican family. That is the best way to understand and appreciate the perspectives of another culture—seeing the world through their eyes!

I know Puerto Rico has many tourist attractions. If it were at all possible, it would be wonderful to visit the agricultural zones of coffee and pineapples to see how these products are harvested. I also know that the colonial zone of San Juan is very historical and picturesque, and since I am a history fanatic, I have to visit that part of the capital. And of course, spending time on Puerto Rico's beautiful beaches would not be a bad idea either!

Once again, I thank you for this opportunity and I await further information about the event. If you need any more information from me, feel free to contact me at your convenience.

A cordial greeting,

Victoria Hirsch

Evaluation

This essay was organized, appropriate, and detailed; it would score a 5. The first paragraph clearly defined the writer's intention (to accept the invitation), the second paragraph talks about the topics that interest her, and the third and fourth paragraphs address specific questions from the prompt email. The closing makes the response even more cohesive. Notice also the breadth of vocabulary (*me dirijo a, contundentes, lidiar, cuenta con, fanática, claro está, sírvase de*) and grammar (*subjunctive, si clauses, formal commands, preterite, conditional*). This is also an important part that graders examine. The response is well presented and not repetitive. Notice also that the writer showed she knew information about the country (coffee and pineapples, the beach, the colonial district). This is very important to demonstrate here and in the presentational speaking section. In order to write a native-sounding letter, you might want to view examples of formal writing online, and try to incorporate several elements you observe in them, not your repertoire. Don't worry if you can't produce this lengthy of a response. If you can duplicate parts of it, and mimic some of the grammar and style, you will be in good shape.

PRESENTATIONAL WRITING

The second composition in the free-response section is a formal presentational writing sample. In this section, you will be required to read two sources and hear one audio piece and then respond to a written prompt. All resources will be related and must be referred to when you write your formal composition. You will have 7 minutes to read the scripts and 3 minutes to listen to the audio piece. After you have finished, you will have 5 minutes to organize your thoughts and plan your response. Finally, you will have 40 minutes to write your formal piece for a total of 55 minutes.

Preparation for this section of the exam is much more extensive than the informal section because we naturally have more practice with informal writing through e-mails, diary entries, and other such writing. Unless you expose yourself to formal writing regularly, this could be a challenging section for you. Exposing yourself to certain media before the exam is an absolute must. Think of social and cultural topics that may appear in an exam. There could be questions on poverty, global warming, social unrest, or literary implications across Latin America and Spain, or there could be questions based on music, food, and clothing trends. Making yourself as well rounded as possible and actively seeking Spanish printed and audio material will greatly help your score on this part.

So how do you plan for topics that are apparently limitless? Take the time to read newspapers from different areas of Latin America and Spain. Surely, you know how to use the Internet. Just do searches for *noticias latinoamericanas* or *periódicos chilenos* (*argentinos/españoles/peruanos*, and so on.) and choose an article that is more challenging for you and grasp its message the best you can. It's not expected for you to understand every word in an article, but if you can read the article's title, skim over it, then read through it, you'll certainly be able to deduce its meaning. Read several articles and follow this procedure as you plan for the exam.

In order to train yourself for the audio prompt of this section, you will need to practice with dialects and search for meaning in a message. A fantastic and fun way to practice with dialects would be to turn on a Spanish soap opera (telenovela) or a movie in Spanish, lie back, and just listen. Some students choose an hour to watch television in Spanish and keep a notebook nearby. They jot down words they don't know or even full sentences they would like to include in their repertoire. Another way you can practice for this section is to download some podcasts. Change your Internet browser into Spanish so you can see and read what is happening in the Spanish-speaking world. Listen to Spanish-speaking radio stations; music is an amazing way to learn vocabulary and improve comprehension. Listen to speeches or interviews in Spanish and start somewhere in the middle of the selection and pay close attention to detail. Take notes as you listen. Be sure to get materials from both Spain and Latin America, as the AP loves to include listening passages with a Spanish accent, which can be a little difficult to understand if you are not used to hearing it.

By reading various selections and listening to diverse audio samples, you begin to build a vocabulary and you enhance your ability to make connections to meaning. These are essential tools to write a thorough formal composition. When you write the essay, be sure to make references to all three resources. When making references to the resources, that does not mean to repeat something written or said in the selections; rather, you make an assertion or connection and use the materials to support your point of view. In your introduction you will explain your goal or position in reference to the topic question. In the paragraphs that follow, be sure to have a topic sentence in each to guide your thoughts and support your ideas with information from the sources. In your conclusion, do not repeat what you said in your introduction; rather, let it serve as a summation of your ideas throughout the essay. If you have time, proofread your composition and make sure you place accents when necessary and check your spelling. If you need to change a thought or idea, do not use correction fluid or try to erase what you wrote; just cross it out. You will not be penalized for doing this. Of course, this may sound silly, but try to be as neat as possible, as a well-presented essay is viewed favorably by graders.

Scoring Guidelines

Writing samples are graded on their degree of task completion, topic development, and use of language. As AP graders are grading large numbers of compositions, make sure yours stands out with creative and memorable vocabulary and content. Scores are awarded on a 1 to 5 scale, just like the overall scores of the AP are given. Here are the rubrics for receiving scores from 5 to 1.

Five: Demonstrates Excellence

For a response to merit a 5, students must fully address and complete the task, and must integrate all sources into the essay. Responses should be relevant, thorough, well-organized, and referenced culturally and socially. There should be significant synthesis of the information rather than mere summarizing or citing of the information. Vocabulary and grammar are rich, high level, and virtually error-free. There should be demonstrated command of orthography, sentence structure, paragraphing, and punctuation.

Four: Demonstrates Command

Responses appropriately address and complete the task; it references and integrates all sources into the essay. Responses are well-developed and generally well-organized, and are generally culturally and socially appropriate. The response is accurate and shows more synthesis than citation. There is use of complex vocabulary and grammar, but there are a few errors. Vocabulary, pronunciation, and overall fluency are very good. Orthography, sentence structure, paragraphing, and punctuation are generally correct.

Three: Demonstrates Competence

To achieve this score, students must address the task and refer to most if not all sources in the essay. Answers are adequately relevant, organized, and generally socially and culturally appropriate. There is more summarizing or citation rather than synthesis. Grammatically, the student shows mastery of simple structures, but struggles with more complex forms. There is good vocabulary, but some English influence may be detected. There may be errors in spelling and structure.

Two: Suggests Lack of Competence

Responses in this category only partially complete or address the task. Only some of the sources are referred to in the essay. Parts of the response may have some irrelevancies; answers may lack organization and social and cultural appropriateness. There is very little evidence of synthesis in the response. Responses show limited control of the simple grammatical and vocabulary structures: limited breadth of vocabulary, frequent English influence, and frequent grammatical and structural errors.

One: Lack of Competence

Student does not complete the task and refers poorly to only one or two sources. Most responses are irrelevant, disorganized, and are not socially and culturally appropriate. The information is limited and inaccurate. There are frequent grammar and vocabulary errors, frequent English influence, and poor comprehension which make understandability difficult.

Zero

Answer is in a language other than Spanish, blank or nearly blank, completely off topic, or simply a restatement of the question.

Sample Question

Directions: The following question is based on the accompanying sources 1-3. The sources include both print and audio material. First, you will have 7 minutes to read the printed material. Afterward, you will hear the audio material; you should take notes while you listen. Then, you will have 5 minutes to plan your response and 40 minutes to write your essay. Your essay should be at least 200 words in length.

This question is designed to test your ability to interpret and synthesize different sources. Your essay should use the information from the sources to support your ideas. You should refer to ALL of the sources. As you refer to the sources, identify them appropriately. Avoid simply summarizing the sources individually.

Instrucciones: La pregunta siguiente se basa en las Fuentes 1-3. Las fuentes comprenden material tanto impreso como auditivo. Primero, dispondrás de 7 minutos para leer el material impreso. Después escucharás el material auditivo; debes tomar apuntes mientras escuches. Luego, tendrás 5 minutos para preparar tu respuesta y 40 minutos para escribir tu ensayo. El ensayo debe tener una extensión mínima de 200 palabras.

El objetivo de esta pregunta es medir tu capacidad de interpretar y sintetizar varias fuentes. Tu ensayo debe utilizar información de TODAS las fuentes, citándolas apropiadamente. Evita un simple resumen de cada una de ellas.

¿Por qué nos urge mejorar las condiciones de vivir de los niños latinoamericanos?

Fuente No. 1

Fuente: Este artículo apareció en la revista mexicana *Auge* en 2009.

A través del continente americano, a pesar de los enormes avances tanto en la tecnología agrícola como en las mismas técnicas de arar la tierra, los niveles de nutrición de varios países siguen estancados a niveles tan reducidos que se ven comprometidas la estatura física, la habilidad de poder trabajar una jornada completa y, peor aún, las capacidades intelectuales de sus ciudadanos. La Organización de Desarrollo y Fomento Internacional reporta que, según cifras de los gobiernos latinoamericanos, el consumo de calorías de la región alcanza un promedio de unas 2680 por día (comparado con unas 3450 en los Estados Unidos), y peor aun en los países centroamericanos apenas sobrepasa las 2250 calorías diarias. En los países de mayor actividad económica, como Argentina, Brasil y México, las diferencias regionales han dejado a ciertas zonas marginadas en condiciones similares. La malnutrición se empeora por la falta de servicios de salud, el desempleo y la alta tasa de enfermedad que resulta de la escasez de debido a los escasos servicios sanitarios adecuados.

Los efectos de la modernización y la caída económica mundial requieren una mano de obra de tiempo completo listo para trabajar horas extensas, y a los niveles de nutrición actuales muchos adultos apenas contarán con la energía necesaria para trabajar las 40 o más horas necesarias semanalmente. Entre el 40% de la población adulta clasificada como "pobre" (con un ingreso diario equivalente a unos $2.50 estadounidenses), la falta de nutrición es un factor constante que les aqueja muy a menudo.

No faltan de los esfuerzos para aliviar el problema, sino que lo que ha variado es la magnitud de su alcance y su eficacia en condiciones sociales y económicas sumamente inhóspitas. Se han registrado victorias en algunas áreas (como el programa Salta de Vitarte en Perú, que se concentró en las personas más pobres y les facilitó 3 servicios básicos) pero el obstáculo más formidable es la irremediable realidad económica en la que vive la población. Los programas de bienestar público intentan repartir certificados a las familias de bajo ingreso—parecido al programa de Cupones de Alimentos en los Estados Unidos—pero no existen ni los recursos ni la infraestructura para sostener el programa a largo plazo. Otros programas tienen como meta enfatizar la educación de salud y nutrición, pero los esfuerzos se hacen en balde ya que los ingresos familiares no generan lo suficiente para sostener dietas mejor balanceadas. Ningún esfuerzo ha logrado tener el impacto necesario para lidiar con el problema en toda su magnitud.

Fuente: Este artículo apareció en *Páginas Escolares*, una revista juvenil colombiana.

EL CÍRCULO DE AMOR

Cuando uno piensa en Guatemala, tal vez le llegue a la mente la imagen de un país pobre donde predomina la agricultura, o tal vez recuerde a la famosa Rigoberta Menchú, ganadora del Premio Nobel de La Paz en 1992 y con ella la gran tradición indígena que por siglos ha representado un papel omnipresente en la historia guatemalteca. Pero si conoce a Maria Giammarino, de Mahwah, Nueva Jersey, entonces lo primero que sabrá de Guatemala es sobre El Círculo de Amor.

El Círculo de Amor fue fundado por Giammarino en 2001, pero su interés en los guatemaltecos proviene desde los años 90, cuando visitaba el país por su trabajo de aeromoza en una línea aérea americana. Así nos cuenta su experiencia: "Durante unas cuantas estadías en el país, tuve la oportunidad de recorrer muchas de las zonas rurales más pobres. Una vez hicimos una excursión en canoa cerca de Livingston, que nos llevó a una aldea prácticamente olvidada por el mundo. Vimos una pobreza que me partió el alma. Llegamos a un pueblo retirado, y de repente vi a unas niñas de edad escolar vendiendo caramelos y cigarrillos en el muelle. ¡Les correspondía estar en la escuela! Una me llamó la atención: llevaba su ropita harapienta y andaba pata pelada, pero me ofreció una sonrisa dulce e inocente. Una mirada hacia el pueblo me confirmó lo peor: unas covachas con techo de estaño, y el desagüe en la calle cuyo olor perduraba y perduraba. Ni Dante hubiera vislumbrado un mundo así".

Después de cultivar una amistad, Giammarino empezó por enseñarle a tejer a la niña. Le obsequió el material y pronto la novata creó chompas de algodón no sólo para su familia, sino también para la venta. Giammarino le alquiló un pequeño puesto donde vendían la mercancía. Y así se inició El Círculo de Amor. Su aerolínea también le dio la mano, lanzando el programa "Quédate con el vuelto", que les pide a pasajeros norteamericanos que vuelven a su tierra que donen los quetzales sobrantes de su estudía en Guatemala. La campaña ha recaudado más de 10.000 dólares desde su inicio. Ahora hay talleres de tejer, los cuales les ayudan a las mujeres a aprender un oficio ya que juegan éstas un papel esencial en la estrategia de la sobrevivencia de las familias. Hay una pequeña cantina que sirve almuerzos a los residentes del pueblo. Y este año, gracias a la bondadosa ayuda de varios auspiciadores, se presenció la apertura de un pequeño consultorio médico que otorga un servicio de salud básico a los 1200 habitantes del pueblo.

El Círculo de Amor tiene como meta principal procurar el bienestar de las niñas guatemaltecas, muchas veces las más explotadas y marginadas de la sociedad. Las contribuciones también se destinan a la educación femenina, porque según Giammarino "a la gente sin acceso a la educación básica se les priva la voz". Por sólo 30 dólares mensuales, un patrocinador puede mandar a una niña a la escuela. El Círculo de Amor pone atención especial en reclutar a las niñas más pequeñas de una familia para que asistan a la escuela, lo cual es un privilegio reservado mayormente para los niños varones. La estrategia de elegir a la niña menor viene de la perspectiva de que mientras más joven sea ella al iniciar los estudios, más probabilidad tendrá de continuarlos en el futuro.

Fuente No. 3: Audio Selection

El siguiente discurso lo ofreció Alesandro Dávila, decano de la escuela de Economía de la Pontificia Universidad Católica del Perú en La X Asamblea del Pacto Andino, celebrado en Cajamarca, Perú el año pasado. Se titula "Declive de inversiones gubernamentales con la crisis económica andina".

AUDIO CD: Track 4

Lo que puedo pronosticar con certeza es que lo único que cambiará en la región latinoamericana es el clima. Nuestra problemática nacional da muchas vueltas, pero al fin y al cabo, termina siendo lo mismo: somos un país pobre y los más marginados se ven cada vez más atrapados en este círculo vicioso que es la pobreza. La realidad que vivimos es que nuestra deuda externa nos sofoca y hasta quita las ganas de querer progresar. Casi el 50% de nuestro Producto Bruto Interno se destina para satisfacer los pagos a nuestros acreedores europeos y norteamericanos. Nuestros problemas sí están fuertemente arraigados en nuestra relación con el exterior. Queda una cantidad mezquina para programas de planificación familiar, educación y vacunas. No nos alcanza el presupuesto nacional para todo, y nuestros niños están sufriendo lo peor.

Las inversiones en el sector educativo han disminuido en un 50%, y varios recintos (ya en decadencia física) ni siquiera pueden abastecer lo mínimo necesario para sus aulas: libros, pizarras, pisos y agua potable. Y cuando se trata de supervivencia, muchos optan por trabajar en vez estudiar. Como resultado, como región tenemos una de las tasas de analfabetismo más altas del continente.

Uno de los problemas más sentidos, por el cual en este momento está atravesando la población en nuestros países en general y específicamente aquellos grupos más marginados, es la fuerte caída de ingresos. En Lima, la canasta familiar (productos de primera necesidad) aguanta menos pero cuesta más. Y ahora La Liga Leche suspenderá las entregas de este valioso alimento a los jardines infantiles debido a los costos desorbitados. Los almuerzos gratuitos son ya una especie en peligro de extinción. Hace 10 años, todos los niños en las provincias andinas recibían vacunas, exámenes dentales y meriendas en sus escuelas. Ahora con suerte recibirán una de las tres. Las cifras indican la triste realidad: en Bolivia, el presupuesto nacional para programas educativos disminuyó en un 33%, aunque la población estudiante aumentó en un 8%. En Chile, la caída de ingresos por las exportaciones resultó en la eliminación de programas de nutrición, planificación familiar, estudios becados y 4 clínicas gratuitas en las zonas más necesitadas. La conclusión que se puede extraer con confiabilidad es que la desigualdad y la pobreza absoluta han aumentado con la crisis económica. Por desgracia, el mundo es ciego frente al problema. El "bail out", un lujo primer mundista, no nos es una opción.

Para el futuro, por lo que se ve actualmente, es probable que el continente sudamericano experimente un crecimiento negativo, tal como la hiperinflación de la década de los 80, lo cual aumentará las deficiencias nutritivas, la productividad, y tristemente, el potencial de crecimiento y desarrollo del futuro.

Sample Student Response and Translation

¿Por qué nos urge mejorar las condiciones de vivir de los niños latinoamericanos?

Es sumamente importante que mejoremos las condiciones de vivir de los niños latinoamericanos, ya que ellos son esenciales para el bienestar del futuro. Hoy en día, se puede decir que la falta de acceso a servicios básicos es uno de los problemas más grandes que confronta a los niños a través del mundo latinoamericano. Como resultado, los niños son atrapados en una problemática sin salida: la pobreza, la cual trae consigo un menor acceso a la educación, la medicina y la vivienda. El trabajo reemplaza la educación como la primera prioridad. Según la fuente #3, algunos niños latinoamericanos carecen de buena nutrición, vacunas y alfabetismo básico. Esto concuerda con otra triste realidad: el hecho preocupante que la inversión financiera en educación, según la fuente número 3, es mucho menor en América Latina, lo cual es claramente paradójico, ya que es donde más se necesita esta clase de inversión (Fuente 2).

Pienso que si las necesidades básicas de la gente se satisficieran, entonces podrían preocuparse de los lujos como la educación. Como nos explica la fuente #1, la gente hambrienta no puede funcionar en el mundo laboral. Vivir, comer y estar libre de enfermedades son necesidades básicas del hombre. Si esta gente no recibe los servicios básicos, ello puede causar epidemias tal como se presencia en México actualmente. Además, la educación, la planificación familiar, la nutrición y la vivienda adecuadas ayudan a la gente a que contribuyan más a sus países. Y hasta es posible que puedan aportar al futuro de su país al convertirse en políticos o doctores. Se dice que con el apoyo y el deseo todo es posible. El mundo está conectado social, económica y políticamente, entonces es nuestra responsabilidad ayudar a estas personas que, según la fuente 2, "se les priva de voz" en su futuro.

Hemos visto que nuestras acciones sí hacen una diferencia en las vidas de los niños latinoamericanos y, obviamente, se sabe que no hay soluciones rápidas y fáciles. Sin embargo, la señora Giammarino se empeñó en ayudar a una comunidad pequeña guatemalteca, demostrando que los esfuerzos pequeños pueden lograr milagros. Esperamos que otras personas reconozcan la urgencia de ayudar a estas personas necesitadas.

Translation

Why is it urgent for us to help improve the living conditions of children in Latin America?

It is extremely important for us to improve the living conditions of Latin America's children, as they are essential to the well being of the future. Nowadays, it can be said that the lack of access to basic services is one of the formidable problems that confront children throughout the Latin American world. As a result, children are trapped in a problem without solution: poverty that brings with it a reduced access to education, medicine, and shelter. Work replaces education as the first priority. According to source #3, some Latin American children lack good nutrition, vaccinations, and basic literacy. This goes with another sad reality—the frightening fact that the financial investment in education in Latin America is much less—clearly paradoxical as this is precisely where this type of investment is needed (source #2).

I believe that if the basic needs of the people were satisfied, then they would be able to concern themselves with luxuries such as education. As source #1 explains to us, hungry people cannot function in the workplace. Living, eating and being free of illness are basic necessities of Man. If these people don't receive basic services, it could cause epidemics as we have witnessed recently in Mexico. Also, adequate education, family planning, nutrition and housing help people to contribute more to their respective countries. Maybe they might contribute to the future of their countries by becoming politicians or doctors. It is said that with support and desire that anything is possible. The world is connected socially, economically, and politically and thus is our responsibility to help those people, who, according to source #2 "are denied a voice" in their future.

We have seen that our actions do indeed make a difference in the lives of Latin American children. And obviously, we know there are no quick and easy solutions. However, Mrs. Giammarino gave of herself to help a small Latin American community, demonstrating that the small efforts can produce miracles. We can only hope that other people recognize the urgency of helping these needy persons.

Evaluation

This essay had strong vocabulary, grammar, and organization. One of the challenges with the presentational writing section is to try to refer to all the sources, because the AP often includes sources that don't have a clear correlation to each other. It is your responsibility to try to find connections between them, however minor, in order to include all of them in your analysis, your synthesis, and ultimately, your composition. Mentioning ALL the sources will help you score higher. One weakness in this essay was that it needed a greater incorporation of the sources, and possibly a deeper analysis. The writer did make some connections among the materials, although somewhat predictable, but nonetheless it carried an idea from start to finish and used data to back up the conclusions. Summary was kept to a minimum and affirmations referred to information in the readings, which are things to remember when writing your essay. This essay would probably score in the 4 range.

SPEAKING

The directions for the speaking part will be given to you by the master recording. You will be told when to open the booklet containing the material. You will be asked to respond to different prompts and to record your voice. Most directions will be spoken in English, but you will be asked different types of questions in Spanish in the Directed Response part of the exam. There are two sections in the speaking part: a role play conversation where the student listens to a speaker and responds to prompts, and an oral presentation of two minutes based on reading and listening passages. Together these sections comprise approximately 20 percent of your overall score.

SECTION I: INTERPERSONAL SPEAKING (SIMULATED CONVERSATION)

This section integrates both listening and speaking skills in a role play conversation. Students will be asked to interact with the recorded conversation. You will be required to answer either five or six times to various prompts. Each response will be 20 seconds long and will be timed by a beep on the recording. Before beginning, you will have the opportunity to read the outline of the simulated conversation and the instructions.

Sample Question

Directions: You will now participate in a simulated conversation. First, you will have 30 seconds to read the outline of the conversation. Then, you will listen to a message and have one minute to read again the outline of the conversation. Afterward, the conversation will begin, following the outline. Each time it is your turn, you will have 20 seconds to respond; a tone will indicate when you should begin and end speaking. You should participate in the conversation as fully and appropriately as possible.

Instrucciones: Ahora participarás en una conversación simulada. Primero, tendrás 30 segundos para leer el esquema de la conversación. Luego, escucharás un mensaje y tendrás un minuto para leer de nuevo el esquema de la conversación. Después, empezará la conversación, siguiendo el esquema. Siempre que te toque un turno, tendrás 20 segundos para responder; una señal te indicará cuando debes empezar y terminar de hablar. Debes participar en la conversación de la manera más completa y apropiada posible.

(A) Imagina que recibes un mensaje del Departamento de Estudios para Extranjeros de una universidad latinoamericana. El director te llama para invitarte a acudir a su oficina para una entrevista sobre tu solicitud de beca.

[You will hear the message on the recording.
Escucharás el mensaje en la grabación.]

(B) La conversación

[The shaded lines reflect what you will hear on the recording.
Las líneas en gris reflejan lo que escucharás en la grabación.]

Entrevistador	Te saluda
Tú	Salúdalo y preséntate
Entrevistador	Te explica por qué te hace la entrevista y te hace una pregunta
Tú	Responde a la pregunta
Entrevistador	Continúa la conversación
Tú	Responde a la pregunta
Entrevistador	Continúa la conversación
Tú	Responde a la pregunta
Entrevistador	Continúa la conversación
Tú	Responde a la pregunta
Entrevistador	Continúa la conversación
Tú	Haz una pregunta

Scoring of Directed Response Speaking

Students' responses will be evaluated using a 5-point scale, similar to the way the overall AP score is generated. The three variables that are evaluated are task completion, topic development, and language use. Here are the criteria for achieving each score.

Five: Demonstrates Excellence

For a response to merit a 5, students must fully address and complete the task, and respond completely or almost completely to all the parts/prompts of the conversation. Responses should be thorough, well-organized, and culturally and socially appropriate. Vocabulary and grammar are rich, high level, and virtually error-free. Pronunciation is excellent as well.

Four: Demonstrates Command

Responses appropriately address and complete the task, and responds fully or almost fully to the parts/prompts of the conversation. Responses are well-developed and generally well-organized, and are generally culturally and socially appropriate. There is use of complex vocabulary and grammar, but there are a few errors. Vocabulary, pronunciation, and overall fluency are very good.

Three: Demonstrates Competence

To achieve this score, students must address the task and adequately answer most parts/prompts of the conversation. Answers are adequately relevant, organized, and generally socially and culturally appropriate. Grammatically, the student shows mastery of simple structures, but struggles with more complex forms. There is good vocabulary, but some English influence may be detected. Fluency and pronunciation are good, with some hesitation and correction of errors.

Two: Suggests Lack of Competence

Responses in this category only partially complete or address the task. Some responses to certain parts of the conversation may be irrelevant or inappropriate. Parts of the conversation may have some irrelevancies; answers may lack organization and social and cultural appropriateness. Responses show limited control of the simple grammatical and vocabulary structures: limited breadth of vocabulary, errors, frequent English influence, and fair pronunciation and minimal overall fluency.

One: Lack of Competence

Student does not complete the task and does not respond appropriately to most parts of the conversation. Most responses are irrelevant, disorganized, and are not socially and culturally appropriate. There are frequent grammar and vocabulary errors, frequent English influence, and poor comprehension which make understandability difficult.

Zero

Answer is in a language other than Spanish, completely off topic, or simply a restatement of the question.

Here's How to Crack It

This section is testing your ability to initiate, sustain and conclude a conversation in a given situation as well as use language that is culturally, semantically, grammatically and socially correct. In other words, are you using the correct *Usted* and *tú* forms? Are you being culturally appropriate in a social setting by using correct markers in your conversation, such as the subjunctive and formal commands, when necessary? Many of these situations involve traveling or studying overseas or applying for jobs, internships, and scholarships. So it would be smart to study up on some of the vocabulary involved in job applications, college courses, scholarships, internships, and so on.

Remember that you have only 20 seconds to respond to each prompt. Do not restate the question in your answer, as it wastes valuable time. Speak clearly and slowly. Don't worry if you get cut off in mid-sentence by the tone. Make it your goal to provide interesting and high level answers that address the question or situation with correct grammar and pronunciation. Try to incorporate certain phrases that can help you introduce your answers: *Me es importante, Quisiera, Si fuera posible,* for example. The higher level structure and vocabulary you use, the higher your score will be. Also, try not to use the simple way to say things, use the higher order vocabulary. For example use, *dirigirse* or *acudir* instead of *ir*. Try to use all 20 seconds as it will enable you to give two solid, high-level sentences. Remember that if you are using the *Usted* form, which is probably more often than not, you need to have all of the verbs, possessive pronouns and especially the object pronouns in the corresponding forms. Pay attention to the Student Answers on the sample script with Student Response as these are the kinds of answers that will get your high scores.

Sample Script with Student Response and Translation

Narrador:	Imagina que recibes un mensaje telefónico de parte del director del Departamento de Estudios para Extranjeros de una universidad latino-americana. El director te llama para invitarte a acudir a su oficina para una entrevista sobre tu solicitud de beca.
	Imagine that you receive a phone message from the director of the Depart-ment of Foreign Student Studies at a Latin American university. The director calls you to invite you to his office for an interview about your scholarship application.
MA:	[Answering machine] [Beep] Buenos días, le habla el señor Guill-ermo Butrón director del programa de Estudios para Extranjeros. Quisiera que pasara por mi oficina mañana para una entrevista sobre la solicitud que usted nos envió. Tengo algunas preguntas que quisiera hacerle.
	Good morning, this is Mr. Guillermo Butrón, director of the Foreign Student Studies program. I would like you to pass by my office tomorrow for an inter-view concerning the application you submitted. I have a few questions I would like to ask you.
Narrador:	Ahora tienes un minuto para leer el esquema de la conversación
	Now you have one minute to read the conversation outline.
	Ahora imagina que te encuentres en la oficina del señor Butrón para realizar una entrevista.
	Now imagine that you are in Mr. Butrón's office for an interview.
Entre:	Buenos días. Me es muy grato conocerle en persona. Soy Guillermo Butrón, director del programa de Estudios para Extranjeros y de becas en la región latinoamericana. Por favor, pase y siéntese.
	Good morning. It is a pleasure to meet you in person. I am Guillermo Butrón, director of the Foreign Student Studies program and scholarships in Latin America. Please, come in and sit down.

Tú:	Es un verdadero gusto conocerle también, Señor Butrón. Soy Michael Randello de Nueva York.
	It is real pleasure to meet you also, Mr. Butrón. I am Michael Randello, from New York.
Entre:	Tengo su solicitud para una beca de estudios y necesito hacerle algunas preguntas para saber un poco más sobre usted. ¿Por qué le interesa estudiar en Latinoamérica?
	I have your scholarship study application and I need to ask you some questions to find out a little more about you. Why are you interested in studying in Latin America?
Tú:	Siempre me han llamado la atención la cultura y el idioma de esa región. Como quisiera trabajar en un empleo relacionado con América Latina, necesito hablar mejor el español y entender más a fondo su cultura y costumbres.
	I have always been interested in both the culture and language of that region. Since I would like to work in a position that relates to Latin America, I need to speak Spanish better and understand in depth its culture and customs.
Entre:	Ah, muy interesante. Se nota que tiene un verdadero interés en estudiar en el extranjero. ¿Dónde en Latinoamérica le gustaría estudiar y vivir, y por qué?
	Ah, very interesting. I see that you have a real interest in studying abroad. Where in Latin America would you like to study and live, and why?
Tú:	Definitivamente me interesaría estar en Argentina. Encuentro tanto la historia como la cultura fascinante. Además, ahí podría perfeccionar el español.
	I would definitely like to be in Argentina. I find both the history and culture fascinating. In addition, there I would be able to perfect my Spanish.
Entre:	Si fuera a recibir la beca, ¿qué le gustaría estudiar y por qué?
	If you were to receive the scholarship, what would you like to study and why?
Tú:	Bueno, obviamente necesitaría estudiar el español, pero como quisiera trabajar en negocios internacionales, sería buena idea que estudiara comercio, relaciones internacionales, e historia.
	Well, obviously I would need to study Spanish, but as I would like to work in international business, it would be a good idea that I study commerce, international relations, and history.
Entre:	Además de sus responsabilidades académicas, los estudiantes que reciben becas deben participar en actividades culturales. ¿Qué aspectos de la cultura del país que visitará le interesan?

In addition to their academic responsibilities, the students who receive scholarships must participate in cultural activities. What aspects of the culture interest you in your country of choice?

Tú: Siempre me ha fascinado el tango. La historia y el significado del tango me son muy interesantes. Siempre soñé con aprender a bailar el tango, así que tomaré clases.

The tango has always fascinated me. The history and meaning of the tango are very interesting. I always dreamed about learning to dance the Tango, so I will take classes.

Entre: ¡Qué bien! Y para terminar, ¿qué preguntas tiene sobre la beca o sobre nuestro programa en general?

How nice. And to conclude, what questions do you have about the scholarship or about our program in general?

Tú   Por favor, dígame: ¿Cuándo empezará el programa? ¿Viviré con una familia o en una residencia estudiantil? ¿Cuándo me informarán sobre la beca?

Please tell me: When does the program begin? Will I live with a family or in a student residence? When will I be informed about the scholarship?

Evaluation

The responses by the student were rich, varied, and complete; he used excellent grammatical and vocabulary structures: conditional, subjunctive, and future tenses. The student also fulfilled the requirement of being socially appropriate by using the *Usted* command "*Dígame*" in the last response. Be sure to get one example of that in your response. The responses enriched and advanced the conversation; notice how the topics were addressed and developed with creative and interesting answers: the student showed an understanding of university courses, culture, and studying overseas. You should be sure to have an understanding of several Spanish speaking countries as you may need to discuss their culture in one of these types of questions. This response would certainly score in the 4 or 5 level.

Section II: Presentational Speaking: Cultural Comparison

This section is brand new for the 2014 exam. It requires you to make a presentation on a specific topic. You are given 4 minutes to read the question and plan your answer, and then 2 minutes to actually deliver your presentation. Although you are not given any material on which to base your answer, you need to reflect on the cultural knowledge you have acquired about the Spanish-speaking world, as well as the knowledge you have acquired about the community in which you live.

Sample Question

Directions: You will deliver an oral presentation to your class on a given cultural topic. You will have 4 minutes to read the presentation topic and formulate your presentation. Then you will have 2 minutes to record your presentation.

In your presentation, you should compare the community in which you reside to an area of the Hispanic world that you have studied. You will need to demonstrate an understanding of the cultural aspects of the Hispanic world. Your presentation should also be organized appropriately.

Instrucciones: Usted dará una presentación oral a su clase sobre un tema cultural. Dispondrá de 4 minutos para leer el tema de la presentación y formular su repuesta.

En su presentación, debe comparar la comunidad en la cual vive con una del mundo hispánico que haya estudiado. Tendrá que demostrar tu comprensión de los aspectos culturales del mundo hispánico. Su presentación debe ser organizada de manera clara.

¿Cómo ha afectado la tecnología la vida de las personas en su comunidad?

Compara sus observaciones sobre las comunidades en las cuales ha estado con las de una región del mundo hispanohablante que haya estudiado. Puede referirse a lo que haya estudiado, vivido, observado, escuchado, etc.

Scoring of Cultural Comparison

Students' responses will be evaluated using a 5-point scale, similar to the way the overall AP score is generated. The three variables that are evaluated are task completion, topic development, and language use. Here are the criteria for achieving each score.

Five: Demonstrates Excellence

For a response to merit a 5, students must fully address and complete the task, and completely or almost completely address and develop the topic. Responses should be thorough, well-organized, and culturally and socially appropriate. Vocabulary and grammar are rich, high level, and virtually error-free. Pronunciation is excellent as well.

Four: Demonstrates Command

Responses appropriately address and complete the task, and fully or almost fully address and develop the topic. Responses are well-developed and generally well-organized, and are generally culturally and socially appropriate. There is use of complex vocabulary and grammar, but there are a few errors. Vocabulary, pronunciation, and overall fluency are very good.

Three: Demonstrates Competence

To achieve this score, students must address the task and adequately develop the topic. Answers are adequately relevant, organized, and generally socially and culturally appropriate. Grammatically, the student shows mastery of simple structures, but struggles with more complex forms. There is good vocabulary, but some English influence may be detected. Fluency and pronunciation are good, with some hesitation and correction of errors.

Two: Suggests Lack of Competence

Responses in this category only partially complete or address the task. Some responses to certain parts of the conversation may be irrelevant or inappropriate. Parts of the conversation may have some irrelevancies; answers may lack organization and social and cultural appropriateness. Responses show limited control of the simple grammatical and vocabulary structures: limited breadth of vocabu¬lary, errors, frequent English influence, and fair pronunciation and minimal overall fluency.

One: Lack of Competence

Student does not complete the task and does not appropriately address or develop the topic. Most responses are irrelevant, disorganized, and are not socially and culturally appropriate. There are frequent grammar and vocabulary errors, frequent English influence, and poor comprehen¬sion, which make understandability difficult.

Zero

Answer is in a language other than Spanish, completely off topic, or simply a restatement of the question.

Here's How to Crack It

This section is challenging since there are no prompts to use as a basis for your answer. It is testing your ability to produce an oral report for an extended period of time, to expound on familiar topics that require some sort of research, and to demonstrate and understand aspects of the target culture (geography, art, music, and social, economic, and political elements). There also should be some sort of comparing and contrasting going on in your response; this is an example of higher-order thinking, and the graders like to see that. The best way to prepare for this section is to become completely familiar with several countries in the Spanish-speaking world. Pick one from each major region: the Carib-bean, Mexico and Central America, Andean region, the Southern Cone, and Spain. This way you have knowledge of the different ethnic groups, history, and customs. Often you will be asked to compare and contrast cultures, so practice doing that on your own by looking for similarities and differences when reading and comparing articles or other media. Use specific vocabulary to voice similarities and differences: *por otra parte, se parecen, se diferencian, vale mencionar que mientras una*_____, *la otra* _____, and so on.

Sample Student Answer and Evaluation

Les voy a hablar sobre cómo la tecnología ha empeñado un papel sumamente importante en las vidas de las personas tanto en mi comunidad como en la comunidad hispanohablante.

Yo diría que en mi comunidad la tecnología ha enriquecido la educación en las escuelas. Gracias al Internet, tenemos acceso a recursos para el estudio de idiomas- periódicos de cualquier país de Latinoamérica o España. Inclusive podemos escuchar noticieros y ver programas televisivos a cualquier hora. Hasta hemos abandonado los diccionarios, ya que podemos usar páginas Web desde los teléfonos para descifrar palabras y entender su uso correcto en la gramática. Como resultado, mi rendimiento como estudiante ha mejorado.

En mi comunidad, veo que hay padres que pueden vigilar sus casas, empleados, niños—todo desde su teléfono celular. Los policías pueden usar tecnología especial para rastrear a niños perdidos o secuestrados a través de las torres de teléfonos celulares.

La tecnología también ha tenido efectos positivos en los países de América Latina. En Argentina, por ejemplo, la tecnología ha ayudado a conservar al medioambiente. Durante un viaje allá, presencié el uso de hidrógeno en los carros en vez de gasolina. Este uso especializado ha ayudado a que la gente use menos combustible y es económicamente beneficioso ya que combate el alto costo del petróleo. Argentina es uno de los pocos países de Sudamérica que no cuenta con vastos campos petrolíferos. También vi el uso de la tecnología en el campo médico. En Argentina hay muchas zonas retiradas y aisladas cuya población no puede acudir al servicio médico. Ahora hay trenes que viajan a través del paisaje y llevan equipo médico portátil y hasta usan el Internet para consultar con expertos en Buenos Aires, para diagnosticar al paciente por la Red. Ese programa se llama "El tren de la Esperanza" y fue creado por jóvenes médicos argentinos que se preocupaban por el bienestar de los niños. Hace 10 años nada de eso fue posible.

Hay centenares de ejemplos más; pero si tuviera que elegir un cambio tecnológico que ha revolucionado al mundo, diría que es el teléfono celular. Los teléfonos de hoy ahora nos hablan, nos guían, nos traducen, y nos conectan al Red. Gracias a la tecnología, los sueños de hace sólo un par de años de verdad pueden convertirse en realidad.

Translation

I'm going to speak to you about how technology has played an important role in the lives of people in both my community and in the Spanish-speaking community.

I would say that in my community, technology has enriched the education in schools. Thanks to the Internet, we have access to resources for the study of language—newspapers from any Latin American country or Spain. We can even listen to news broadcasts or watch television at any time. We've stopped using dictionaries since we can use web pages from our phones to decipher words and understand their correct grammatical usage. As a result, my performance as a student has improved.

In my community, I see that parents can watch their homes, employees, children—all from a cell phone. The police can use special technology to track lost or kidnapped children through cell phone towers.

Technology has also had positive effects in Latin America. In Argentina, for example, technology has helped save the environment. During a trip there, I witnessed the use of hydrogen in cars instead of gasoline. This specialized use has helped people use less fuel and it is economically beneficial because it combats the high price of oil. Argentina is one of the few countries in South America that does not possess vast oil fields. I also saw the use of technology in the medical field. In Argentina there are many isolated areas where the population doesn't have access to medical services. There are now trains that travel through the countryside and bring portable medical equipment and even use the Internet to consult with experts in Buenos Aires to diagnose the patient over the Internet. This program is called the "Train of Hope" and was created by young Argentinean doctors who were concerned about the wellbeing of children. Ten years ago, none of this was possible.

There are hundreds of examples more; but if I had to choose one technological change that has revolutionized the world, I would say it would have to be the cell phone. The phones of today speak to us, they guide us, translate for us, and connect us to the Internet. Thanks to technology, the dreams from just a few years ago can now become reality.

Evaluation

This was a tough question, as it was so open ended. Although it seemed that the student was grasping at straws at first, it turned out to be a pretty good response. Overall, there was a lack of contrasting, and the two applications of technology didn't really have a common thread. However, the student clearly demonstrated knowledge of the target culture and did apply the variable of technology to both societies in a very creative way. The answer also flowed well and even gave a surprise at the end with a personal evaluation of technology's greatest contribution. It would probably score a 4, possibly a 5, given the strong grammar and organization it demonstrated.

REVIEW OF SPANISH VERB AND GRAMMAR FORMS

Time does not permit us to review every grammar topic covered on the AP Spanish Language and Culture Exam. Your best bet is to assume that you need to know all the grammar that you have studied. In the following pages, we will highlight the topics you should have mastered by test day. We strongly urge you to study your textbook and class notes for a more comprehensive review of grammar. If there is a topic that you don't fully understand and is not covered here, be sure to go through your textbook and ask your teacher about it well before test day. This is intended as a brief grammatical overview. It is *not* a comprehensive review. Keep in mind, however, that while there may be many grammar details to keep track of, they are not all complex or difficult topics. In other words, if you review the verb forms and grammar rules carefully and thoroughly, it can translate into higher quality responses on the exam.

BASIC TERMS

Although you won't see the following terms on the test, they are important because they will come up later in the chapter. Knowing these terms will allow you to understand the rules of grammar that you're about to review.

Noun: a person, place, or thing

EXAMPLES: Abraham Lincoln, New Jersey, a taco

Pronoun: a word that replaces a noun

EXAMPLES: Abraham Lincoln would be replaced by "he," New Jersey by "it," and a taco by "it." You'll see more about pronouns later.

Adjective: a word that describes a noun

EXAMPLES: cold, soft, colorful

Verb: an action—a word that describes what is being done in a sentence

EXAMPLE: Ron *ate* the huge breakfast.

Infinitive: the original, unconjugated form of a verb

EXAMPLES: to eat, to run, to laugh

Auxiliary Verb: the verb that precedes the past participle in the perfect tense

EXAMPLE: He *had* eaten his lunch.

Past Participle: the appropriate form of a verb when it is used with the auxiliary verb

EXAMPLE: They have *gone* to work.

Adverb: word that describes a verb, adjective, or another adverb, just like an adjective describes a noun

EXAMPLES: slowly, quickly, happily (In English, adverbs often, but don't always, end in -ly.)

Subject: the person or thing (noun) in a sentence that is performing the action

EXAMPLE: *John* wrote the song.

Compound Subject: a subject that's made up of two or more subjects or nouns

EXAMPLES: *John and Paul* wrote the song together.

Object: the person or thing (noun or pronoun) in the sentence that the action is happening to, either directly or indirectly

EXAMPLES: Mary bought *the shirt*. Joe hit *him*. Mary gave a gift to *Tim*.

Direct Object: the thing that receives the action of the verb

EXAMPLE: I see *the wall*. (The wall "receives" the action of seeing.)

Indirect Object: the person who receives the direct object

EXAMPLE: I wrote *her* a letter. (She receives a letter.)

Preposition: a word that marks the relationship (in space or time) between two other words

EXAMPLES: He received the letter *from* her. The book is *below* the chair.

Article: a word (usually a very small word) that precedes a noun

EXAMPLES: *a* watch, *the* room

That wasn't so bad, was it? Now let's put all those terms together in a few examples.

Dominic	spent	the	entire	night	here.
subject	verb	article	adjective	dir. obj.	adverb

Margaret	often	gives	me	money.
subject	adverb	verb	indir. obj. pronoun	dir. obj.

Alison and Rob	have	a	gorgeous	child.
compound subject	verb	article	adjective	dir. obj.

PRONOUNS

You already learned that a pronoun is a word that takes the place of a noun. Now you'll review what pronouns look like in Spanish. There are three basic types.

SUBJECT PRONOUNS

These are the most basic pronouns and probably the first ones you learned. Just take a moment to look them over to make sure you haven't forgotten them. Then spend some time looking over the examples that follow until you are comfortable using them.

yo	me	**nosotros/as**	us
tú	you (singular)	**vosotros/as**	you (plural)
él, ella, Ud.	him, her, you (singular)	**ellos, ellas, Uds.**	them, you (plural)

When to Use Subject Pronouns

A subject pronoun (like any other pronoun) replaces the noun that is the subject of the sentence.

Marco no pudo comprar el helado.

Marco couldn't buy the ice cream.

Who performs the action of this sentence? Marco, so he is the subject. If we wanted to use a subject pronoun in this case, we'd replace "Marco" with **"él."**

Él no pudo comprar el helado.

He couldn't buy the ice cream.

DIRECT OBJECT PRONOUNS

Direct object pronouns replace (you guessed it) the direct object in a sentence.

me	me	**nos**	us
te	you (*tú* form)	**os**	you (*vosotros* form)
lo/la	him, it (masc.)/you (*Ud.* form)/ her, it (fem.)	**los/las**	them (masc./fem.)/ you (*Uds.* form)

When to Use Direct Object Pronouns

Now let's see what it looks like when we replace the direct object with a pronoun in a sentence.

> *Marco no pudo comprar el helado.*

What couldn't Marco buy? Ice cream. Since ice cream is what's receiving the action, it's the direct object. To use the direct object pronoun, you'd replace **helado** with **lo**:

> *Marco no pudo comprar**lo**.* or *Marco no **lo** pudo comprar.*

When the direct object pronoun is used with the infinitive of a verb, it can either be tacked on to the end of the verb (the first example), or it can come before the conjugated verb in the sentence (the second example). Here is another example.

*Voy a ver**lo**.*	I'm going to see it.
***Lo** voy a ver.*	(Both sentences mean the same thing.)

The direct object pronoun also follows the verb in an affirmative command, for example.

*¡Cóme**lo**!*	Eat it!
*¡Escúcha**me**!*	Listen to me!

INDIRECT OBJECT PRONOUNS

These pronouns replace the indirect object in a sentence. Keep in mind that in Spanish, when the object is indirect, the preposition is often implied, not explicitly stated. So how can you tell the difference? In general, the indirect object is the person who receives the direct object.

me	me	**nos**	us
te	you (*tú* form)	**os**	you
le	him, her, you (*Ud.* form)	**les**	them, you (*Ud.* form)

When to Use Indirect Object Pronouns

This may seem a bit strange, but in Spanish the indirect object pronoun is often present in a sentence that contains the indirect object noun.

> *Juan **le** da el abrigo al viejo.*
>
> Juan gives the old man the coat.

Notice that the sentence contains the indirect object noun (**viejo**) and the indirect object pronoun (**le**). This is often necessary to clarify the identity of the indirect object pronoun, or to emphasize that identity. Typically, an expression of clarification is used with the pronouns **le** and **les** and **se** (see below), but is not used with other pronouns.

*María **nos** ayudó.*	María helped us.
*Juan **me** trae el suéter.*	Juan brings me the sweater.

The identity of the indirect object is obvious with the choice of pronoun in these examples and so is not necessary for clarification. It may be used, however, to emphasize the identity of the indirect object.

*No **me** lo trajeron a mí; **te** lo trajeron a ti.*	They didn't bring it to **me**; they brought it to **you.**

We would change our intonation to emphasize these words in English. This doesn't happen in Spanish; the expressions **a mí** and **a ti** serve the same function.

Se is used in place of **le** and **les** whenever the pronoun that follows begins with **l.**

*¿**Le** cuentas la noticia a María?*	Are you telling Maria the news?
*Sí, **se** la cuento **a María.***	Yes, I'm telling it to her.
*¿**Les** prestas los guantes a los estudiantes?*	Do you lend gloves to the students?
*No, no **se** los presto **a ellos.***	No, I don't lend them to them.

Notice that **le** changes to **se** in the first example and **les** to **se** in the second because the direct object pronoun that follows begins with an **l.** Notice also the inclusion of **a María** and **a ellos** to clarify the identity of **se** in each example.

PREPOSITIONAL PRONOUNS

As we mentioned earlier, there are some pronouns that take an explicitly stated preposition, and they're different from the indirect object pronouns. The prepositional pronouns are as follows.

mí	me	**nosotros/nosotras**	us
ti/Ud.	you (*tú* form-*Ud.* form)	**vosotros/vosotras/Uds.**	you (plural)
él/ella/Ud.	him/her	**ellos/ellas/Uds.**	them

When to Use Prepositional Pronouns

Consider the following examples:

1. *Cómprale un regalo de cumpleaños.*	Buy him a birthday present.
2. *Vamos al teatro sin él.*	We're going to the theater **without** him.

Notice that in the first example, "him" is translated as **le,** whereas in the second, "him" is translated as **él.** What exactly is the deal with that?! Why isn't it the same word in Spanish as in English? In Spanish, the different pronouns distinguish the different functions of the word within the sentence.

In the first example, "him" is the indirect object of the verb "to buy" (Buy the gift for whom? For him—"him" receives the direct object), so we use the indirect object pronoun **le.** In the second example, however, "him" is the object of the preposition "without," so we use the prepositional pronoun **"él."** Here are some more examples that involve the prepositional pronouns. Notice that they all have explicitly stated prepositions.

*Las flores son **para** ti.*	The flowers are **for** you.
*Estamos enojados **con** él.*	We are angry **with** him.
*Quieren ir de vacaciones **sin** Uds.*	They want to go on vacation **without** you.

In two special cases, when the preposition is **con** and the object of the preposition is **mí** or **ti,** the preposition and the pronoun are combined to form **conmigo** (with me) and **contigo** (with you).

*¿Quieres ir al concierto **conmigo**?*	Do you want to go to the concert **with me?**
*No, no puedo ir **contigo**.*	No, I can't go **with you.**

When the subject is **él, ella, ellos, ellas, Ud.,** or **Uds.,** and the object of the preposition is the **same** as the subject, the prepositional pronoun is **sí,** and is usually accompanied by **mismo/a** or **mismos/as:**

*Alejandro es muy egoísta. Siempre habla de **sí mismo.***
Alejandro is very egotistical. He always talks about **himself.**
*Ellos compran ropa para **sí mismos** cuando van de compras.*
They buy clothes for **themselves** when they go shopping.

POSSESSIVE ADJECTIVES AND PRONOUNS

Possessive adjectives and pronouns are used to indicate ownership. When you want to let someone know what's yours, use the following pronouns or adjectives:

STRESSED POSSESSIVE ADJECTIVES

mío/mía	mine	**nuestro/nuestra**	ours
tuyo/tuya	yours (fam.)	**vuestro/vuestra**	yours
suyo/suya	his, hers, yours (for *Ud.*)	**suyo/suya**	theirs, yours (for *Uds.*)

UNSTRESSED POSSESSIVE ADJECTIVES

mi	my	**nuestro/nuestra**	our
tu	your (fam.)	**vuestro/vuestra**	yours
su	his/her/your (for *Ud.*)	**su**	their, your (for *Uds.*)

When to Use Possessive Adjectives

The first question is, "When do you use an unstressed adjective, and when do you use a stressed adjective?" Check out these examples, and then we'll see what the rule is.

*Ésta es **mi** casa.*	*Esta casa es **mía.***
This is **my** house.	This house is **mine.**
*Aquí está **tu** cartera.*	*Esta cartera es **tuya.***
Here is **your** wallet.	This wallet is **yours.**

The difference between stressed and unstressed possessive adjectives is emphasis, as opposed to meaning. Saying "This is my house" puts emphasis on the house, while saying "This house is mine," takes the focus off of the house and stresses the identity of its owner—me. To avoid getting confused, just remember that unstressed is the Spanish equivalent of "my" and stressed is the Spanish equivalent of "mine."

In terms of structure, there is an important difference between the two types of adjectives, but it's an easy one to remember: Stressed adjectives come after the verb, but unstressed adjectives come before the noun. Notice that neither type agrees with the possessor; they agree with the thing possessed.

If it's not clear to you why these are adjectives when they look so much like pronouns, consider their function. When you say "my house," the noun "house" is being described by "my." Any word that describes a noun is an adjective, even if that word looks a lot like a pronoun. The key is how it's being used in the sentence.

POSSESSIVE PRONOUNS

Possessive pronouns look like stressed possessive adjectives, but they mean something different. Possessive pronouns *replace* nouns; they don't *describe* them.

When to Use Possessive Pronouns

This type of pronoun is formed by combining the article of the noun that's being replaced with the appropriate stressed possessive adjective. Just like stressed possessive adjectives, possessive pronouns must agree in gender and number with the nouns they replace.

Mi bicicleta es azul.	*La mía es azul.*
My bicycle is blue.	**Mine** is blue.

Notice how the pronoun not only shows possession, but also replaces the noun. Here are some more examples.

Mis zapatos son caros.	*Los míos son caros.*
My shoes are expensive.	**Mine** are expensive.
Tu automóvil es rápido.	*El tuyo es rápido.*
Your car is fast.	**Yours** is fast.
No me gustaban los discos que ellos trajeron.	*No me gustaban los suyos.*
I didn't like the records they brought.	I didn't like **theirs.**

REFLEXIVE PRONOUNS

Remember those reflexive verbs you learned about in class (**ponerse, hacerse,** and so on)? Those all have a common characteristic, which is that they indicate the action is being done to or for oneself. When those verbs are conjugated, the reflexive pronoun (which is always **se** in the infinitive) changes according to the subject.

me	myself	**nos**	ourselves
te	yourself (fam.)	**os**	yourselves (fam.)
se	him/herself/yourself (for *Ud.*)	**se**	themselves/yourselves (for *Uds.*)

Reflexive pronouns are used when the subject and indirect object of the sentence are the same. This may sound kind of strange, but after you see some examples it ought to make more sense.

> *Alicia se pone el **maquillaje**.*
>
> **Alicia** puts on makeup.
>
> What does she put on? **Makeup**—direct object.
>
> Who receives the makeup? **Alicia**—she's also the subject.

The action is thus *reflected* back upon itself: Alicia does the action and then receives it. No outside influences are involved.

Another meaning for reflexive verbs is literally that the person does something directly to or for him/herself.

> *Rosa **se cortó** con el cuchillo.*
>
> Rosa **cut herself** with the knife.
>
> *Roberto tiene que **comprarse** una libreta nueva.*
>
> Roberto has to **buy himself** a new notebook.

THE RELATIVE PRONOUNS (QUE, QUIEN, AND QUIENES)

Relative pronouns connect a noun or pronoun to a clause that describes the noun or pronoun. They may represent people or things or ideas, and they may function as subjects, direct or indirect objects, or as objects of prepositions. Unlike English, the relative pronouns cannot be omitted in Spanish.

Let's look at some examples with relative pronouns in their various functions.

Remember that **que** is used to refer to people and things. **Quien(es)** is used to refer only to people.

1. As a subject:	*Busco el libro que estaba en mi mochila.*
	I am looking for the book that was in my bookbag.
2. As a direct object:	*Hicimos la tarea que la profesora nos asignó.*
	We did the assignment that the professor gave us.
3. As an indirect object:	*No conozco a la prima a quien le mandé la invitación.*
	I don't know the cousin to whom I sent the invitation.
4. As an object of a preposition:	*Ud. no conoce a los alumnos de quienes hablo.*
	You don't know the students who I am talking about.

The relative pronoun **cuyo** acts as an adjective and agrees with the noun it introduces, not the possessor.

> *El alumno, cuyas notas son excelentes, es un chico muy simpático.*
>
> The student, whose grades are excellent, is a very nice boy.

INTERROGATIVE WORDS

You probably know most of your interrogative words in Spanish by this time, but it wouldn't hurt for you to review them. Remember that they all have an accent when used as part of a question. Let's look briefly at one common student mistake: **Cuál** (meaning *which* or *what*) is used when a choice is involved. It's used in place of **que** before the verb **ser**, and it has only two forms: singular (**cuál**) and plural (**cuáles**). Both **cuál** and the verb **ser** must agree in number with the thing(s) being asked about.

¿Cuál es tu ciudad favorita?	**What** is your favorite city?
¿Cuáles son nuestros regalos?	**Which** presents are ours?

ADJECTIVES

Demonstrative pronouns have an accent on the first "**e.**" The adjectives don't. First, learn the construction and meaning.

este/esta	this (one)	**estos/estas**	these
ese/esa	that (one)	**esos/esas**	those
aquel/aquella	that (one over there)	**aquellos/aquellas**	those (over there)

Adjective or Pronoun—Which Is It?

If the demonstrative word comes before a noun, then it is an adjective.

Este plato de arroz con pollo es mío.	**This** plate of chicken and rice is mine.
Ese edificio es de mi hermano.	**That** building is my brother's.

If the demonstrative word takes the place of a noun, then it's a pronoun.

Dije que éste es mío.	I said that this one is mine.
Sabemos que ése es de mi hermano.	We know **that one** is my brother's.

When used as adjectives, these words mean *this*, *that*, and so on. When used as pronouns, they mean *this one*, *that one*, and so on.

PRONOUN SUMMARY

You should know the following types of pronouns: subject, object (direct and indirect), possessive, prepositional, reflexive, and demonstrative.

- Don't just memorize what the different pronouns look like! Recognizing them is important, but it's just as important that you understand how and when to use them.

- When selecting your final answer choices, don't forget about POE. Something simple (like the gender of a pronoun) is easy to overlook if you're not on your toes. Before you start thinking about grammar, cancel answers that are wrong based on flagrant stuff like gender, singular versus plural, and so on.

- If all else fails, your ear can sometimes be your guide. In learning Spanish, you probably spoke and heard the language on a pretty regular basis, and so you have a clue as to what correct Spanish sounds like. You don't want to use your ear if you can eliminate answers based on the rules of grammar, but if you've exhausted the rules and you're down to two answers, one of which sounds a lot better than the other, choose the correct-sounding one. The fact is many grammatical rules were born out of a desire to make the language sound good.

QUIZ: HOW WELL DO YOU KNOW YOUR PRONOUNS?

1. Si él puede hacerlo solo, yo no _____ tengo que ayudar.

    (A) la

    (B) lo

    (C) le

    (D) los

2. Pedimos asientos cerca de una ventanilla, pero _____ dieron éstos.

    (A) nos

    (B) les

    (C) nuestros

    (D) me

3. Cuando sus estudiantes se portan mal, la profesora _____ castiga.

    (A) las

    (B) los

    (C) les

    (D) le

4. ¿Son _____ aquellos guantes que están sobre la butaca?

    (A) mío

    (B) mía

    (C) míos

    (D) mías

5. Para tus cumpleaños _____ daré un caballo nuevo.

    (A) le

    (B) te

    (C) a ti

    (D) me

6. ¿ _____ es tu cantante favorito?

    (A) Quién

    (B) Cuál

    (C) Quiénes

    (D) Qué

7. ¿ _____ prefieres? ¿El azul o el rojo?

    (A) Qué

    (B) Cuál

    (C) Cuáles

    (D) Ese

VERBS

You probably learned what felt like a zillion different verbs and tenses in Spanish class. For the purposes of the AP Spanish Language and Culture Exam, you should focus on recognizing clues in the sentences that suggest certain tenses, and then finding the answer in the appropriate tense. Even if you don't know which answer is in the tense that corresponds to the sentence, you can still cancel answers that definitely aren't correct. Use POE! A brief review of the tenses that show up on the test is probably a good place to begin, so let's get right to it.

THE PRESENT TENSE (A.K.A. THE PRESENT INDICATIVE)

The present tense is the easiest, and probably the first, tense that you ever learned. It is used when the action is happening in the present, as in the following example:

> *Yo **hablo** con mis amigos cada día.*
>
> I **speak** with my friends each day.

You should know the present tense inside and out if you are enrolled in an AP Spanish class, but take a quick glance at the following verb conjugations just to refresh your memory:

	trabajar	vender	escribir
yo	trabaj**o**	vend**o**	escrib**o**
tú (fam.)	trabaj**as**	vend**es**	escrib**es**
él/ella/Ud.	trabaj**a**	vend**e**	escrib**e**
nosotros/nosotras	trabaj**amos**	vend**emos**	escrib**imos**
vosotros/vosotras (fam.)	trabaj**áis**	vend**éis**	escrib**ís**
ellos/ellas/Uds.	trabaj**an**	vend**en**	escrib**en**

THE PAST TENSE (A.K.A. THE PRETERITE)

> *Ayer yo **hablé** con mis amigos.*
>
> Yesterday I **spoke** with my friends. (The action began and ended.)

There are many different tenses that are considered past tenses—all of which describe actions that took place at various points in the past. There are, for example, different tenses for saying "I spoke," "I was speaking," "I have spoken," and so on. Let's start by reviewing the most basic of these: the plain past tense.

	trabajar	vender	escribir
yo	trabaj**é**	vend**í**	escrib**í**
tú (fam.)	trabaja**ste**	vend**iste**	escrib**iste**
él/ella/Ud.	trabaj**ó**	vend**ió**	escrib**ió**
nosotros/nosotras	trabaj**amos**	vend**imos**	escrib**imos**
vosotros/vosotras	trabaj**asteis**	vend**isteis**	escrib**isteis**
ellos/ellas/Uds.	trabaj**aron**	vend**ieron**	escrib**ieron**

The easiest forms to spot are the first and third person singular (**yo** and **él/ella/Ud.** forms) because of the accent.

THE FUTURE TENSE

The future tense is used to describe things that will *definitely* happen in the future. The reason we stress definitely is that there is a different verbal mode (the dreaded subjunctive) used to describe things that *may* happen in the future. In Spanish, just as in English, there is a difference between being certain ("I will go") and being uncertain ("I may go"), and different forms are used for the different degrees of certainty. You'll see the fancier stuff later. First take a look at the regular future tense.

*Mañana yo **hablaré** con mis amigos.*

Tomorrow I **will speak** with my friends.

Notice that what takes two words to say in English (**will speak**) takes only one word to say in Spanish (**hablaré**). The future is a nice, simple tense (no auxiliary verb, only one word), which is easy to spot thanks to the accents and the structure. The future is formed by tacking on the appropriate ending to the infinitive of the verb *without dropping the -ar, -er, or -ir.*

	trabajar	vender	escribir
yo	trabajar**é**	vender**é**	escribir**é**
tú (fam.)	trabajar**ás**	vender**ás**	escribir**ás**
él/ella/Ud.	trabajar**á**	vender**á**	escribir**á**
nosotros/nosotras	trabajar**emos**	vender**emos**	escribir**emos**
vosotros/vosotras	trabajar**éis**	vender**éis**	escribir**éis**
ellos/ellas/Uds.	trabajar**án**	vender**án**	escribir**án**

THE PRESENT PERFECT

The present perfect is used to refer to an action that began in the past and is continuing into the present (and possibly beyond). It is also used to describe actions that were completed very close to the present. Compare these sentences.

> 1. *Ayer **hablé** con mis amigos.*
>   Yesterday **I spoke** with my friends.
>
>   ***Decidiste** no ir al cine.*
>   **You decided** not to go to the movies.
>
> 2. ***He hablado** mucho con mis amigos recientemente.*
>   **I have spoken** a lot with my friends lately.
>
>   ***Has decidido** hacerte abogado.*
>   **You have decided** (recently) to become a lawyer.

The first examples are just the plain past tense: You started and finished talking with your friends yesterday, and you completed the process of deciding not to go to the movies. In the second examples, the use of the present perfect tense moves the action to the very recent past, instead of leaving it in the more distant past. The present perfect, then, is essentially a more precise verb form of the past, used when the speaker wants to indicate that an action happened very recently in the past.

Spotting the perfect tenses is rather easy. This is a compound tense, meaning that it is formed by combining two verbs: a tense of the auxiliary (or helping) verb **haber** (present, imperfect, future, conditional) and the past participle of the main verb.

	trabajar	vender	escribir
yo	**he** trabaj**ado**	**he** vend**ido**	**he** escrito
tú (fam.)	**has** trabaj**ado**	**has** vend**ido**	**has** escrito
él/ella/Ud.	**ha** trabaj**ado**	**ha** vend**ido**	**ha** escrito
nosotros/nosotras	**hemos** trabaj**ado**	**hemos** vend**ido**	**hemos** escrito
vosotros/vosotras	**habéis** trabaj**ado**	**habéis** vend**ido**	**habéis** escrito
ellos/ellas/Uds.	**han** trabaj**ado**	**han** vend**ido**	**han** escrito

Most past participles are formed by dropping the last two letters from the infinitive and adding **-ido** (for **-er** and **-ir** verbs) or **-ado** (for **-ar** verbs). **Escribir** has an irregular past participle, as do some other verbs, but don't worry about it. This is no problem, since the irregulars still look and sound like the regulars, and, with respect to this tense, you still know it's the present perfect because of **haber.**

THE IMPERFECT

The imperfect is yet another past tense. It is used to describe actions that occurred continuously in the past and exhibited no definitive end at that time. This is different from the preterite, which describes "one-time" actions that began and ended at the moment in the past that is being described. Look at the two together, and the difference between them will become clearer.

*Ayer **yo hablé** con mis amigos y luego **me fui.***

Yesterday **I spoke** with my friends and then left.

(The act of speaking obviously ended, because I left afterward.)

*Yo **hablaba** con mis amigos mientras **caminábamos.***

I spoke with my friends while we walked.

(The act of speaking was **in progress** at that moment, along with walking.)

The imperfect is also used to describe conditions or circumstances in the past, since these are obviously ongoing occurrences.

Era una noche oscura y tormentosa.

It was a dark and stormy night.

*Cuando **tenía** diez años…*

When **I was** ten years old…

In the first example, it didn't just start or just stop being a stormy night, did it? Was the dark and stormy night already a past event at that point? No. The dark and stormy night was **in progress** at that moment, so the imperfect is used, not the preterite.

In the second example, did I start or stop being ten years old at that point? Neither. Was being ten already a past event at the moment I am describing? No. I was simply in the process of being ten years old at that moment in the past, so the imperfect is the more precise tense to use.

Make sense? Good; now check out the conjugation.

	trabajar	vender	escribir
yo	trabaj**aba**	vend**ía**	escrib**ía**
tú (fam.)	trabaj**abas**	vend**ías**	escrib**ías**
él/ella/Ud.	trabaj**aba**	vend**ía**	escrib**ía**
nosotros/nosotras	trabaj**ábamos**	vend**íamos**	escrib**íamos**
vosotros/vosotras	trabaj**abais**	vend**íais**	escrib**íais**
ellos/ellas/Uds.	trabaj**aban**	vend**ían**	escrib**ían**

Although the imperfect is similar to the other past tenses you've seen (e.g., the preterite and the present perfect), because it speaks of past actions, it looks quite different. That's the key since half of your job is just to know what the different tenses look like. The toughest part will be distinguishing the preterite from the imperfect.

BACK TO THE FUTURE: THE CONDITIONAL

Remember the future tense? (It's the one that is used to describe actions that are *definitely* going to happen in the future.) Well, now you will learn the other future tense you need to know; the one that is used to describe things that *may* happen in the future.

The conditional describes what could, would, or may happen in the future.

> Me **gustaría** hablar con mis amigos cada día.
>
> I **would like** to talk to my friends each day.
>
> Con más tiempo, **podría** hablar con ellos el día entero.
>
> With more time, I **could** speak with them all day long.
>
> Si gastara cinco pesos, solamente me **quedarían** tres.
>
> If I spent (were to spend) five dollars, I **would have** only three left.

It can also be used to make a request in a more polite way.

> ¿**Puedes** prestar atención?   ¿**Podrías** prestar atención?
>
> **Can you** pay attention?   **Could you** pay attention?

The conditional is formed by taking the future stem of the verb (which is the infinitive) and adding the conditional ending.

	trabajar	vender	escribir
yo	trabajar**ía**	vender**ía**	escribir**ía**
tú (fam.)	trabajar**ías**	vender**ías**	escribir**ías**
él/ella/Ud.	trabajar**ía**	vender**ía**	escribir**ía**
nosotros/nosotras	trabajar**íamos**	vender**íamos**	escribir**íamos**
vosotros/vosotras	trabajar**íais**	vender**íais**	escribir**íais**
ellos/ellas/Uds.	trabajar**ían**	vender**ían**	escribir**ían**

To avoid confusing the conditional with the future, concentrate on the conditional endings. The big difference is the accented **í**, which is in the conditional, but not in the future.

FUTURE	CONDITIONAL
trabajaré	trabajaría
venderán	venderían
escribiremos	escribiríamos

THE SUBJUNCTIVE

Don't give up now! Just two more verb modes (not tenses—the subjunctive is a different *manner* of speaking) and you'll be done with all this verb business (give or take a couple of special topics).

The Present Subjunctive

The present subjunctive is used in sentences that have *two distinct subjects* in *two different clauses*, generally (on this test, at least) in four situations.

1. When a *desire* or *wish* is involved.
   *Quiero que **comas** los vegetales.*
   I want you **to eat** the vegetables.
   *Ordenamos que Uds. nos **sigan.***
   We order you (pl.) **to follow** us.

2. When *emotion* is involved.
   *Me alegro que **haga** buen tiempo hoy.*
   I am happy that the weather **is** nice today.
   *Te enoja que tu novio nunca te **escuche.***
   It makes you angry that your boyfriend never **listens** to you.

3. When *doubt* is involved.
   *Ellos no creen que **digamos** la verdad.*
   They don't believe that **we are telling** the truth.
   *Jorge duda que su equipo **vaya** a ganar el campeonato.*
   Jorge doubts that his team **is going** to win the championship.

4. When an *impersonal expression* or *subjective commentary* is made.
   *Es ridículo que no **pueda** encontrar mis llaves.*
   It's ridiculous that I **can't** find my keys.
   *Es importante que los estudiantes **estudien** mucho.*
   It's important that students **study** a lot.

The subjunctive is formed by taking the **yo** form of the present tense, dropping the **-o**, and adding the appropriate ending.

	trabajar	vender	escribir
yo	trabaj**e**	vend**a**	escrib**a**
tú (fam.)	trabaj**es**	vend**as**	escrib**as**
él/ella/Ud.	trabaj**e**	vend**a**	escrib**a**
nosotros/nosotras	trabaj**emos**	vend**amos**	escrib**amos**
vosotros/vosotras	trabaj**éis**	vend**áis**	escrib**áis**
ellos/ellas/Uds.	trabaj**en**	vend**an**	escrib**an**

Commands are very similar to the present subjunctive form, perhaps because they are an obvious attempt to tell someone what to do. Let's look briefly at the formation of the regular commands.

	hablar	comer	subir
tú (fam.)	habla, no hables	come, no comas	sube, no subas
él/ella/Ud.	hable	coma	suba
nosotros/nosotras	hablemos	comamos	subamos
vosotros/vosotras	hablad, no habléis	comed, no comáis	subid, no subáis
ellos/ellas/Uds.	hablen	coman	suban

Remember: The affirmative **tú** (accent) form derives from the third person present singular tense, except for the verbs that are irregular in the **tú** (accent) form. The affirmative **vosotros** form comes from the infinitive, so the 'r' is dropped and the 'd' is added. All other command forms come from the subjunctive. ¡*Muy fácil*!

¡Trabaja con tu padre!	**¡Vende** el coche!	**¡Escribe** la carta!
Work with your father!	**Sell** the car!	**Write** the letter!

The Imperfect Subjunctive

This version of the subjunctive is used with the same expressions as the present subjunctive (wish or desire, emotion, doubt, impersonal commentaries), but it's used in the *past tense*.

*Quería que **comieras** los vegetales.*

I wanted you **to eat** the vegetables.

*Me alegré que **hiciera** buen tiempo ayer.*

I was happy that the weather **was** nice yesterday.

*No creían que **dijéramos** la verdad.*

They didn't believe that **we told** the truth.

*Era ridículo que no **pudiera** encontrar mis llaves.*

It was ridiculous that **I couldn't** find my keys.

One very important thing to notice in the examples above is that because the *expression* is in the past, you use the imperfect subjunctive. If you're looking at a sentence that you know takes the subjunctive, but you're not sure whether it's present or imperfect, focus on the expression. If the expression is in the present, use the present subjunctive. If the expression is in the past, use the imperfect subjunctive.

The imperfect subjunctive is also always used after the expression **como si,** which means "as if." This expression is used to describe hypothetical situations.

*Él habla como si **supiera** todo.*

He speaks as if **he knew** it all.

*Gastamos dinero como si **fuéramos** millonarios.*

We spend money as if **we were** millionaires.

The imperfect subjunctive is formed by taking the **ellos/ellas/Uds.** form of the preterite (which you already know, right?) and adding the correct ending.

	trabajar	vender	escribir
yo	trabajara	vendiera	escribiera
tú (fam.)	trabajaras	vendieras	escribieras
él/ella/Uds.	trabajara	vendiera	escribiera
nosotros/nosotras	trabajáramos	vendiéramos	escribiéramos
vosotros/vosotras	trabajarais	vendierais	escribierais
ellos/ellas/Uds.	trabajaran	vendieran	escribieran

Verbs that are in the imperfect subjunctive shouldn't be too tough to spot when they show up in the answer choices. The imperfect subjunctive has completely different endings from the preterite. It's not a compound tense, so you won't confuse it with the present perfect. The stems are different from the present subjunctive, so distinguishing between those two shouldn't be a problem.

SPECIAL TOPICS

Ser versus Estar

The verbs **ser** and **estar** both mean "to be" when translated into English. You may wonder, "Why is it necessary to have two verbs that mean exactly the same thing?" Good question. The answer is that in Spanish, unlike in English, there is a distinction between temporary states of being (e.g., "I am hungry") and fixed, or permanent states of being (e.g., "I am Cuban"). Although this difference seems pretty simple and easy to follow, there are some cases when it isn't so clear. Consider the following examples:

> El señor González _____ mi doctor.

> Cynthia _____ mi novia.

Would you use **ser** or **estar** in these two sentences? After all, Cynthia may or may not be your girl-friend forever, and the same goes for Mr. González's status as your doctor. You may get rid of both of them tomorrow (or one of them may get rid of you)! So which verb do you use?

In both cases, the answer is **ser**, because in both cases there is no *foreseeable* end to the relationships described. In other words, even though they may change, nothing in either sentence gives any reason to think they will. So whether you and Cynthia go on to marry or she dumps you tomorrow, you would be correct if you used **ser**. When in doubt, ask yourself, "does this action/condition have a definite end in the near or immediate future?" If so, use **estar**. Otherwise, use **ser.** Try the following drill:

Fill in the blank with the correct form of **ser** or **estar**.

1. Pablo _está_ muy cansado.

2. El automóvil _está_ descompuesto.

3. No puedo salir de casa esta noche porque _es_ castigado.

4. Mi hermano _es_ muy gracioso.

5. Mis profesores _es_ demasiado serios.

6. Ayer salí sin abrigo, y hoy _estoy_ enfermo.

7. Los tacos que mi madre cocina _están_ ricos.

8. ¡No podemos empezar! Todavía no _estamos_ listos.

Answers: 1) está 2) está 3) estoy 4) es 5) son 6) estoy 7) son 8) estamos

Don't assume that certain adjectives (like **enfermo**, for example) necessarily take **estar**. If you're saying someone is sick as in "ill," then **estar** is appropriate. If you're saying that someone is sick, as in, "a sickly person," then **ser** is correct.

Unfortunately, usage is not the only tough thing about **ser** and **estar.** They are both irregular verbs. Spend a little time reviewing the conjugations of **ser** and **estar** before you move on.

estar

>**present:** estoy, estás, está, estamos, estáis, están
>
>**preterite:** estuve, estuviste, estuvo, estuvimos, estuvistéis, estuvieron
>
>**pres. subj.:** esté, estés, esté, estemos, estéis, estén
>
>**imp. subj.:** estuviera, estuvieras, estuviera, estuviéramos, estuvierais, estuvieran

The other tenses of **estar** follow the regular patterns for **-ar** verbs.

ser

>**present:** soy, eres, es, somos, sois, son
>
>**imperfect:** era, eras, era, éramos, erais, eran
>
>**preterite:** fui, fuiste, fue, fuimos, fuistéis, fueron
>
>**pres. subj.:** sea, seas, sea, seamos, seáis, sean
>
>**imp. subj.:** fuera, fueras, fuera, fuéramos, fuerais, fueran

The other tenses of **ser** follow the regular patterns for **-er** verbs.

Conocer versus *Saber*

As you probably remember from Spanish I, there is another pair of verbs that have the same English translation but are used differently in Spanish. However, don't worry; these two have (for the most part) regular conjugations, and knowing when to use them is really very straightforward.

The words **conocer** and **saber** both mean "to know." In Spanish, knowing a person or a thing (basically, a noun) is different from knowing a piece of information. Compare the uses of **conocer** and **saber** in these sentences.

>*¿Sabes cuánto cuesta la camisa?*
>
>**Do you know** how much the shirt costs?
>
>*¿Conoces a mi primo?*
>
>**Do you know** my cousin?
>
>*Sabemos que Pelé era un gran futbolista.*
>
>**We know** that Pelé was a great soccer player.
>
>*Conocemos a Pelé.*
>
>**We know** Pelé.

When what's known is a person, place, or thing, use **conocer.** It's like the English, "acquainted with." When what's known is a fact, use **saber.** The same basic rule holds for questions.

¿Sabe a qué hora llega el presidente?

Do you know at what time the president arrives?

¿Conoce al presidente?

Do you know the president?

Now that you know how they're used, take a look at their conjugations.

conocer

present: conozco, conoces, conoce, conocemos, conocéis, conocen

pres. subj.: conozca, conozcas, conozca, conozcamos, conozcáis, conozcan

The other tenses of **conocer** follow the regular **-er** pattern.

saber

present: sé, sabes, sabe, sabemos, sabéis, saben

preterite: supe, supiste, supo, supimos, supistéis, supieron

future: sabré, sabrás, sabrá, sabremos, sabréis, sabrán

conditional: sabría, sabrías, sabría, sabríamos, sabríais, sabrían

pres. subj.: sepa, sepas, sepa, sepamos, sepáis, sepan

imp. subj.: supiera, supieras, supiera, supiéramos, supiéráis, supieran

In the following drill, fill in the blanks with the correct form of **conocer** or **saber:**

1. ¡Él _sabe_ cocinar muy bien!

2. ¿ _Sabes_ el libro que ganó el premio? (tú)

3. Las mujeres _saben_ bailar como si fueran profesionales.

4. ¿Es verdad que _conoces_ a Michael Jackson? (ustedes)

5. Es importante _sabe_ nadar.

6. No _saber_ cómo voy a ganar la carrera.

7. ¿Cómo puede ser que tú no _se_ la casa donde viviste?

8. Los dos abogados no se _conocen_ el uno al otro porque nunca han trabajado juntos.

9. _Sé_ que vamos a divertirnos en el circo esta noche. (yo)

VERB SUMMARY

The tenses you need to know are the present, past, future, and perfect tenses; both subjunctive forms; and the command forms. You also need to know the subjunctive mode (both present and imperfect as well as the commands). In terms of memorizing and reviewing them, we think the best approach is to lump them together in the following way:

Present Tenses	Past Tenses	Future Tenses	Subjunctive	Commands
Present	Preterite	Future	Present	
	Imperfect	Conditional	Imperfect	
	Present perfect			

By thinking in terms of these groupings, you'll find that eliminating answers is a snap once you've determined the tense of the sentence. That is your first step on a question that tests your knowledge of verb tenses: Determine the tense of the sentence (or at least whether it's a past, present, or future tense), and cancel.

When memorizing the uses of the different tenses, focus on clues that point to one tense or another.

- There are certain expressions (wish or desire, emotion, doubt, and impersonal commentaries) that tell you to use the subjunctive, and whether the expression is in the present or the past will tell you which subjunctive form to use.

- To distinguish between future and conditional, focus on the certainty of the event's occurrence.

- The three past tenses are differentiated by the end (or lack thereof) of the action and when that end occurred (if it occurred at all). If the action had a clear beginning and ending in the past, use the regular past. If the action was a continuous action in the past, use the imperfect. If the action began in the past and is continuing into the present, or ended very close to the present, use the present perfect.

- Recognizing the different tenses shouldn't be too tough if you focus on superficial characteristics.

- Certain tenses have accents, while others do not.

- Review all the verb forms by studying your textbook.

Quiz: How Well Do You Know Your Verbs?

1. Cuando tenga dinero, te _____ un automóvil de lujo.

   (A) compraré

   (B) compré

   (C) compraría

   (D) compraste

2. Quiero que _____ la tarea antes de acostarte.

   (A) hiciste

   (B) hace

   (C) haga

   (D) hagas

3. El año pasado nosotros _____ a México para las vacaciones.

   (A) iremos

   (B) fuimos

   (C) iríamos

   (D) vamos

4. Si tuvieran tiempo, ellos _____ el tiempo relajándose.

   (A) pasan

   (B) pasaban

   (C) pasen

   (D) pasarían

5. Esperaba que Uds. _____ a construir el barco.

   (A) ayudarían

   (B) ayudaran

   (C) ayudaron

   (D) ayudan

6. Carlos _____ mucho tiempo estudiando la biología últimamente.

   (A) pasó

   (B) pasaría

   (C) pasaba

   (D) ha pasado

PREPOSITIONS

Prepositions are those little words that show the relationship between two other words. In English, they're words such as to, from, at, for, about, and so on. In Spanish, they're words like *a*, *de*, *sobre*, and so on.

Part of what you need to know about prepositions is what the different ones mean. That's the easy part. The other thing you need to know is how and when to use them. You need to know which verbs and expressions take prepositions and which prepositions they take. This isn't too difficult to learn, but it can be tricky.

COMMON PREPOSITIONS AND THEIR USES

- **a:** to; at

  ¿Vamos a la obra de teatro esta noche?

  Are we going to the play tonight?

  Llegamos a las cinco.

  We arrived at 5:00.

- **de:** of; from

  Son las gafas de mi hermano.

  Those are my brother's glasses. (Literally, the glasses of my brother.)

  Soy de la Argentina.

  I am from Argentina.

- **con:** with

  Me gusta mucho el arroz con pollo.

  I like chicken with rice a lot.

- **sobre:** on; about; over

  La chaqueta está sobre la mesa.

  The jacket is on the table.

  La conferencia es sobre la prevención del SIDA.

  The conference is about AIDS prevention.

  Los Yankees triunfaron sobre los Braves en la serie mundial.

  The Yankees triumphed over the Braves in the World Series.

- **antes de:** before

  Antes de salir quiero ponerme un sombrero.

  Before leaving I want to put on a hat.

- **después de:** after

  Después de la cena me gusta caminar un poco.

  After dinner I like to walk a little.

- **en:** in

    Regresan en una hora.

    They'll be back in an hour.

    Alguien está en el baño.

    Someone is in the bathroom.

- **entre:** between

    La carnicería está entre la pescadería y el cine.

    The butcher shop is between the fish store and the cinema.

    La conferencia duró entre dos y tres horas.

    The conference lasted between two and three hours.

- **durante:** during; for

    Durante el verano me gusta nadar cada día.

    During the summer I like to swim each day.

    Trabajé con mi amigo durante quince años.

    I worked with my friend for fifteen years.

- **desde:** since; from

    He tomado vitaminas desde mi juventud.

    I've been taking vitamins since childhood.

    Se pueden ver las montañas desde aquí.

    The mountains can be seen from here.

PARA versus *POR*

The prepositions **para** and **por** both mean "for" (as well as other things, depending on context), but they are used for different situations, and so they tend to cause a bit of confusion. Luckily, there are some pretty clear-cut rules as to when you use **para** and when you use **por** because they both tend to sound fine even when they're being used incorrectly. Try to avoid using your ear when choosing between these two.

When to Use *Para*

The following are examples of the most common situations in which **para** is used. Instead of memorizing some stuffy rule, we suggest that you get a feel for what types of situations imply the use of **para,** so that when you see those situations come up on your AP Spanish Language and Culture Exam, you'll recognize them.

The preposition **para,** in very general terms, expresses the idea of *destination*, but in a very broad sense.

- **Destination in time**
  *El helado es **para** mañana.*
  The ice cream is for tomorrow. (Tomorrow is the ice cream's destination.)

- **Destination in space**
  *Me voy **para** el mercado.*
  I'm leaving for the market. (The market is my destination.)

- **Destination of purpose**
  *Compraste un regalo **para** Luis.*
  You bought a gift for Luis. (Luis is the destination of your purchase.)
  *Estudiamos **para** sacar buenas notas.*
  We study to get good grades. (Good grades are the destination of our studies.)

- **Destination of work**
  *Trabajo **para** IBM.*
  I work for IBM. (IBM is the destination of my work.)

Two uses of **para** do not indicate a sense of destination.

- **To express opinion**
  ***Para** mí, el lunes es el día más largo de la semana.*
  For me, Monday is the longest day of the week.

- **To qualify or offer a point of reference**
  ***Para** un muchacho joven, tiene muchísimo talento.*
  For a young boy, he has a lot of talent.

When to Use *Por*

Chances are, if you're not discussing destination in any way, shape, or form, or the other two uses of **para,** then you'll need to use **por.** If this general rule isn't enough for you, however, study the following possibilities and you should have all the bases covered.

- **To express how you got somewhere (by)**
  *Fuimos a Italia **por** barco.*
  We went to Italy by boat.
  *Pasamos **por** esa tienda ayer cuando salimos del pueblo.*
  We passed by that store yesterday when we left the town.

- **To describe a trade (in exchange for)**
  *Te cambiaré mi automóvil **por** el tuyo este fin de semana.*
  I'll trade you my car for yours this weekend.

- **To lay blame or identify cause (by)**
  *Todos los barcos fueron destruidos **por** la tormenta.*
  All the boats were destroyed by the storm.

- **To identify gain or motive (for; as a substitute for)**

  *Ella hace todo lo posible **por** su hermana.*

  She does everything possible for her sister.

  *Cuando Arsenio está enfermo, su madre trabaja **por** él.*

  When Arsenio is ill, his mother works (as a substitute) for him.

IR A AND ACABAR DE

Ir a is used to describe what the future will bring, or, in other words, what is going to happen. The expression is formed by combining the appropriate form of **ir** in the present tense (subject and verb must agree) with the preposition **a**.

> *Mañana **vamos a** comprar el árbol de Navidad.*
>
> Tomorrow we are going to buy the Christmas tree.
>
> *¿**Vas a** ir a la escuela aun si te sientes mal?*
>
> You're going to go to school even if you feel ill?

Acabar de is the Spanish equivalent of "to have just," and is used to talk about what has just happened. It is formed just like **ir a**, with the appropriate form of **acabar** in the present tense followed by **de**.

> ***Acabo de** terminar de cocinar el pavo.*
>
> I have just finished cooking the turkey.
>
> *Ellos **acaban de** regresar del mercado.*
>
> They have just returned from the supermarket.

OTHER PREPOSITIONS TO REMEMBER

Other prepositions and prepositional phrases you should know follow. Notice that many of these are merely adverbs with **a** or **de** tacked on to the end to make them prepositions.

hacia	toward
enfrente de	in front of
frente a	in front of
dentro de	inside of
fuera de	outside of

a la derecha de	to the right of
a la izquierda de	to the left of
debajo de	underneath
encima de	above, on top of
alrededor de	around, surrounding
en medio de	in the middle of
hasta	until
tras	behind
cerca de	near
lejos de	far from
detrás de	behind
(a) delante de	in front of
al lado de	next to

PREPOSITION SUMMARY

- Much of your work with prepositions boils down to memorization: which expressions and verbs go with which prepositions, and so on.

- You should concentrate on the boldfaced examples at the beginning of the preposition section since those are the most common. Once you're comfortable with them, the subsequent list should be a snap because many of those expressions are merely adverbs with **a** or **de** after them.

- Some verbs take prepositions all the time, some never do, and others sometimes do. This isn't as confusing as it may sound, however, because prepositions (or lack thereof) change the meaning of verbs. Consider the following:

Voy a tratar _____ despertarme más temprano.

(A) a

(B) de

(C) con

(D) sin

Which one of these goes with **tratar**? Actually, each of them does, depending on what you are trying to say. In this case you want to say "try to," so **de** is the appropriate preposition. **Tratar con** means "to deal with," and **tratar sin** means "to try/treat without," while **tratar a** doesn't mean anything unless a person is mentioned afterward; in which case it means "to treat." None of them makes sense in this sentence. The moral of the story is don't try to memorize which verbs go with which prepositions; concentrate on meaning.

Quiz: How Well Do You Know Your Prepositions?

1. Quiero llegar a la fiesta _____ María.

    (A) antes de

    (B) antes de que

    (C) a

    (D) sin que

2. Todos mis alumnos estuvieron _____ acuerdo conmigo.

    (A) entre

    (B) en

    (C) con

    (D) de

3. Estamos apurados, y por eso tenemos que viajar _____ el camino más corto.

    (A) dentro de

    (B) por

    (C) alrededor de

    (D) para

4. Los paraguas se usan _____ evitar la lluvia.

    (A) en medio de

    (B) hacia

    (C) para

    (D) por

5. La próxima semana ellos van _____ tocar aquí.

    (A) a

    (B) de

    (C) con

    (D) por

6. No me gusta ver las películas de horror _____ la noche.

    (A) tras de

    (B) sobre

    (C) en

    (D) durante

7. Salieron hace un rato, así que deben regresar _____ unos cinco minutos.

    (A) alrededor de

    (B) en vez de

    (C) en

    (D) después de que

ANSWERS AND EXPLANATIONS FOR QUIZZES

HOW WELL DO YOU KNOW YOUR PRONOUNS? (PAGE 75)

1. If he can do it alone, I don't have to help _____ .
   - (A) her
   - **(B) him (direct object)**
   - (C) him (indirect object)
   - (D) them

Whom do I have to help? **Him,** which is the direct object, therefore (B) is the answer.

2. We asked for window seats, but they gave _____ these.
   - **(A) us**
   - (B) them (indirect object)
   - (C) ours
   - (D) me

Pedimos tells you that the subject of the sentence is **nosotros.** Since you are trying to say, "they gave us these," the correct pronoun is **nos.**

3. When her students misbehave, the professor punishes _____ .
   - (A) them (f., direct object)
   - **(B) them (m., direct object)**
   - (C) to them (indirect object)
   - (D) to him (indirect object)

Estudiantes is masculine and plural, so choices (A) and (D) are incorrect. (Remember that in Spanish the masculine pronoun is used whenever the gender of a group is mixed, even if the majority of the group is female. Also, when the gender of the people in the group is unknown [like in this question] the male pronoun is used.) Whom does the professor punish? **Them,** which is the direct object; therefore (B) is the answer.

4. Are those gloves that are on the armchair _____ ?
   - (A) mine (m., sing.)
   - (B) mine (f., sing.)
   - **(C) mine (m., pl.)**
   - (D) mine (f., pl.)

Guantes is a masculine plural word, so the correct form of the possessive adjective is **míos,** which is choice (C).

5. For your birthday, I'll give _____ a new horse.

   (A) him (indirect object)

   (B) you

   (C) to you

   (D) me

The person whose birthday it is in the sentence is **tú,** so **te** is the correct indirect object pronoun. It is indirect in this case because it receives the direct object "horse." Choice (C) is incorrect because it is an expression of emphasis that complements an indirect object pronoun. However, there is no indirect object pronoun to complement, so it can't be right. The indirect object pronoun itself is necessary, so (B) is the best answer.

6. _____ is your favorite singer?

   (A) Who

   (B) Which

   (C) Who (pl.)

   (D) What

Since the question refers to a single person (**el cantante**), **quién** is the correct pronoun.

7. _____ do you prefer? The blue one or the red one?

   (A) What

   (B) Which

   (C) Which (pl.)

   (D) That one

In this question a choice is being given, so **cuál** is used instead of **qué. Cuáles** is incorrect because the choice is between two singular things.

How Well Do You Know Your Verbs? (Page 88)

1. When I have money, I _____ you a luxury car.

   (A) will buy (future)

   (B) bought (past, *yo* form)

   (C) would buy (conditional)

   (D) bought (past, *tú* form)

The sentence refers to something that will happen in the future. It is an example of the present subjunctive (**tenga**) used with the future tense to express an action that will happen if another action is fulfilled. In this case, the intent to buy the car is certain (I will buy you a luxury car). Therefore, the future, or choice (A), is correct.

2. I want you to _____ the homework before going to bed.

   (A) did (past, *tú* form)

   (B) does (present, *él* form)

   (C) do (present subjunctive, *él* form)

   (D) do (present subjunctive, *tú* form)

Quiero que is one of those expressions that tells you to use the subjunctive. In this case, the expression is in the present tense, so the present subjunctive is correct. If the expression were in the past (**quería que**), you'd use the imperfect subjunctive. The reason (D) is correct is that **te** is the reflexive pronoun in the sentence that tells you to use the **tú** form of the verb.

3. Last year we _____ to Mexico for vacation.

   (A) will go (future)

   (B) went (past)

   (C) would go (conditional)

   (D) go (present)

El año pasado (last year) is a big hint that the answer will be in one of the past tenses. There is only one answer choice with the past tense, choice (B).

4. If they had (were to have) time, they _____ the time relaxing.

   (A) spend (present)

   (B) spent (imperfect)

   (C) spend (present subjunctive)

   (D) would spend (conditional)

Si tuvieran tells you to use the conditional. In fact, **si** + the imperfect subjunctive often precedes the use of the conditional because it introduces a condition that doesn't currently exist. The only answer that's in the conditional is (D), **pasarían**.

5. I hoped that you _____ build the boat.
    (A) would help (conditional)
    (B) would help (imperfect subjunctive)
    (C) helped (past)
    (D) help (present)

Esperaba que is another one of those expressions of desire that tells you to use the subjunctive, but this time the expression is in the past, so the correct tense is the imperfect subjunctive. The tense of the expression is what tells you whether to use the present or the imperfect subjunctive.

6. Carlos _____ much time studying biology lately.
    (A) spent (past)
    (B) would spend (conditional)
    (C) spent (imperfect)
    (D) has spent (present perfect)

"Lately" suggests the past tense, but a more recent past tense. Answers (A) and (C) place the action too far in the past, while (B) is not a past tense. Therefore, (D) is the answer.

How Well Do You Know Your Prepositions? (Page 94)

1. I want to arrive at the party _____ María.

   (A) before

   (B) before (preceding a verb)

   (C) at, to

   (D) without (preceding a verb)

Answer choice (C) makes no sense in the context, so you can eliminate it right away. Because choices (B) and (D) both include a **que,** they imply another conjugated verb in the second part of the sentence, which is not there. Thus the correct answer is (A), **antes de.**

2. All of my students were _____ agreement with me.

   (A) between

   (B) in

   (C) with

   (D) in

This is a tough question, especially if you haven't seen the expression **estar de acuerdo.** In English we say that two people are "in agreement" with each other, but unfortunately the Spanish translation isn't the literal equivalent of the English expression. In Spanish two people **están de acuerdo.** (We know this isn't on your list, but that list is only a start: If you find new expressions that you don't know, add them to your list!)

3. We're in a rush, so we must travel _____ the shortest route.

   (A) inside of

   (B) by

   (C) around

   (D) for

This is the old **para** versus **por** trap, which is definitely tricky. In this case you want to say "travel by," and **por** is the preposition that sometimes means "by." **Para** is never used to mean "by."

4. Umbrellas are used _____ avoid the rain.

   (A) in the middle of

   (B) towards

   (C) in order to

   (D) for

Here it is again: **para** versus **por.** The other choices are pretty clearly wrong based on meaning, which leaves us with (C) and (D). In what sense are we saying "for" in this sentence? Is it "for the purpose of" (which would tell you to use **para**) or "for," as in a period of time or cause of action (which would tell you to use **por**)? In this case, "for the purpose of," or "in order to," fits pretty neatly, and so **para** is correct.

5. Next week they are going _____ play here.
   (A) **to**
   (B) of
   (C) with
   (D) for

Nice and easy, no tricks or traps, and it translates straight from English. This is an example of the use of **ir a.** Notice that **ir** is conjugated to agree with the subject of the sentence (**ellos**).

6. I don't like to see horror films _____ the night.
   (A) behind
   (B) on
   (C) in
   (D) **during**

Pretty tough call between (C) and (D) because both sound fine in the blank, but one of them makes a little more sense than the other if you think carefully about the difference in meaning between the two. Do you see films in (as in, "inside") the night, or during the night? They're sort of close, and the exact English would be "at night," but "during" makes a bit more sense.

7. They left a while ago, so they should return
   _____ about five minutes.
   (A) around
   (B) instead of
   (C) **in**
   (D) after

Basically what you're trying to say is that they'll be back soon, and "in five minutes" says that. "Around" would be fine if it were preceded by "in," or if "from now" were tacked on to the end of the sentence, but neither is the case here. Choice (B) doesn't really make sense. For choice (D), "que" eliminates the possibility of being a correct answer since it suggests verb usage after its use.

PART II

PRACTICE TESTS

6

PRACTICE TEST 1

Note to Reader

Following are the audio track numbers for Practice Test 1.

- Track 6: Dialogue 1

- Track 7: Dialogue 2

- Track 8: Dialogue 3

- Track 9: Narrative 1

- Track 10: Narrative 2

- Track 11: Selection 1

- Track 12: Selection 2

- Track 13: Presentational Writing (Fuente No. 3)

- Track 14: Interpersonal Speaking

Good luck!

AP® Spanish Language and Culture

SECTION I: Multiple-Choice Questions

DO NOT OPEN THIS BOOKLET UNTIL YOU ARE TOLD TO DO SO.

At a Glance

Total Time
1 hour and 35 minutes
Number of Questions
62
Percent of Total Grade
50%
Writing Instrument
Pencil required

Instructions

Section I of this examination contains 62 multiple-choice questions. Fill in only the ovals for numbers 1 through 62 on your answer sheet.

Indicate all of your answers to the multiple-choice questions on the answer sheet. No credit will be given for anything written in this exam booklet, but you may use the booklet for notes or scratch work. After you have decided which of the suggested answers is best, completely fill in the corresponding oval on the answer sheet. Give only one answer to each question. If you change an answer, be sure that the previous mark is erased completely. Here is a sample question and answer.

Sample Question   Sample Answer

Chicago is a   Ⓐ ● Ⓒ Ⓓ Ⓔ
(A) state
(B) city
(C) country
(D) continent
(E) village

Use your time effectively, working as quickly as you can without losing accuracy. Do not spend too much time on any one question. Go on to other questions and come back to the ones you have not answered if you have time. It is not expected that everyone will know the answers to all the multiple-choice questions.

About Guessing

Many candidates wonder whether or not to guess the answers to questions about which they are not certain. Multiple choice scores are based on the number of questions answered correctly. Points are not deducted for incorrect answers, and no points are awarded for unanswered questions. Because points are not deducted for incorrect answer, you are encouraged to answer all multiple-choice questions. On any questions you do not know the answer to, you should eliminate as many choices as you can, and then select the best answer among the remaining choices.

This page intentionally left blank.

Part A

Directions: You will now listen to three dialogues. After each one, you will be asked some questions about what you have heard. Choose the best answer to each question from among the four choices printed in your test booklet and darken the corresponding oval on your answer sheet.

Instrucciones: Ahora oirás tres diálogos breves. Después de cada narración oirás varias preguntas sobre lo que acabas de oír. Elige la mejor respuesta de las cuatro posibles respuestas impresas en tu libreta de examen y rellena el óvalo correspondiente en la hoja de respuestas.

NOW HERE IS THE FIRST DIALOGUE.

> Dialogue number 1
> AUDIO CD: Track 6

1. (A) el parque
   (B) el café
   (C) la estación de tren
   (D) la cocina

2. (A) Quiere tomar una merienda.
   (B) Quiere sentarse en el salón.
   (C) Quiere tomar el sol.
   (D) Quiere leer el periódico.

3. (A) la tarta de manzana
   (B) la tarta de chocolate
   (C) chocolate con churros
   (D) bizcochuelos

4. (A) Hace frío.
   (B) Llueve.
   (C) Está nublado.
   (D) Hace calor.

> Dialogue number 2
> AUDIO CD: Track 7

5. (A) Es la línea aérea.
   (B) Es la compañía de abogados.
   (C) Es el nombre del aeropuerto.
   (D) Es el nombre de la señora.

6. (A) Es azafata.
   (B) Trabaja en el mostrador de la línea aérea.
   (C) Es abogada.
   (D) Es la jefa de administración.

7. (A) Viaja a Londres.
   (B) Viaja a Barcelona.
   (C) Viaja a Burgos.
   (D) Viaja al mostrador de la línea aérea.

> Dialogue number 3
> AUDIO CD: Track 8

8. (A) Porque se murió su esposo.
   (B) Porque se murió su madre.
   (C) Porque se murió su tío.
   (D) Porque se murió su hermana.

9. (A) viajar
   (B) estudiar
   (C) trabajar
   (D) ir al cine

10. (A) Van al cine y después van a cenar.
    (B) Van a casa.
    (C) Van a una fiesta.
    (D) Van a trabajar.

GO ON TO THE NEXT PAGE.

Directions: You will now listen to two narratives. After each one, you will be asked some questions about what you have heard. Choose the best answer to each question from among the four choices printed in your test booklet and darken the corresponding oval on your answer sheet.

Instrucciones: Ahora oirás dos narraciones breves. Después de cada narración oirás varias preguntas sobre lo que acabas de oír. Elige la mejor respuesta de las cuatro posibles respuestas impresas en tu libreta de examen y rellena el óvalo correspondiente en la hoja de respuestas.

NOW GET READY FOR THE FIRST NARRATIVE.

Narrative number 2
AUDIO CD: Track 10

Narrative number 1
AUDIO CD: Track 9

11. (A) nuevo y moderno
    (B) pintoresco
    (C) histórico y prestigioso
    (D) innovador

12. (A) Hacía un tiempo agradable.
    (B) Hacía calor.
    (C) Nevaba.
    (D) Hacía un tiempo tempestuoso.

13. (A) Se sintió frustrado.
    (B) Se sintió muy a gusto.
    (C) Se sintió nostálgico.
    (D) Se sintió triste.

14. (A) Jugaba golf con su padre.
    (B) Acompañaba a su abuelo en el campo de golf.
    (C) Jugaba golf con su hermana.
    (D) Jugaba golf con su abuela.

15. (A) a la innovación de la construcción
    (B) a los elefantes y las jirafas
    (C) a la recaudación de dinero
    (D) a la preservación de los animales

16. (A) Costó diez millones de dólares.
    (B) Es muy grande y contiene aspectos de su hábitat natural.
    (C) Es muy limpio.
    (D) Ofrece cursos para la educación.

17. (A) Director del parque y naturalista.
    (B) El veterinario principal.
    (C) El agente de publicidad.
    (D) El gobernador de Virginia.

GO ON TO THE NEXT PAGE.

Directions: You will now hear two selections of about five minutes in length. You should take notes in the blank space provided, though your notes will not be graded. At the end of the narration, you will read a number of questions about what you have heard. Based on the content of the narration, choose the BEST answer for each question from among the four choices printed in your test booklet and darken the corresponding oval on the answer sheet.

Instrucciones: Ahora oirás dos selecciones de unos cinco minutos. Se debe tomar apuntes en el espacio en blanco de esta hoja. Estos apuntes no serán calificados. Al final de la narración, leerás unas cuantas preguntas sobre lo que acabas de oír. Basándote en el contenido de la narración, elige la MEJOR respuesta de las cuatro posibles respuestas a cada pregunta impresa en tu libreta de examen y rellena el óvalo correspondiente en la hoja de respuestas.

Write your notes on this page.

GO ON TO THE NEXT PAGE.

Selection number 1
AUDIO CD: Track 11

18. ¿Cómo interpretan algunos el movimiento feminista en España?

(A) Una lucha política

(B) Una cuestión artística

(C) Una competencia entre iguales

(D) Un concurso de belleza

19. ¿Cuál característica de la cultura española se puede considerar como el opuesto del movimiento feminista?

(A) El marianismo

(B) La honra

(C) La dignidad

(D) El machismo

20. Según la conferencia, ¿cúal es el objetivo ideológico del movimiento feminista?

(A) El triunfo de la mujer sobre el hombre

(B) La aceptación del marianismo en todo el mundo

(C) Una identidad individual para la mujer

(D) La apreciación de la cultura tradicional

21. Según la conferencia, ¿qué pensamiento surgió en la época de Franco?

(A) Un pensamiento radical

(B) Un pensamiento tradicional

(C) Un pensamiento progresivo

(D) Un pensamiento feminista

22. Según la conferencia, ¿qué debemos guardar de la sociedad tradicional machista?

(A) El papel de la mujer como madre

(B) El marianismo

(C) El papel de la mujer subordinada al hombre

(D) El machismo

GO ON TO THE NEXT PAGE.

23. ¿Cómo se interesó Alejandro Martínez en los juegos olímpicos especiales?

 (A) Siempre había participado en los juegos especiales.

 (B) Su hermano participaba en los juegos especiales.

 (C) Su hijo respondió favorablemente a los deportes.

 (D) Su esposa está muy metida en los juegos especiales.

24. ¿Cuándo se dedica Alejandro completamente a los juegos especiales?

 (A) Los fines de semana

 (B) Durante las vacaciones escolares

 (C) En invierno

 (D) En verano

25. Según la entrevista, ¿por qué no trabaja exclusivamente con los juegos especiales?

 (A) Porque no gana suficiente dinero

 (B) Porque es maestro de matemáticas

 (C) Porque su hija le ocupa mucho tiempo

 (D) Porque no podría soportarlo

26. ¿Por qué le gusta a Alejandro trabajar con los niños?

 (A) Porque son jóvenes

 (B) Porque son honestos

 (C) Porque tienen mucho interés

 (D) Porque tienen más habilidad

27. Según la entrevista, ¿por qué es terapéutico el ejercicio físico?

 (A) Porque practican ejercicios especiales

 (B) Porque los entrenadores tienen educación en terapia física

 (C) Porque es divertido

 (D) Porque les hace sentir mejor a los niños mentalmente y físicamente

28. ¿Cómo se caracteriza el espíritu colectivo de los niños?

 (A) No saben colaborar con el grupo.

 (B) Entienden instintivamente cómo colaborar.

 (C) No saben funcionar físicamente.

 (D) Hay mucha competencia entre los grupos.

29. Según la entrevista, ¿cuál característica describe mejor a los niños que participan en los juegos olímpicos especiales?

 (A) Son muy delgados.

 (B) Son muy delicados.

 (C) Son muy dedicados.

 (D) Son delegados a los juegos especiales.

30. ¿Qué recomienda Alejandro a las familias que no quieren participar en los juegos?

 (A) Que se enteren de los eventos planeados

 (B) Que sigan su corazón

 (C) Que organicen sus propios juegos con los juegos especiales

 (D) Que no participen

GO ON TO THE NEXT PAGE.

Part B

Directions: Read the following selections carefully for comprehension. Each selection is followed by a series of questions. Choose the BEST answer based on the passage and fill in the corresponding oval the answer sheet. There is no sample for this part.

Instrucciones: Lee con cuidado cada una de las selecciones siguientes. Cada selección va seguida de una serie de preguntas. Elige la MEJOR respuesta según la selección y rellena el óvalo correspondiente en la hoja de respuestas. No hay ejemplo en esta parte.

SECCIÓN UNO

Nosotros llegamos al aeropuerto Charles de Gaulle a las seis de la mañana del viernes. Llevábamos mucho tiempo de viaje y estábamos rendidos de cansancio. La *Línea* combinación de los asientos incómodos, el aire reciclado
5 y la comida genérica nos dejó en un estado de sueño nebuloso e irreal. Nos sentíamos sucios y malolientes. Después de esperar dos horas más (y ¿qué son dos horas más después de casi diez horas de viaje?) en el reclamo de equipaje, por fin supimos que nuestro equipaje se
10 había perdido. Bueno, en realidad el equipaje no se había perdido. Solamente optó por otra ruta y estaba a punto de llegar al aeropuerto Heathrow, en Londres. De acuerdo, el equipaje tenía que pasar primero por Londres. Estaría en el primer avión que sale para Charles de Gaulle. No tenía
15 sentido enfadarnos con los empleados. Ellos no entendían el estado soporífero en que nos encontrábamos. Tampoco les importaba mucho nuestra crisis. Ellos pudieron ducharse esta mañana. Seguramente tomaron su café habitual de las mañanas y su desayuno. Quizás llegaron al
20 trabajo sin ningún atasco ni otro problema de tráfico. Pero para nosotros la vida esta mañana no era tan fácil. ¡Con lo que nos encanta viajar! Decidimos irnos del aeropuerto y buscar el hotel. Luego un mozo nos llevaría el equipaje al hotel. ¡Qué servicial! Nos daba miedo pensar en la
25 propina que estaríamos obligados a regalarle. De todos modos, salimos del aeropuerto en busca de un taxi. Todo el mundo nos miraba de una forma rara. Seguramente querían saber dónde estaba nuestro equipaje. Por fin econtramos la parada de taxis. El señor que nos tocó era
30 mayor, pero con una cara muy amable. "Vamos al hotel Washington, por favor", declaró mi marido casualmente en su mejor francés. El taxista nos miró en el espejo como un lobo cuándo ve una manada de ovejas a través de las ramas de un árbol. Asintió con la cabeza y emprendió el
35 viaje a París.

31. ¿De qué se trata esta selección?
   (A) Las dificultades de unos viajeros
   (B) La vida de un piloto y su esposa
   (C) El aeropuerto Charles de Gaulle en París
   (D) El mejor equipaje para viajes cortos

32. ¿Cuál es el punto de vista de esta selección?
   (A) El punto de vista del piloto
   (B) El punto de vista de la azafata
   (C) El punto de vista de la esposa
   (D) El punto de vista del taxista

33. ¿Por qué se sentían sucios y malolientes?
   (A) No se ducharon antes de subir al avión.
   (B) Hacía mucho calor.
   (C) Había aire reciclado en la cabina del avión y comida mala.
   (D) Porque llevaban mucho tiempo esperando.

GO ON TO THE NEXT PAGE.

34. ¿Qué pasó con el equipaje?

    (A) Algunas maletas llegaron rotas.

    (B) No llevaban equipaje.

    (C) Se perdió.

    (D) No había ningún problema con el equipaje.

35. ¿Por qué no se enfadaron con los empleados?

    (A) Porque todos son amigos

    (B) Porque los empleados son unos imbéciles

    (C) Porque los empleados no están

    (D) Porque a los empleados no les importa su problema

36. ¿A qué se refiere el "estado soporífero" de la línea 16?

    (A) El no poder respirar bien

    (B) El sentirse sucios

    (C) El cansancio

    (D) El estado de crisis

37. ¿Cómo imagina el narrador la vida de los empleados?

    (A) Siguen su rutina diaria sin problemas.

    (B) Tienen mucha tensión en la vida.

    (C) Se desayunan gratis en el aeropuerto.

    (D) Se interesan mucho en la vida de los que pasan por el aeropuerto.

38. La siguiente oración se puede añadir al texto: "Nos tratará de estafar seguramente". ¿Dónde serviría mejor la oración?

    (A) Posición A   (línea 12)

    (B) Posición B   (línea 24)

    (C) Posición C   (línea 30)

    (D) Posición D   (línea 34)

SECCIÓN DOS

Mi abuela tendría entonces unos doce años. Vino con su madre. Las dos habían abandonado para siempre su país natal y la familia, o lo que quedaba de la familia, después de empezar la guerra. Vinieron a vivir a Estados Unidos.
Línea
5 Era su primera vez en Estados Unidos y su primera vez en Nueva York. Mi abuela quedó muy impresionada con la muchedumbre apurada. Todos parecían marchar al ritmo de un reloj secreto que ella no entendía. Pero no era una impresión negativa. No se sentía ofendida por
10 los trajes grises que se le adelantaban en la acera de la avenida Park. Más bien se sentía como una hormiguita curiosa que acaba de descubrir un almuerzo completo abandonado al lado de un arroyo apacible. Tenía todo el tiempo que necesitaba para explorar el universo de
15 Nueva York. De hecho, pasaría su vida entera explorando las esquinas y agujeros de esa ciudad famosa en todo el mundo. Su madre trabajaba como costurera en un almacén grande y famoso. Mi abuela se pasaba las mañanas en el piso y las tardes en el parque cuidando de
20 niños ajenos. Su madre había conocido a una señora rica que tenía dos niños pequeños y quien siempre quería que mi abuela fuera a su casa para jugar con ellos, llevarlos al parque o a alguna excursión especial. Pagaba bien para lo que era entonces, unos cincuenta centavos por hora. Lo
25 mejor era que siempre llevaba a mi abuela a los museos, al teatro, a las tiendas y a los mejores restaurantes. Mi abuela sólo tenía que ocuparse de los niños y asegurar que se portaran bien. La señora rica le compraba vestidos bonitos, zapatos nuevos y siempre pagaba las entradas en
30 los museos, al teatro y las comidas en los restaurantes. Mi abuela era como la hija mayor de la familia. Y los niños la adoraban. Los dos siguen en contacto con ella y la tratan como a una tía querida.

39. ¿Por qué vino la abuela a Estados Unidos?

    (A) Vino de vacaciones.

    (B) Huía de la guerra en su país natal.

    (C) Se murieron sus hermanos.

    (D) Vino para estudiar.

40. ¿Cuál era la impresión de la abuela de Nueva York?

    (A) Tenía una impresión negativa.

    (B) Se asustaba con la cantidad de gente en Nueva York.

    (C) Se sentía cómo un insecto pequeño.

    (D) Veía muchas oportunidades y cosas nuevas que le interesaban.

GO ON TO THE NEXT PAGE.

41. ¿De qué vivían la abuela y su madre?

   (A) Vivían en las esquinas y agujeros.

   (B) La abuela cuidaba niños y su madre trabajaba en un almacén.

   (C) Vivían en la avenida Park.

   (D) Vivían en la pobreza.

42. ¿Cómo pasaba la abuela su tiempo en Nueva York?

   (A) Pasaba las tardes en el parque con los niños que cuidaba.

   (B) Trabajaba en el almacén.

   (C) Estudiaba en el colegio.

   (D) Trabajaba en la avenida Park.

43. ¿Qué se puede inferir de la abuela?

   (A) Que no era muy culta antes de conocer a la señora rica.

   (B) Que de día ayudaba a su mamá en el trabajo.

   (C) Que no asistió a la escuela.

   (D) Que su sueldo fue una gran ayuda a la familia.

44. ¿Por qué iba la abuela al teatro, las tiendas, los museos y los mejores restaurantes?

   (A) Porque la señora rica la invitaba para acompañar a los niños

   (B) Porque buscaba trabajo

   (C) Porque tenía mucho interés

   (D) Porque su madre quería que fuera

45. ¿Que relación tenía la abuela al final con los niños de la señora rica?

   (A) La odiaban mucho.

   (B) La trataban muy mal.

   (C) La ignoraban.

   (D) La amaban mucho.

SECCIÓN TRES

No me podía dormir. Estaba tan obsesionado con la idea de la inauguración del nuevo restaurante el próximo sábado que millones de ideas pasaban por mi cabeza. *Línea* ¿Había invitado a todos los amigos del club deportivo? 5 ¿Había invitado a todos los hermanos y primos de Eliza? No quería ofender a nadie, ni mucho menos a la familia de mi esposa. Escuchaba el ritmo lento de la respiración tranquila de ella. Era tan hermosa y me encantaba verla dormir. Parecía tan serena, como un 10 lirio blanco. En comparación, yo me sentía al punto de un ataque cardíaco. Había tantos detalles y yo estaba seguro de que se me olvidaba algo importante. Había llamado a los críticos de la prensa local. Había hablado con los cocineros y los camareros. Pedí toda la comida 15 para el bufé. ¿Reviso otra vez el menú? Para empezar, tendremos calamares, mejillones, ostras, jamón serrano, canapés, albóndigas suecas y espárragos bañados en crema y caviar. Luego tendremos un cordero asado y un salmón escalfado. También tendremos ensalada y patatas 20 asadas. De postre, tendremos varios sorbetes, una tarta de manzana exquisita y unos chocolates de trufa. La música, ah, la música. ¡Eso sí que se me olvidaba! Se me olvidó llamar al conjunto clásico para confirmar la hora. Los llamo ahora mismo. ¿Qué hora es? Ah, son las tres de la 25 madrugada. No pasa nada, los puedo llamar mañana.

46. ¿Por qué no puede dormir el narrador?

   (A) Está enfermo.

   (B) No tiene sueño.

   (C) Está nervioso.

   (D) Está triste.

47. ¿Por qué se siente así el narrador?

   (A) Va a abrir un nuevo restaurante.

   (B) Va a hablar en público.

   (C) Va a tocar música.

   (D) Va a cocinar.

48. ¿Cómo describe a su mujer?

   (A) Como una persona dormida

   (B) Como una madre ejemplar

   (C) Como una flor

   (D) Como una sirena

GO ON TO THE NEXT PAGE.

49. ¿Qué significa en la líneas 10–11 cuando dice que se siente "al punto de un ataque cardíaco"?

    (A) Va a morir.

    (B) Está deprimido.

    (C) Está ansioso.

    (D) Está enfermo.

50. Todas las siguientes comidas son mariscos MENOS:

    (A) calamares

    (B) mejillones

    (C) ostras

    (D) albóndigas

51. ¿Qué carne va a servir de plato principal?

    (A) Jamón serrano

    (B) Canapés

    (C) Salmón

    (D) Cordero

52. ¿Qué había olvidado el narrador?

    (A) Poner el despertador

    (B) Llamar al conjunto musical

    (C) Poner la mesa

    (D) Llamar a la prensa

53. La siguiente oración se puede añadir al texto: "¿Y cómo podría olvidarme de los damascos y arándanos para la macedonia?" ¿Dónde serviría mejor la oración?

    (A) Posición A (línea 16)

    (B) Posición B (línea 19)

    (C) Posición C (línea 21)

    (D) Posición D (línea 22)

54. ¿Qué va a hacer el narrador mañana?

    (A) Dormir la siesta

    (B) Comer mucho

    (C) Llamar a los músicos

    (D) Llamar a los críticos

SECCIÓN CUATRO

Cuando el tren número 65 se detuvo en la pequeña estación situada entre los kilómetros 171 y 172, casi todos los viajeros de segunda y tercera clase se quedaron durmiendo dentro de los coches, porque el frío penetrante de la madrugada no les permitió a pasear por el desamparado andén. El único viajero de primera clase que venía en el tren bajó apresuradamente, y dirigiéndose a los empleados, les preguntó si aquella era la estación de Villahorrenda.

—En Villahorrenda estamos—repuso el conductor, cuya voz se confundió con el cacarear de las gallinas que en aquel momento estaban debajo del furgón—. Creo que ahí le esperan a usted con los caballos.

—¡Pero hace aquí un frío de tres mil demonios!—dijo el viajero envolviéndose en su manta—. ¿No hay en la estación algún sitio donde descansar y reponerse antes de emprender un viaje a caballo por este país de hielo?

No había terminado de hablar, cuando el conductor, llamado por las apremiantes obligaciones de su oficio, se marchó, dejando a nuestro desconocido caballero con la palabra en la boca. Vio éste que se acercaba otro empleado con un farol pendiente de la mano derecha, el cual se movía al compás de la marcha.

—¿Hay fonda o dormitorio en la estación de Villahorrenda?—preguntó el viajero al del farol.

—Aquí no hay nada—respondió éste secamente.

—Lo mejor será salir de aquí a toda prisa—dijo el caballero para su capote—. El conductor me anunció que ahí estaban los caballos. El hombre salió con la manta en las manos.

Línea

5

10

15

20

25

30

55. ¿De qué se trata esta selección?

    (A) Las ventajas de viajar por tren.

    (B) Las desventajas de viajar por tren.

    (C) Dos amigos viajando por tren con animales.

    (D) El viaje de un hombre descontento.

56. ¿Qué busca el caballero en la estación Villahorrenda?

    (A) Un lugar para descansar

    (B) Sus amigos y sus animales

    (C) Un trabajo y un hogar

    (D) Los empleados del tren

GO ON TO THE NEXT PAGE.

57. Según las conversaciones entre el caballero y el conductor, ¿qué adjetivo caracteriza mejor la actitud del conductor?

    (A) Amable

    (B) Desencantado

    (C) Ocupado

    (D) Dudoso

58. El narrador describe Villahorrenda como un lugar:

    (A) Desamparado

    (B) Peligroso

    (C) Tranquilo

    (D) El narrador no describe Villahorrenda.

59. ¿A quién se dirige el caballero cuando dice, "Lo mejor será salir de aquí a toda prisa"? (linea 27)

    (A) A las gallinas

    (B) Al conductor

    (C) A sí mismo

    (D) Al otro empleado

60. ¿Quiénes son los que esperan con los caballos?

    (A) Los empleados

    (B) Las mujeres de Villahorrenda

    (C) Los hombres de Villahorrenda

    (D) Las personas desconocidas

61. ¿Por qué se envuelve el viajero con su manta?

    (A) Porque está muy frío.

    (B) Porque necesita dar la manta a los empleados del tren.

    (C) Porque cacarean las gallinas debajo del tren.

    (D) Porque tiene miedo de los demonios.

62. La siguiente oración se puede añadir al texto: "No le apetecía la idea de una cabalgata de 2 días por sierras ajenas con sus ráfagas, chaparrones y nevadas". ¿Dónde serviría mejor la oración?

    (A) Posición A   (línea 6)

    (B) Posición B   (línea 17)

    (C) Posición C   (línea 21)

    (D) Posición D   (línea 31)

END OF SECTION I

IF YOU FINISH BEFORE TIME IS CALLED, YOU MAY CHECK YOUR WORK ON THIS SECTION

GO ON TO THE NEXT PAGE.

This page intentionally left blank.

SPANISH LANGUAGE AND CULTURE

SECTION II

Total Time—85 minutes

50% of total grade

Part A

INTERPERSONAL WRITING: EMAIL REPLY

Instrucciones: Para la siguiente pregunta, escribirás una carta. Tendrás 15 minutos para leer la pregunta y escribir tu respuesta.

Introducción: Este mensaje es de su profesor/a del colegio. Ha recibido este mensaje porque recientemente le había pedido que le escribiera una carta de recomendación para su solicitud de ingreso a la universidad. Tendrás 15 minutos para leer la carta y escribir su respuesta.

Estimado/a y muy recordado/a estudiante:

He recibido su pedido para una carta de recomendación; me alegro mucho que haya decidido solicitar ingreso a la universidad que tanto le gustaba. Fue uno de mis estudiantes favoritos y me es muy grato escribirle esa carta. Ya que quisiera escribirle la mejor recomendación posible, por favor me gustaría saber lo siguiente sobre Usted:

- ¿Qué recuerda más de mi clase, y cómo le servirá en el futuro?

- ¿Cuáles son sus metas para los próximos años en la universidad?

- ¿Cuáles han sido algunas actividades extracurriculares en que ha participado y qué ha aprendido de éstas?

Por favor, contésteme en detalle estas preguntas en un correo electrónico a la mayor brevedad posible. Al recibir su información, le prepararé la carta y se la enviaré tanto por correo cómo por correo electrónico.

Reciba mis mejores deseos y hasta entonces.

Señor Santo Palacios, Profesor de Idiomas

GO ON TO THE NEXT PAGE.

Directions: The following question is based on the accompanying sources 1-3. The sources include both print and audio material. First, you will have 7 minutes to read the printed material. Afterward, you will hear the audio material; you should take notes while you listen. Then, you will have 5 minutes to plan your response and 40 minutes to write your essay. Your essay should be at least 200 words in length.

This question is designed to test your ability to interpret and synthesize different sources. Your essay should use the information from the sources to support your ideas. You should refer to ALL of the sources. As you refer to the sources, identify them appropriately. Avoid simply summarizing the sources individually.

Instrucciones: La pregunta siguiente se basa en las Fuentes 1-3. Las fuentes comprenden material tanto impreso como auditivo. Primero, dispondrás de 7 minutos para leer el material impreso. Después escucharás el material auditivo; debes tomar apuntes mientras escuches. Luego, tendrás 5 minutos para preparar tu respuesta y 40 minutos para escribir tu ensayo. El ensayo debe tener una extensión mínima de 200 palabras.

El objetivo de esta pregunta es medir tu capacidad de interpretar y sintetizar varias fuentes. Tu ensayo debe utilizar información de TODAS las fuentes, citándolas apropiadamente. Evita un simple resumen de cada una de ellas.

¿Cómo nos afecta la vida el calentamiento global?

GO ON TO THE NEXT PAGE.

Fuente No. 1

Fuente: Este artículo apareció en un sitio de Internet de España en mayo de 2008.

Las consecuencias del calentamiento global asociadas con un aumento en el nivel de mar

Con la destrucción de la capa de ozono, observamos una mayor penetración de rayos solares al planeta. Estos, a su vez, contribuyen a una expansión térmica de los océanos y el derretimiento de grandes números de montañas glaciares y de los casquetes de hielo ubicados en las partes orientales de las Tierras Antárticas y Groenlandia. Ya con estos niveles elevados del mar, se pronosticarán graves cambios para el porvenir del planeta.

El nivel del mar ya aumentó en entre 4 y 8 pulgadas en el siglo pasado. Se predice que los niveles del mar podrían aumentar en desde 10 hasta 23 pulgadas para el año 2100. Lamentablemente los niveles vienen creciendo más de lo previsto—la capa de hielo de Groenlandia ha disminuido en la última década. Este declive contribuye aproximadamente una centésima de pulgada anualmente al aumento del nivel del mar. La cifra parece ser minima a primera vista, pero hay que tener en cuenta que Groenlandia cuenta con alrededor de 10% de la masa total del hielo mundial. Si el hielo de Groenlandia fuera a derretirse, los niveles del mar mundiales podrían aumentar en hasta 21 pies. Este año, por primera vez, los barcos pudieron pasar por las aguas árticas sin la ayuda de un barco rompehielos. O sea, que las predicciones de los científicos que el hielo empezaría a derretirse han acontecido 25 años por adelantado. Esto también significará graves consecuencia para el planeta. Ya se pronostica que el oso polar, los lobos marinos y ciertas especies de pingüinos estarán al borde de la extinción en pocos años.

Con la destrucción de los glaciares y casquetes del hielo, más agua dulce entra al mar, y así aumentando los niveles actuales. Estos derretimientos provocarán inundaciones severas en áreas costeñas. Si el nivel de mar subiera apenas 6 metros, arrasaría con lugares como Miami, Florida y San Francisco, California en los Estados Unidos; en China dejaría hundidas a ciudades como Shangai y Beijing, y en India, la ciudad de Calcuta estaría bajo agua. Estos últimos tres centros urbanos figuran entre las ciudades más pobladas del mundo.

GO ON TO THE NEXT PAGE.

Fuente No. 2

Fuente: Este artículo apareció en la prensa argentina en julio de 2008.

Advertencia: El calentamiento global traerá consigo graves consecuencias sobre la vida y la salud humana

"No es ninguna especulación – es una realidad. Los días del planeta están contados. Ya es hora de actuar y poner en marcha programas de planificación y contingencia", comentó Francisco García, director general de la Organización de Preservación Mundial, en rueda de prensa durante la undécima convocatoria general de La Semana del Planeta celebrada en Buenos Aires, Argentina. Representantes de más de 35 países se reunieron en la capital argentina para discutir, analizar data, y formular planes de acción para que las organizaciones internacionales y nacionales entendieran con mayor profundidad las consecuencias del calentamiento global. Es su esperanza, que una vez armados con esta información los países adopten programas para evitar un desastre que, según García, "está al acecho".

Una de las charlas más alarmantes dio a conocer las cifras actuales sobre enfermedades y desastres por el mundo. El doctor alemán Martin Teuscher, profesor de la Universidad de Tübingen, explicó que el ser humano ya ha sido expuesto a varias enfermedades causadas por cambios o exageraciones del clima. "Es una realidad que hemos estado viviendo durante este siglo. Pero fíjense que con el cambio climático, las bajas serán aún mayores. Intensificarán el balance delicado entre el desastre y la prosperidad, entre tener hogar y ser desamparado, y finalmente, entre la vida y la muerte". Señaló, en concreto, que mundialmente mueren más de 4 millones de personas por la malnutrición, más de 2 millones por enfermedades diarreicas, y 1,2 millones por enfermedades como la malaria. Indudablemente, estas cifras aumentarán con el cambio del clima mundial. Dijo Teuscher que no estaría fuera de lo posible que esas cifras triplicaran en apenas 5 ó 10 años.

Los descensos no pararán ahí. Con las temperaturas más cálidas, los insectos y otros organismos maléficos tendrán más oportunidad de desarrollarse y contagiar a los seres humanos como resultado. Se espera que ocurrirán más brotes de dengue y epidemias de malaria. Ambas enfermedades se trasmiten por la picadura de mosquitos. El calentamiento global favorece a estos insectos portadores de enfermedades. Otro resultado del calentamiento global son las inundaciones, las cuales proveen el ambiente ideal para la cría de mosquitos y las temidas pandémicas de cólera. Los recientes estudios realizados por los científicos ilustran la gravedad del problema del calentamiento global. En apenas 15 años, el número de personas en el continente de África expuesta a la malaria podrá llegar a las 100 millones. Globalmente, el dengue podrá amenazar a casi unos 2.000 millones de personas.

El calentamiento global ha traído trastornos en los climas mundiales, y cada año se manifiestan cambios y matices climáticos jamás vistos anteriormente. Por ejemplo, las olas de calor en Europa y los Estados Unidos significan miles de muertos cada año y los huracanes cada vez se vuelvan más devastadores y potentes. "El huracán Katrina de 2005 y El Huracán Mitch de en 1998 destrozaron grandes partes del territorio americano", puntualizó Felipe Fonseca, meteorólogo mexicano que habló sobre los cambios sufridos en el Golfo de México por el calentamiento global. "Estos efectos sociales, económicos, y políticos, aún se sienten. En 50 años podríamos encontrar partes del América del Norte bajo agua".

Las emisiones ocasionadas por los automóviles, camiones, y aviones envenenan el aire que respiramos. Esa contaminación del aire causa casi un millón de muertes al año. Según los estimados citados por los expertos, por cada grado centígrado que aumente la temperatura global, habrá casi 30.000 muertos anuales adicionales por enfermedades cardiorrespiratorias. Con los recientes aumentos de precio de los combustibles, la demanda no ha disminuido lo suficiente para reducir la contaminación del aire. Muchos temen que con el crecimiento de las economías emergentes de Asia, más el gran número de chóferes que tendrán acceso a automóviles, el daño ambiental continúe perjudicando cualquier intento de conservar el medioambiente.

GO ON TO THE NEXT PAGE.

"El individuo sí tiene el poder para hacer una diferencia", explica Rachel Johnson, estudiante alemana y miembro de GreenWatch, un movimiento estudiantil que educa a jóvenes sobre la conservación y el reciclaje. "Esa bolsa plástica que arrojas a la basura sin pensarlo tardará un centenar en descomponerse. La gasolina y el petroleo influencian casi todos los aspectos de nuestra vida, y al mismo tiempo perjudican al nuestro bienestar y el del planeta. Tenemos que cambiar nuestra manera de pensar y actuar ahora. En mi país hay un dicho que dice: *Macht es jetzt! Warte nicht auf bessere Zeiten*. (¡Hazlo ahora! No esperes mejores momentos). Si no hacemos el esfuerzo ahora, nuestras futuras generaciones se condenarán a una vida sin vida".

GO ON TO THE NEXT PAGE.

Fuente No. 3: Audio Selection

Este informe, que se titula "Los expertos señalan mayores riesgos de salud por el calentamiento global" se emitió por la emisora hispanoamericana Enteramérica en julio de 2005.

AUDIO CD: Track 13

END OF PART A

IF YOU FINISH BEFORE TIME IS CALLED, YOU MAY CHECK YOUR WORK ON PART A.

SPANISH LANGUAGE AND CULTURE

SECTION II

Part B

AUDIO CD: Track 14

Directions: You will now participate in a simulated conversation. First, you will have 30 seconds to read the outline of the conversation. Then, you will listen to a message and have one minute to read the outline of the conversation again. Afterward, the conversation will begin, following the outline. Each time it is your turn, you will have 20 seconds to respond; a tone will indicate when you should begin and end speaking. You should participate in the conversation as fully and appropriately as possible.

Instrucciones: Ahora participarás en una conversación simulada. Primero, tendrás 30 segundos para leer el esquema de la conversación. Luego, escucharás un mensaje y tendrás un minuto para leer de nuevo el esquema de la conversación. Después, empezará la conversación, siguiendo el esquema. Siempre que te toque un turno, tendrás 20 segundos para responder; una señal te indicará cuando debes empezar y terminar de hablar. Debes participar en la conversación de la manera más completa y apropiada posible.

(A) Has solicitado una posición de aprendiz en una empresa multinacional latinoamericana. Imagina que recibes una llamada telefónica del director del Departamento de Recursos Humanos para hablar sobre la posición que has solicitado.

(B) La conversación

[The shaded lines reflect what you will hear on the recording.
Las líneas en gris reflejan lo que escucharás en la grabación.]

GO ON TO THE NEXT PAGE.

Entrevistador	Te saluda
Tú	Contesta la pregunta
Entrevistador	Te hace una pregunta
Tú	Responde a la pregunta
Entrevistador	Continúa la conversación
Tú	Responde a la pregunta
Entrevistador	Continúa la conversación
Tú	Contesta que no es posible y ofrece una alternativa
Entrevistador	Continúa la conversación
Tú	Responde a la pregunta
Entrevistador	Continúa la conversación
Tú	Despídete

GO ON TO THE NEXT PAGE.

Directions: You will deliver an oral presentation to your class on a given cultural topic. You will have 4 minutes to read the presentation topic and formulate your presentation. Then you will have 2 minutes to record your presentation.

In your presentation, you should compare the community in which you reside to an area of the Hispanic world that you have studied. You will need to demonstrate an understanding of the cultural aspects of the Hispanic world. Your presentation should also be organized appropriately.

Instrucciones: Usted dará una presentación oral a su clase sobre un tema cultural. Dispondrá de 4 minutos para leer el tema de la presentación y formular su repuesta.

En su presentación, debe comparar la comunidad en la cual vive con una del mundo hispánico que haya estudiado. Tendrá que demostrar tu comprensión de los aspectos culturales del mundo hispánico. Su presentación debe ser organizada de manera clara.

Se sabe que los idiomas enriquecen la vida de uno. Explique de qué manera los idiomas han influenciado la sociedad en que Usted vive y en otra ciudad hispanohablante que usted haya observado, estudiado, o visitado.

Compara sus observaciones sobre las comunidades en las cuales ha estado con las de una región del mundo hispanohablante que haya estudiado. Puede referirse a lo que haya estudiado, vivido, observado, escuchado, etc.

STOP

END OF EXAM

7

Practice Test 1: Answers and Explanations

ANSWER KEY

Section I: Part A

1.	B	11.	C	21.	B
2.	A	12.	D	22.	A
3.	A	13.	A	23.	C
4.	D	14.	B	24.	D
5.	A	15.	D	25.	B
6.	C	16.	B	26.	B
7.	B	17.	A	27.	D
8.	A	18.	A	28.	B
9.	A	19.	D	29.	C
10.	A	20.	C	30.	A

Section I: Part B

31.	A	44.	A	57.	C
32.	C	45.	D	58.	D
33.	C	46.	C	59.	C
34.	C	47.	A	60.	D
35.	D	48.	C	61.	A
36.	C	49.	C	62.	B
37.	A	50.	D		
38.	D	51.	D		
39.	B	52.	B		
40.	D	53.	C		
41.	B	54.	C		
42.	A	55.	D		
43.	C	56.	A		

Section II

See explanations beginning on page 155.

SECTION I: PART A

DIALOGUES (PAGE 108)

Dialogue 1: Translation

(NARRATOR) In a café

(WOMAN) Good afternoon. I would like to have a bite to eat. Is there seating on the terrace?

(MAN) Yes, madam. What would you like to have? We have hot chocolate with churros, coffee, tea, iced lemon slush, ice creams, cakes, soaked sponge cakes.

(WOMAN) I would like to have a coffee with something sweet. What type of cakes have you got?

(MAN) Well, I have rich, homemade apple pie. I also have lemon cake, cheesecake, and chocolate cake.

(WOMAN) A piece of apple pie, please.

(MAN) Okay, and how would you like your coffee?

(WOMAN) I would like a black iced coffee, please. It's so hot I feel as though I will melt.

(MAN) Yes, it is dreadfully hot. So, a piece of apple pie and a black iced coffee, correct?

(WOMAN) Yes, thank you.

Dialogue 1: Translated Questions and Explanations

1. Where does this conversation take place?
   - (A) In the park
   - **(B) In the café**
   - (C) In the train station
   - (D) The kitchen

   The narrator clearly states at the beginning of the dialogue that the conversation takes place in a café. If you missed that, you may have been tempted to pick choice (D) because of the many references to food. You should, however, have picked up enough to know that choice (B) is the correct answer.

2. What does the woman want?
   - **(A) She wants to have a bite to eat.**
   - (B) She wants to sit in the reception area.
   - (C) She wants to sit in the sun.
   - (D) She wants to read the newspaper.

   The correct answer is choice (A): She wants to have a bite to eat. The woman does ask to be seated on the terrace, but that doesn't necessarily mean that she'll be sitting in the sun. Nothing about newspapers or a reception area is mentioned in the narrative.

3. What does the waiter suggest?

(A) Apple pie

(B) Chocolate cake

(C) Hot chocolate with churros

(D) Sponge cakes

The correct answer is choice (A). The waiter says that the homemade apple pie is rich and homemade. He simply states that they also have chocolate cake, hot chocolate with churros, and sponge cakes.

4. What is the weather like?

(A) It is cold.

(B) It is raining.

(C) It is cloudy.

(D) It is hot.

The correct answer is choice (D). It is so hot, the woman feels as if she will melt.

Dialogue 2: Translation

(NARRATOR) In the airport

(MAN) Excuse me madam, but would you know where the ticket counter for AeroEspaña is?

(WOMAN) Where are you going?

(MAN) I am going to Barcelona, and I am in a big hurry because I believe the plane leaves within twenty minutes.

(WOMAN) That's right. There is a plane that leaves for Barcelona this morning. The ticket counter for AeroEspaña is at the end of this hallway on your right.

(MAN) Do you have the time?

(WOMAN) Yes, it is nine o'clock. I will accompany you to the counter if you wish. I am also going to Barcelona this morning.

(MAN) Well yes, of course, it would be my pleasure. I am Ricardo Herrero.

(WOMAN) Delighted to meet you. I am Teresa Vara.

(MAN) Are you by chance the attorney for the Arturo Águila Company?

(WOMAN) Yes, I am. And you are the chief financial officer. We have met before, haven't we?

(MAN) Yes, I think we met at the annual meeting last year in London. What a coincidence!

(WOMAN) I suppose that you are going to the meeting in Barcelona with the president of the company?

(MAN) Of course, what a small world!

Dialogue 2: Translated Questions and Explanations

5. What is AeroEspaña?

   (A) It is the airline.

   (B) It is the law firm.

   (C) It is the name of the airport.

   (D) It is the woman's name.

AeroEspaña is the name of the airline, answer choice (A). We know this because once inside the airport, the man asks the woman where the ticket counter is for the airline he is taking to Barcelona.

6. What work does the woman do?

   (A) She is a flight attendant.

   (B) She works at the ticket counter.

   (C) She is an attorney.

   (D) She is the head of administration.

Choice (C) is the correct answer. The woman is an attorney for the Arturo Águila Company.

7. Where is the woman going?

   (A) She is going to London.

   (B) She is going to Barcelona.

   (C) She is going to Burgos.

   (D) She is going to the ticket counter.

This should be an easy one for you. Barcelona is mentioned several times in the dialogue, so if you picked (B), you had your ears open! London is mentioned in the dialogue as well, but only in reference to the fact that the two had met there last year.

Dialogue 3: Translation

(NARRATOR) A telephone conversation

(WOMAN A) Hello?

(WOMAN B) Aunt Mari-Carmen? It's Ángela.

(WOMAN A) Angelina, how are you?

(WOMAN B) I'm well, and how are things with you? Are you very lonely?

(WOMAN A) You see, my dear, since your Uncle Manolo died I am lonelier, yes. But it is not that bad. And furthermore, your mother calls me every day to chat. How are your classes going at the university?

(WOMAN B) Pretty good. Now I'm on vacation until September. I am going to look for a summer job. But I would like to come and see you before starting to work. I wanted to take you out to the movies.

(WOMAN A) Great, I would love that! When are you coming?

(WOMAN B) How about next Sunday? Why don't we go to the cinema? I think they are showing the new Italian film in the Metropol Cinema, which is near your house.

(WOMAN A) What a good idea. What time should we meet?

(WOMAN B) Why don't we meet around 7:00 at your house? I'll pick you up, and we can go directly to the movie theater.

(WOMAN A) Very well, and after the movie, I will treat you to dinner at the Italian restaurant that is next door to the house.

(WOMAN B) Excellent. So let's plan to meet at 7:00 at your house on Sunday.

Dialogue 3: Translated Questions and Explanations

8. Why is Mari-Carmen very lonely?

  (A) Because her husband died.

  (B) Because her mother died.

  (C) Because her uncle died.

  (D) Because her sister died.

The correct answer is (A), because her husband died. There is no mention of her mother, (B), nor of her sister, (D). Choice (C) may trick you since Mari-Carmen refers to Manolo as *tu tío Manolo*. But remember that Manolo is the husband of Mari-Carmen, and she is the one who is lonely.

9. What is Ángela going to do this summer?

(A) Travel

(B) Study

(C) Work

(D) Go to the movies

The correct answer is (C), she is going to work. There is no mention made of travel, so you can cancel choice (A). She studies at the university during the school year but not in the summer, which eliminates (B). She is talking about going to the movies with her aunt next Sunday, but not for the entire summer, which eliminates (D).

10. What are Ángela and Mari-Carmen going to do on Sunday?

(A) They are going to the movies and then to dinner.

(B) They are going home.

(C) They are going to a party.

(D) They are going to work.

The correct answer is (A), they are going to the movies and then to dinner. Ángela tells her aunt she wants to take her to see the new Italian film at the Metropol Cinema, and then Mari-Carmen is going to take Ángela to an Italian restaurant.

NARRATIVES (PAGE 109)

Narrative 1: Translation

(NARRATOR) The Argentine, Alfonso García, wins the golf championship in Scotland.

(WOMAN) The tumultuous and cold weather here in St. Andrew's, Scotland, yesterday was the catalyst for some extraordinarily high scores in the international golf championship, which was won by the young Argentine, Alfonso García. García, who is only twenty-two years old, is the first Argentine who has won this championship at St. Andrew's, the most historic and perhaps the most prestigious golf course in the world. The efforts of the golfers were complicated throughout the three-day tournament by an implacable wind and intermittent rain squalls.

"I have never experienced such a violent and tempestuous wind," the young Argentine said yesterday. And when he was asked how the weather affected his game, García replied, "At the beginning, I didn't know how to adapt well to the wind and calculate it into each shot. Later, the rain squalls bothered me quite a bit. The first day when I scored a 75, I was feeling very frustrated. But during the second day, when I realized that the other players were also struggling, it was much easier for me to concentrate. I began to think I might actually be able to win this tournament."

García, who comes from a family of athletes, is the first of his family to play golf at the professional level. His father was a tennis champion in the seventies and his younger sister, Patricia, is also a tennis player. Alfonso spends the majority of his time traveling on the PGA tour, but when he is not traveling, he lives with his parents in Buenos Aires. They say that he acquired his passion for golf from his maternal grandfather, who used to take him out on the golf course regularly.

Certainly, Alfonso García is a new star in the sport of golf.

Narrative 1: Translated Questions and Explanations

11. What is the golf course like in St. Andrews, Scotland?

    (A) New and modern

    (B) Picturesque

    (C) Historic and prestigious

    (D) Innovative

The correct answer is (C). The golf course is said to be historic and prestigious. Something historic is certainly not new and modern, so that eliminates (A). The golf course may be picturesque, choice (B), but it is not described that way in the narrative. Choice (D), innovative, is never mentioned.

12. What was the weather like during the tournament?

    (A) The weather was nice.

    (B) The weather was hot.

    (C) It was snowing.

    (D) The weather was tempestuous.

The correct answer is (D). There are various references to the tempestuous weather, primarily the wind and the rain squalls.

13. How did Alfonso García react to the variable weather in Scotland?

    (A) He felt frustrated.

    (B) He felt very happy.

    (C) He felt nostalgic.

    (D) He felt sad.

The correct answer is (A); he felt very frustrated initially. Later, he realized that the other players were experiencing the same challenges, and he was able to regain his focus.

14. How did Alfonso García become interested in golf?

    (A) He played golf with his father.

    (B) He accompanied his grandfather to the golf course.

    (C) He played golf with his sister.

    (D) He played golf with his grandmother.

The correct answer is (B). It is stated in the narrative that he accompanied his maternal grandfather to the golf course frequently. Reference is made to his father and his sister, but not in reference to golf, so (A) and (C) are eliminated. His grandmother is never mentioned, which easily eliminates (D).

Narrative 2: Translation

(NARRATOR) The modern zoological park "My House"

(MAN) At its grand opening yesterday, March 12, the zoo "My House," which is located in the northern part of the state of Virginia, was named the most innovative zoo in the country. Arthur Richardson, the director of the park, declared that the park is devoted to the preservation of animals in natural, clean, and animal-friendly environments. The construction of the habitats took three years to complete and cost more than ten million dollars. The elephant habitat has received much attention because it includes more than two hectares of land and includes other animals that are part of the elephants' natural habitat such as the African cranes and giraffes. Richardson, who is a naturalist known for his work with "Freedom for Animals" and other naturalist organizations, has devoted himself entirely to this project from its inception to its completion. At the moment, he is working as director of the park while he tries to establish a series of educational courses offered to the public in zoological and preservation studies.

Narrative 2: Translated Questions and Explanations

15. According to the narrative, to what cause is the park "My House" devoted?

    (A) Innovation of construction

    (B) Elephants and giraffes

    (C) Fund-raising

    (D) Preservation of animals

Choice (D) is the correct answer. The park is devoted to the preservation of animals. Choice (A) may seem logical because it is a new zoo and makes use of recent technological capabilities, but that is not the zoo's goal, which cancels (A). The narrative talks about the elephants and giraffes, but they are not the sole focus of the zoo, which eliminates (B). Fund-raising is never mentioned in the narrative, which cancels (C).

16. The elephant habitat received a lot of attention because

    (A) it cost ten million dollars

    (B) it is very big and contains elements of their natural habitat

    (C) it is very clean

    (D) it offers educational courses

The correct answer is (B). The elephant habitat received a lot of attention because it is very big, more than two hectares of land. It alone did not cost ten million dollars; the entire zoo did, which eliminates (A). The cleanliness of the elephant habitat is never mentioned, so that cancels (C). Of course, the elephant habitat would not be offering educational courses, which cancels (D).

17. Arthur Richardson is

    (A) director of the park and a naturalist

    (B) the local veterinarian

    (C) a publicist

    (D) governor of Virginia

Even if you missed this part of the narrative, common sense should guide you to the correct answer, choice (A).

FIVE-MINUTE NARRATIVES (PAGES 110–112)

Selection 1: Translation

Feminism in Spain is a strong force. For some it is a political battle. For others it is an economic struggle. Yet others search for a theoretical liberation, including a sexual liberation. One thing is certain: It is a movement that continues growing with increasing force. What interests us here is the situation in Spain today. We will examine how the peninsular movement sprang out of Spanish culture and what directions it is likely to take. It is very important that we look at this brand of feminism as a product of the Spanish culture. Of course, there is a universal movement going on outside of Spain. However, there are some specific characteristics of the movement in Spain that play a key role in its development there. Let's examine a few facets of Spanish culture and later turn our attention to the current state of feminism in Spain today.

One characteristic well-rooted in the Spanish culture, and perhaps the most opposed to feminism, is "machismo." Historically, in Spanish society, it is the man who makes decisions. It seems that the informal social laws are written by men to favor men. The concepts of honor and dignity are also very important. What comes out of all of this, then, is the idea of the strong and dignified man, who protects and assures the future of the woman. Similarly, the concept of "marianismo" establishes the desired qualities in the ideal Spanish woman. Also influenced by the ideas of honor and dignity, "marianismo" defines the domain of the woman in the home. Subordinated by the man, the woman personifies the qualities of obedience and self-sacrifice. Almost as if she were to exist through her association with the man, the woman is seen as fulfilled by her union in marriage to the man. After leaving the home of her father, the woman moves on to the home of her husband. Historically, in this culture there was no room for feminist independence.

The reverberations of these basic concepts from the Spanish culture provide the foundation for the feminist movement today. According to its own ideology, the feminist movement looks for an individual identity for the woman. Feminists want to reject the traditional concepts of "machismo" and "marianismo." The difficult part, however, is penetrating deeply into a culture that has a long history with these cultural values.

Now, let us turn our attention to the contemporary situation in Spain today. The reign of Franco marks a period of rigid censure. This oppressive regime reinforced the traditional values of the Spanish culture. It was almost as if it had resuscitated the concepts of "machismo" and "marianismo" in the society of the forties. Or perhaps they never died. In any case, there is most decidedly an important cultural foundation. What comes out of the Franco period are the reverberations of thought that have carried over from the Middle Ages. For that reason, the feminist movement was faced with a monumental obstacle. The feminists in Spain were looking for a way to express and communicate their protest. There are, among the feminist movement in Spain, those who want greater social or political freedom while others seek the complete elimination of traditional roles for women. There are militant groups and intellectual groups. Thus, the feminist movement in Spain is diverse and growing.

How can we evaluate such a movement? Surely, the extremes and excesses of a "machista" society should be eliminated. It is also essential that the independent identity of the woman be recognized. But with a radical approach, are we also prepared to lose all of the characteristics of femininity? It would seem that there are some traditional feminine roles worth maintaining, such as the nurturing mother figure, even in a society that is not gender biased. A search for complete equality, without limits or distinctions, it seems, would be a great loss. The role of women in the family, as mentioned above, is uniquely, distinctly, and positively feminine. Furthermore, the characteristics typically considered feminine, such as sensitivity, have a value for society in and of themselves. It is important, of course, that in this search for the true feminine identity, we don't lose femininity itself.

Selection 1: Translated Questions and Explanations

18. How do some interpret the feminist movement in Spain?

    (A) As a political battle

    (B) As an artistic issue

    (C) As a competition between equals

    (D) As a beauty pageant

The correct answer choice is (A), a political battle. There is no reference made to artistic issues, which eliminates (B). It is clearly not a competition between equals, which cancels choice (C). Choice (D) goes against all of the ideals described in the selection regarding a feminine identity.

19. Which characteristic of the Spanish culture can be considered as opposed to the ideals of the feminist movement?

    (A) *Marianismo*

    (B) Honor

    (C) Dignity

    (D) *Machismo*

The correct answer is (D). It should be pretty clear that honor and dignity would not go against feminist ideals, so choices (B) and (C) should be eliminated immediately. That leaves *marianismo* and *machismo*. If you understood what was said about *marianismo*, you know that *marianismo* defines the role of women in the home and idealizes the qualities of obedience and sacrifice. While these ideals do not seem to support the feminist movement, they are minor in comparison with the ideals that go along with *machismo*. In reality, both terms refer to cultural attitudes that clash with the modern feminist movement. However, the more obvious choice is *machismo*, which the selection, in fact, describes as "opposed to the feminist movement."

20. According to the selection, what is the ideological objective of the feminist movement?

    (A) The victory of the woman over the man

    (B) The acceptance of *marianismo* in all parts of the world

    (C) The individual identity for women

    (D) The appreciation of the traditional culture

The correct answer is (C), the individual identity for women. Choice (A) is extreme, and the selection did not advocate extremist measures. Choice (B) may be tempting because it uses the term *marianismo*, but *marianismo* is really a cultural view of women that grew out of the veneration of the Virgin Mary, and should not be confused with the feminist movement. Choice (D) is actually the opposite of what the selection is describing. The baggage of the traditional culture must be shed to find an individual identity for women.

21. According to the selection, what type of thinking surfaced during the Franco era?

    (A) Radical thinking

    (B) Traditional thinking

    (C) Progressive thinking

    (D) Feminist thinking

The correct answer is (B), traditional thinking. Franco was very traditional and very conservative. That cancels choices (A) and (C). Feminist thinking, (D), came about much later in Spain.

22. According to the selection, what should we keep from the traditional *machista* society?

(A) The role of the woman as mother

(B) *Marianismo*

(C) The role of the woman as subordinated to the man

(D) *Machismo*

The correct answer is (A), the role of the woman as mother. Both *marianismo* and *machismo* need to be overcome to move on to a greater state of gender equality, which cancels out both (B) and (D). Choice (C) is clearly one of the reasons to create a feminist movement and would most certainly not be desirable in a culture free of gender bias.

Selection 2: Translation

(NARRATOR)   Now you are going to hear an interview with Alejandro Martínez, victorious coach from the recent competition of the Special Olympic Games held in Vermont last April.

(MAN A)   Alejandro, first of all, how did you get involved with the world of the Special Olympic Games?

(MAN B)   Well, I have always been interested in sports. When I was in college, I played four sports during all four years, so sports have been a fundamental part of my life. The other fundamental part of my life, in chronological order, not order of importance, is my son, Carlos. Carlos was born eight years ago with a mild form of cerebral palsy. I noticed that with increased movement and physical activity, he felt better. For that reason, I have devoted myself to Special Olympics. We have met other children like Carlos and other families like ourselves. It has been a very positive experience.

(MAN A)   Do you work with the Special Olympics all year long?

(MAN B)   I wish I could devote myself to the Special Olympics 100 percent, but I also have a job. I am a high school mathematics teacher. So I work with the Special Olympics during the weekends and during the summer all week, which is the busiest time for us.

(MAN A)   It seems that you are drawn to professions that deal with children. Do you have any other children?

(MAN B)   Yes, I have a daughter who just turned four last month. It is true that I enjoy working with children. They are more innocent and honest than adults.

(MAN A)   What would you say is the most difficult part of your work with the Special Olympics?

(MAN B) Well, we are faced with new obstacles every day. Perhaps the most difficult part for me is recognizing my own limitations. Frequently, I try to do much more than is reasonable in a day. And the worst thing is that the kids are the same way. Once they have become enthused by an idea or a training exercise, for example, they want to practice for hours. They are very dedicated.

(MAN A) It seems that you too are very dedicated. How do you explain the phenomenal success of your teams?

(MAN B) Well, I think there are two important factors. The first factor is that physical exercise has a very positive effect on the mind and body. It is incredibly therapeutic. It makes the kids feel better physically. And mentally, they are more alert. Of course, they also enjoy the benefits that we all gain when we participate in a physical sport. Our kids feel the pride and dignity that medicine or medical treatment cannot give them. The second factor that contributes to our success is the dedication of our kids. The kids are completely dedicated to their team. They understand instinctively the importance of the group and of working together. Each one of them is completely dedicated to the program. Without them, it would never work. Without our kids, the Special Olympics would not exist.

(MAN A) What is Carlos's favorite sport?

(MAN B) Without a doubt, his favorite sport is American football, perhaps because he knows that I played in college.

(MAN A) What would you recommend to other families with children who at the moment do not participate in the Special Olympic games? Maybe they think these games are silly or too juvenile.

(MAN B) I recommend that they call as soon as possible to find out about the upcoming events that are planned. One only has to go to one competition to see the advantages of this program. It's a great organization. The volunteers are very generous and dedicated. It's a very important experience for the children and for the families.

(MAN A) Well, Alejandro Martínez, many thanks for being here with us.

Selection 2: Translated Questions and Explanations

23. How did Alejandro Martínez become interested in the Special Olympic Games?

    (A) He had always participated in the Special Games.

    (B) His brother participated in the Special Games.

    (C) His son responded favorably to sports.

    (D) His wife is very involved in the Special Games.

The correct answer is (C), his son responded favorably to sports. There is no mention of his wife or brother, which eliminates both (B) and (D) easily. Choice (A) is really a restatement of the question and not an answer to the question.

24. When does Alejandro devote himself entirely to the Special Olympics?

    (A) On weekends

    (B) During school vacations

    (C) In the winter

    (D) In the summer

Because Alejandro is a high school teacher, he has his summers off and devotes himself to the Special Olympics. There is no mention made of the school vacations (B), except the summer vacation, which is best described by answer choice (D). It is stated in the narrative that Alejandro spends time working for the Special Olympic Games on weekends, choice (A). However, it's pretty clear that he is *entirely* devoted to the games during the summer.

25. According to the interview, why does he not work full time for the Special Olympics?

    (A) Because he doesn't earn enough money

    (B) Because he is a math teacher

    (C) Because he doesn't have time for everything

    (D) Because he couldn't take it

The correct answer is (B); he mentions that he would dedicate 100% of this time, but he also has a full time job as a math teacher. There is no mention made of money, so that eliminates (A). At first glance, choice (C) would seem possible as children generally occupy a person's time, but this is not stated in the selection. (D) is an excuse that many people make, but Alejandro does not.

26. Why does Alejandro enjoy working with children?

    (A) Because they are young

    (B) Because they are honest

    (C) Because they are very interested

    (D) Because they are gifted

The correct answer is (B), as he mentions that he prefers working with children because they are more "honest and innocent." There are no specific mentions of age, interest level or talents, so the other answers are not correct in this situation.

27. According to the interview, why is physical exercise therapeutic?

(A) Because they practice therapeutic exercises

(B) Because the coaches have studied physical therapy

(C) Because it's fun

(D) Because it makes the kids feel better mentally and physically

The correct answer is (D), because it makes the kids feel better mentally and physically. Choices (B) and (C) may be true, but they are not mentioned in the interview. Choice (A) simply does not answer the question.

28. How is the collective spirit of the kids characterized?

(A) They don't know how to collaborate in a group.

(B) They understand instinctively how to collaborate.

(C) They don't know how to function physically.

(D) There is a lot of competition among the groups.

The correct answer is (B), they understand instinctively how to collaborate. Choice (A) is the exact opposite of the correct answer. Choices (C) and (D) are either completely false, or simply not mentioned in the interview.

29. According to the interview, which characteristic best describes the children who participate in the Special Olympic Games?

(A) They are very thin.

(B) They are very delicate.

(C) They are very dedicated.

(D) They are delegates.

The correct answer is (C), they are very dedicated. The other answer choices are designed to sound and look alike in an effort to confuse you. You, of course, will know your vocabulary and will not be fooled!

30. What does Alejandro recommend to the families who don't participate in the Special Olympic Games?

(A) That they find out about the planned events

(B) That they follow their hearts

(C) That they organize their own games

(D) That they don't participate

The correct answer is (A), that they find out about the planned events. None of the other answers were mentioned in the interview, although they may be true. Be sure to answer the questions according to the interview.

SECTION I: PART B

READING COMPREHENSION (PAGE 113)

Sección Uno: Translated Passage and Questions, with Explanations

We arrived at the Charles de Gaulle airport at six in the morning on Friday. We had spent a long time traveling, and we were exhausted. The combination of the uncomfortable seats, the recirculated air, and the generic food left us in an unreal, dream-like state. We felt dirty and smelly. After waiting two more hours (and what are two more hours after a ten-hour trip?) at the baggage claim, we finally found out that our bags had been lost. Well, in reality they were not lost. They only took a different route than we did and were about to arrive in Heathrow Airport in London. Okay, the baggage had to pass through London first but would soon be en route to us in Paris. It would be on the first plane that leaves for Charles de Gaulle. It didn't make any sense to become angry with the airline employees. They didn't understand the soporific state in which we found ourselves at the moment. Our crisis was of little importance to them. They had been able to have a hot shower this morning. They probably also had their usual morning coffee and their breakfast. Perhaps they arrived at work without encountering any jams or other traffic problems. But life for us this morning was not quite so easy. And how we love to travel! We decided to leave the airport and go look for the hotel. Later that day a bellhop would bring our baggage to the hotel. What service! We were frightened to think of the tip we would have to give him. In any case, we left the airport looking for a taxi. Everyone was looking at us strangely. They probably wanted to know where our baggage was. Finally we found the taxi stand. Our driver was older, but had a friendly face. "We are going to the Washington Hotel, please," my husband declared casually in his best French. The taxi driver looked at us in the mirror like a wolf when it sees a flock of sheep through the branches of a tree. He nodded his head and began our trip into Paris.

31. What is this selection about?

    (A) The difficulties of some travelers

    (B) The life of a pilot and his wife

    (C) The Charles de Gaulle airport in Paris

    (D) The best baggage for short trips

This is a general question asking about the general meaning of the passage. It would be difficult to answer this question without reading the passage. If you misunderstood bits of the passage, you may be fooled by answer choices (B), (C), or (D). Choice (B) is quite obviously a misunderstanding of the narrator and her traveling companion. Choices (C) and (D) are alluded to in the passage: The airport name and the word for "baggage" do appear but are not the focus of the passage.

32. What is the point of view of the selection?

    (A) From the point of view of the pilot

    (B) From the point of view of the flight attendant

    (C) From the point of view of the wife

    (D) From the point of view of the taxi driver

This is a popular type of question, so as you read the passages, be sure to pay attention to point of view. In this passage the key to the correct answer is located at the end of the passage: *declaró mi marido casualmente en su mejor francés*, "my husband declared casually in his best French." The correct answer is (C).

33. Why did they feel dirty and smelly?

   (A) They hadn't showered before getting on the plane

   (B) It was very hot

   (C) Because of the recirculating air in the cabin

   (D) Because they had been waiting for a long time

The best answer is (C). Although answer choices (A) and (B) could be true, neither is explicitly stated in the passage. Choice (D) may be true according to the passage, but it is not a likely answer to the question.

---

34. What happened with the baggage?

   (A) Some bags arrived broken.

   (B) They were not carrying bags.

   (C) It was lost.

   (D) There was no problem with the bags.

Choices (A) and (B) are not mentioned in the passage. Choice (D) can be immediately ruled out because there is clearly a problem with the bags. It is stated that the bags were on a different route to Paris, one that would pass through London first. Choice (C) is correct.

---

35. Why don't they get angry with the airline employees?

   (A) Because they are all friends

   (B) Because the employees are imbeciles

   (C) Because the employees are not there

   (D) Because the employees don't care about their problem

This answer is straightforward. The other answer choices may be true based on your own personal experience or someone else's experience, but are clearly not true according to the passage.

---

36. What does the "soporific state" refer to in line 16?

   (A) Not being able to breathe well

   (B) Feeling dirty

   (C) Tiredness

   (D) The state of crisis

This is a cognate, or word that looks and means the same in both languages. Unfortunately, it may be a vocabulary word that you don't know in English. "Soporific" refers to sleepiness or tiredness.

---

37. How does the narrator imagine the life of the airline employees?

   (A) Following their daily routine without problems

   (B) They have a lot of tension in their lives

   (C) They eat breakfast free in the airport

   (D) They're very interested in the lives of those who pass through the airport

Some of these answers, such as choices (B), (C), and (D) are simply thrown in there to confuse the unsophisticated test taker. You, of course, will not be fooled! Remember that the answer to these questions must come from the passage.

---

38. The following sentence can be added to the text. **"He'll surely try to take advantage of us."** Where would this sentence fit best?

   (A) Position A (line 12)

   (B) Position B (line 24)

   (C) Position C (line 30)

   (D) Position D (line 34)

This type of question is somewhat difficult because it requires you to have a strong grasp on vocabulary, but from some of the context clues, you might be able to deduce that the word *estafar* means *to swindle* or *trick*. This refers to the taxi driver, who has already been described with a negative metaphor. Lines 24 and 30 are mentioning positive comments about helpful or nice people, where the inserted sentence would make no sense. Thus, the correct answer is (D).

Sección Dos: Translated Passage and Questions, with Explanations

My grandmother would have been around twelve years of age. She came with her mother. The two of them had abandoned forever their homeland and their family, or what was left of the family after the beginning of the war. They came to live in America. It was her first time in America and her first time in New York. My grandmother was very impressed by the hurried masses of people. All of them seemed to be following a secret clock that she didn't understand. But it wasn't a negative impression. She didn't feel offended by the gray suits that passed by her on the sidewalk of Park Avenue. She felt more like a curious little ant that had just discovered a complete lunch abandoned on the side of a peaceful stream. She had all of the time she needed to explore New York. In fact, she would spend her entire life exploring the nooks and crannies of this city famous throughout the world. Her mother was working as a seamstress in a large and famous department store. My grandmother spent mornings in the apartment, and in the afternoons she went to the park to care for the children of strangers. Her mother had met a rich lady who had two small children, and she always wanted my grandmother to go to her house to play with them, or to take them to the park or on some special excursion. It paid pretty well for what it was then, about fifty cents an hour. The best part was that she always took my grandmother to the museums, the theater, the shops, and the best restaurants. My grandmother only had to take care of the children and make sure they behaved properly. The rich lady bought her pretty dresses and new shoes, and always paid for the tickets to the museums, the theater, and the meals in the restaurants. My grandmother was like the eldest daughter in the family. And the children adored her. Both of them keep in contact with her today and treat her like a beloved aunt.

39. Why did the grandmother come to America?

    (A) She came over on vacation.

    (B) She fled the war in her native land.

    (C) Her brothers and sisters died.

    (D) She came to study.

This question is very clearly answered in the first part of the passage. Look for answers to first questions in the early part of the passage.

40. What was the grandmother's impression of New York?

    (A) She had a negative impression.

    (B) She was frightened by the large crowd of people in New York.

    (C) She felt like a small insect.

    (D) She saw many opportunities and new things that interested her.

This is a tricky question. Although the passage says she does feel like a little ant, the point of that comparison is the abandoned picnic (of the city of New York) she (the ant) is about to devour. So what it really means is best explained by choice (D). Both (A) and (B) would be misreadings of the passage.

41. How did the grandmother and her mother make money to live?

    (A) They lived on the street corners.

    (B) The grandmother cared for children, and her mother worked in a department store.

    (C) They lived on Park Avenue.

    (D) They lived in poverty.

The text says that the grandmother would spend her life exploring the corners and nooks and crannies of New York, but that doesn't mean she will be living on the street corners, so that eliminates choice (A). Choices (C) and (D) are simply not true. There are various references to the two jobs the women secured.

42. How did the grandmother spend her time in New York?

    (A) She spent the afternoons in the park with the children that she cared for.

    (B) She worked in a department store.

    (C) She studied in the high school.

    (D) She worked on Park Avenue.

Her mother worked in the department store, which cancels (B). There is no mention of school, which cancels (C). There is only a reference to Park Avenue early on in the passage when describing her first impression of the city. That leaves you with the right answer, (A).

43. What can we infer about the grandmother?

    (A) That she wasn't very cultured before meeting the rich woman

    (B) That during the day she helped her mom at her job

    (C) That she didn't attend school

    (D) That her salary was a great help to the family

The inference questions are sometimes tricky because you have to draw conclusions with only limited information. It's best to eliminate answers here. Choice (A) could be true, as she was taken to exciting and cultured places, but it doesn't mean she wasn't cultured. Choice (D) could be an inference, but there is no mention of the family's economic conditions in the passage. Choice (B) has no factual information to prove that she worked during the day, as the article says "she spent mornings in the apartment." This very sentence though, makes (C), the right answer, as she was home instead of being in school.

44. Why did the grandmother used to go to the theater, the stores, the museums, and the best restaurants?

    (A) Because the rich lady used to invite her to accompany the children

    (B) Because she was looking for work

    (C) Because she was very interested in everything

    (D) Because her mother wanted her to go

Other than the correct answer, (A), the only answer choice that appears in the passage above is (C), which is stated early on in the reading, so choices (B) and (D) can be easily eliminated. Choice (A) is clearly the best choice when you reexamine the text.

45. What relationship did the grandmother have later with the children of the rich lady?

    (A) They hated her.

    (B) They treated her poorly.

    (C) They ignored her.

    (D) They loved her very much.

The correct answer, choice (D), stands out because it is the one that is different from the others. When that happens, the one different answer is generally the correct answer.

Sección Tres: Translated Passage and Questions, with Explanations

I wasn't able to fall asleep. I was so obsessed with the idea of the grand opening of the new restaurant next Saturday that millions of ideas were passing through my head. Had I invited all of the friends from the sports club? Had I invited all of the brothers and sisters and cousins of Eliza? I didn't want to offend anyone, much less my wife's family. I was listening to the slow rhythm of her calm breathing. She was so beautiful, and I loved to watch her sleep. She seemed so serene, like a white lily. In comparison, I felt as though I were on the verge of a heart attack. There were so many details, and I was certain that I was forgetting something important. I had called the critics from the local press. I had spoken with the chefs and waiters. I ordered all the food for the buffet. Shall I go over the menu once more in my head? We will start with squid, mussels, oysters, serrano ham, canapes, Swedish meatballs, and asparagus bathed in a cream sauce with caviar. Later, we will have a roast lamb and a poached salmon. We will also have salad and roast potatoes. For dessert, we will have various sorbets, an exquisite apple tart, and some chocolate truffles. The music, ah, the music. That's what I was forgetting! I forgot to call the band to confirm the time. I'll call them right now. What time is it? Oh, it's three in the morning. No problem. I can call them tomorrow.

46. Why can't the narrator sleep?

    (A) He's sick.

    (B) He's not sleepy.

    (C) He's nervous.

    (D) He's sad.

Once again it is important to understand the point of view to answer this question. The second and third sentences almost appear to be thoughts he is thinking out loud. Choices (A) and (D) are not mentioned. Answer choice (B) may be true, but (C) is most accurate.

47. Why does the narrator feel this way?

    (A) He's going to open a new restaurant.

    (B) He's going to speak in public.

    (C) He's going to play some music.

    (D) He's going to cook.

This information comes from the second sentence in the passage. Remember to look for answers to the earlier questions in the beginning of the reading. The correct answer is (A).

48. How does he describe his wife?

    (A) As a sleepy person

    (B) As an exemplary mother

    (C) Like a flower

    (D) Like a siren

He compares her with a *lirio blanco*, which means "white lily." He describes her calm breathing but doesn't describe her as a sleepy person. Choices (B) and (D) are never mentioned.

49. What is meant in lines 10-11 when the narrator says that he feels as if he were on the "verge of a heart attack"?

    (A) He is going to die.

    (B) He is depressed.

    (C) He is anxious.

    (D) He is sick.

He is exaggerating for effect. He is not really on the verge of a heart attack; he is only nervous and anxious. Answer choices (A) and (D) would be more literal readings of the passage. Choice (B) is not mentioned.

50. All of the following foods appear on the menu EXCEPT:

    (A) squid

    (B) mussels

    (C) oysters

    (D) shrimp

This is a detail question. You don't even have to know what the English equivalents of these foods are. A quick review of the items on the menu will reveal the correct answer, choice (A). Shrimp is not offered.

51. What meat will be served as the main course?

    (A) Serrano ham

    (B) Canapes

    (C) Salmon

    (D) Lamb

Remember that the first seven or so foods listed are all starters. The two main courses mentioned are lamb and salmon. Lamb is the only meat mentioned as a main course. The correct choice is (D).

52. What had the narrator forgotten?

    (A) To set the alarm clock

    (B) To call the band

    (C) To set the table

    (D) To call the press

Choice (B) is correct. At the end of the passage, when the narrator reflects upon the music to be played at the restaurant, he realizes that he's forgotten to call the band to confirm the time.

53. The following sentence can be added to the text. **"How could I forget about the apricots and the berries for the fruit salad?"** Where would this sentence fit best?

    (A) Position A (line 16)

    (B) Position B (line 19)

    (C) Position C (line 21)

    (D) Position D (line 22)

This is a vocabulary question testing your knowledge of fruit vocabulary. In Hispanic culture, fruit salad is often served as a dessert, making choice (C) the best place for the sentence, as the narrator is speaking about the desserts.

54. What is the narrator going to do tomorrow?

    (A) Take a nap

    (B) Eat a lot

    (C) Call the band

    (D) Call the critics

Choice (C) is correct. Recall that he wants to call them just when he thinks of it, but soon realizes that it's three in the morning so he decides to call the next day.

Sección Cuatro: Translated Passage and Questions, with Explanations

When train number 65 stopped at the small station located between kilometers 171 and 172, almost all of the second- and third-class passengers remained asleep inside their cars because the penetrating cold of the dawn did not allow them to walk on the abandoned platform. The only first-class passenger to come on the train descended hurriedly, and turning himself to the crew, asked them if that place was the Villahorrenda station.

"We are in Villahorrenda," responded the conductor, whose voice became lost in the clucking of hens, which at that moment were underneath the caboose. "I believe they are there waiting for you with the horses."

"But it's cold as hell here!" said the passenger, wrapping himself in his blanket. "Is there any place in the station where I may rest and recover before I begin a trip by horse through this country of ice?" They had not finished speaking when the conductor, called by the pressing obligations of his job, left, leaving our anonymous gentleman as he was in the middle of his sentence. The passenger saw that another member of the crew was approaching with a lantern hanging from his left hand, which was moving to the rhythm of his walk.

"Is there a room or boarding-house in Villahorrenda station?" asked the passenger to the man with the lantern.

"There is nothing here," he said brusquely.

"It is best to leave here as quickly as possible," said the gentleman to himself. "The conductor told me that the horses were over there." The passenger left with his blanket in his hands.

55. What is this selection about?

(A) The advantages of traveling by train.

(B) The disadvantages of traveling by train.

(C) Two friends traveling by train with animals.

(D) The trip of a discontented man.

If you could not understand the passage, you could have used this question to help you understand the general topic. All four answer choices indicate traveling and (A), (B), and (C) explicitly mention that this traveling is done by train. If the passage were a list of advantages or disadvantages, as in (A) and (B), there would probably not be dialogue and literary description, so you can eliminate those two answer choices without reading much at all. The passage has nothing to do with two friends or traveling with animals, so you can eliminate (C), making (D) the correct answer.

56. What is the gentleman searching for in Villahorrenda?

(A) A place to rest

(B) His friends and their animals

(C) Work and a home

(D) The crew of the train

The conversations between the first-class passenger and the crew repeatedly show that the man is looking for a place to rest and relax, so (A) is the correct answer. There are no friends mentioned, so (B) is out. We have no idea as to what his long term plans are, so (C) is also entirely made up. Answer choice (D) does not make sense considering that the man was talking to the crew, which was still on the train.

57. According the conversations between the gentleman and the conductor, what adjective best characterizes the attitude of the conductor?

(A) Kind

(B) Disenchanted

(C) Busy

(D) Doubtful

The conductor seems hurried and overly busy as a result of his work on the train, so (C) is the correct answer to this question. He has nothing about which to be disenchanted or doubtful, so we can eliminate (B) and (D). His rudeness to the gentleman (leaving him mid-sentence) means that (A) is very weak in light of (C).

58. The narrator describes Villahorrenda as _____ place.

(A) an abandoned

(B) a dangerous

(C) a quiet

(D) The narrator does not describe Villahorrenda.

While you will not see many overtly "trick" questions on the AP exam, keep your eyes open for ETS's deceptive wording. The correct answer here is (D) because the narrator never describes Villahorrenda himself, but allows the characters to describe it through dialogue. The one common adjective used to describe the station is "cold," which, fortunately, is not an answer choice.

59. Whom is the gentleman addressing when he says, "It is best to leave here as quickly as possible"?

(A) The hens

(B) The conductor

(C) Himself

(D) The other member of the crew

The phrase "decir…para su capote" (lines 27–28) is an idiomatic expression meaning "to say to one-self." The correct answer is (C).

60. Who are those waiting with the horses?

(A) The crew

(B) The women of Villahorrenda

(C) The men of Villahorrenda

(D) Unknown people

We are never told of any "women" or "men" of Villahorrenda, so (B) and (C) can be eliminated. Choice (A) seems ridiculous in light of the fact that it was the conductor who told him, so (D) is the only possible answer.

61. Why does he wrap himself in his blanket?

(A) Because it is cold.

(B) Because he needs to give the blanket to the train's crew.

(C) Because the hens are clucking beneath the train.

(D) Because he is afraid of demons.

This is a simple vocabulary and comprehension question, which relies on basic Spanish skills and common sense. Choice (B) is never mentioned in the passage, (C) makes no sense whatsoever, and (D) is an out-of-context and overly literal reading of the passenger's outburst. The correct answer is (A).

62. The following sentence can be added to the text. **"The idea of a two-day horseback ride through unfamiliar mountains with their windstorms, rainstorms, and snowstorms didn't appeal to him."** Where would this sentence fit best?

(A) Position A (line 6)

(B) Position B (line 17)

(C) Position C (line 21)

(D) Position D (line 31)

In this type of question, it is helpful to define the tone of the sentence to see where it would be complementary to other sentences in the passage. Then see where semantically it would make more sense; that is, find a sentence before or after the proposed position that will show flow and topic development. Lines 15-17 are showing the protagonist's desire to rest before a journey. As such, line 17, choice (B), would be the best answer for this question.

SECTION II: PART A

INTERPERSONAL WRITING: EMAIL REPLY (PAGE 185)

Translation

Introduction: This message is from your high school teacher. You have received this message because recently you had asked him to write a letter of recommendation for your college application.

Dear and most remembered student:

I have received your request for a letter of recommendation; I am happy you have decided to apply to the university that you liked so much. You were one of my favorite students and it is a pleasure for me to write this letter. Since I would like to write the best recommendation letter possible for you, I would like to know the following about you:

- What do you remember most from my class and how will it serve you in the future?

- What are some of your goals for the upcoming years in the university?

- What are some of the extracurricular activities in which you have participated and what have you learned from them?

Please answer these questions in detail as soon as possible in an email reply. Upon receiving your information, I will prepare the letter and I will send it you both by mail and by email.

My best wishes and until soon,
Señor Santo Palacios, Teacher

Sample Student Response

Estimado Profesor Palacios:

Es un verdadero placer saludarlo nuevamente. Aunque han pasado un par de años desde que estuve en su clase, recuerdo con mucha nostalgia los buenos momentos que pasamos en el curso. Sobre todo recordaré las lecciones no sólo académicas, sino también las aplicaciones que tuvieron a la vida real. Aprendí a siempre dar mi mejor esfuerzo en todo lo que lleva mi nombre, y que nunca debo darme por vencido ante las situaciones difíciles en la vida.

Me dirijo a usted ya que pienso que usted es el profesor que mejor me conoce y mejor me describirá a la universidad. Puesto que el español será mi concentración en la universidad, mi meta es ser traductor o interprete y trabajar con una impresa multinacional en América Latina. Durante mis años universitarios, me gustaría retarme con cursos en otros idiomas. Otro meta que tengo, y ojalá se haga realidad, es estudiar por un año en una universidad extranjera.

Las actividades extracurriculares que más me impresionaron en el colegio fueron el equipo de tenis, el club de español, y el club de servicio comunitario. En el Club de tenis aprendí la importancia de trabajar en equipo y la importancia de la práctica para mejorar las destrezas de uno. En el club de español, tuve la oportunidad de viajar a España y experimentar la cultura directamente. Viajé solo por primera vez en la vida y creo que representé bien a mi escuela y a mi país. Aprendí también que los estereotipos que mucha gente tiene son falsas, y una meta mía en el futuro es ayudar a combatirlos. Y en el club de servicio comunitario, vi que ayudar a los demás es ayudar a uno mismo.

Le doy las gracias por ser un ejemplo positivo en mi vida académica, y por haberme brindado su conocimiento y sabiduría tras los años.

Un saludo cordial.
Josh Messinger

Translation of Sample Student Response

Dear Professor Palacios:

It is indeed a pleasure to greet you once again. Although a few years have passed since I was last in your class, I remember with great nostalgia the good times we students had in the course. Above all I will remember the lessons; not only academic, but also the applications that they had to real life. I learned to always give my best effort in everything that reflects upon me, and to never give up when facing difficult situations in life.

I am contacting you because I believe you are the teacher that knows me best and who can best describe me to the university. Given that Spanish will be my college major, my goal is to be a translator or interpreter and work with a multinational company in Latin America. During my university studies, I would to challenge myself with classes in other languages. Another goal I have, which I hope comes true, is to study for a year in an overseas university.

The extracurricular activities that most impacted me in high school were the tennis team, the Spanish Club and the Community Service Club. In the tennis club I learned the importance of working with others and the importance of refining one's skills. In the Spanish Club, I had the opportunity to travel to Spain and experience the culture directly. I traveled alone for the first time in my life and I think I represented both my school and my country well. I also learned that stereotypes that many people have are untrue, and my future goal is to help combat them. And finally in the Community Service club, I saw that helping others really is helping oneself.

I thank you for being a positive role model in my academic career and for having bestowed your knowledge and wisdom throughout the years.

Cordial Greetings,

Josh Messinger

Evaluation

Sometimes the AP exam picks topics from "out of left field" which can sometimes catch a student off guard. This essay really forced the writer to reflect on his goals and plans. Perhaps you don't have those defined yet. That doesn't matter. It is okay to make up things to fulfill the answers. The readers are not concerned if you played tennis in high school or not; they are more concerned with how you answered the question. The exam in some way will ask you to talk about yourself or your academic experience, so make sure you have those details clear in your head so you can access them quickly.

Overall, this essay fulfilled all requirements, and maintained good grammar throughout. It also was logically organized and had a clear beginning and showed cultural appropriateness in the opening, closing and in the register used. There was a lack of transition between some of the sentences and a few awkward translations (*retarme con cursos*, *mi concentración*), but it would most likely receive a 4.

Essay Topic (Page 120)

Translation of the Question

How does global warming affect our lives?

Sample Student Essay

El calentamiento global trae consigo graves riesgos al bienestar del planeta. El ritmo al cual han crecido tanto la población mundial como la expansión industrial han puesto en peligro las defensas naturales del planeta. Como resultado, en la Tierra hay una mayor tendencia a ocurrir acontecimientos perjudiciales como desastres naturales, escasez de comida, brotes de enfermedades, y una disminución de recursos vitales para sobrevivir. Por consiguiente, nuestras vidas han cambiado también.

Yo diría que los cambios más drásticos se han presenciado en nuestra vida diaria. Los precios de gasolina, comida, y transportación han aumentado muchísimo recientemente. Por ello, nuestra vida económica cotidiana es más difícil. Muchas personas han sufrido ya que sus sueldos no rinden como antes y les es difícil que su presupuesto les alcance para todo lo necesario. Y como recientemente ha surgido conciencia para preservar el planeta, estamos viendo programas de reciclar, ahorrar energía, compartir viajes, explotar recursos locales, descubrir fuentes de energía, y hasta salvar a los animales que están en peligro de extinción, particularmente en las zonas antárticas. La calidad de nuestras vidas ha bajado también por el calentamiento global. Por ejemplo, en muchos países subdesarrollados, las cifras de muertes causadas por el calentamiento global han crecido. Las enfermedades como la malaria tendrán más víctimas como nunca ya que el calentamiento global permite que los insectos proliferen y sobrevivan con más facilidad. El derretimiento del hielo de Antártica traerá más inundaciones y consigo más casos de cólera y otras enfermedades. Yo mismo he observado el crecimiento de alergias y problemas cardiorrespiratorios entre la gente de mi familia. Y tal como predijeron los expertos, estos problemas están manifestándose ahora. Si hubiéramos hecho caso a las advertencias de los expertos hace años, tal vez no nos habríamos encontrado en esta situación tan desconsolada.

Finalmente, el calentamiento global ha cambiado nuestra forma de pensar. Se han despertado nuevas maneras de planificar el futuro. Los expertos están educando al público para que varíe su forma de pensar y su percepción en el mundo. El individuo se ha dado cuenta de que sí se puede hacer una diferencia al preservar el planeta y consumir más prudentemente. La gente está tratando de hacer lo posible para preservar el medio ambiente. Cada día se ve más programas para ayudar a preservar los recursos naturales, minerales y humanos del planeta. Solo esperamos que no sea demasiado tarde.

En resumen, se reconoce que el planeta en sí es la base de nuestra existencia y supervivencia. El calentamiento global, fenómeno creado por el hombre, ha llegado a tal punto que por fin el mundo ha reconocido su importancia, y como resultado, ha tratado de modificar su forma de pensar y actuar. Sin embargo, el daño es extenso, y requiere que también los gobiernos apoyen toda opción necesaria para salvar al mundo. Solo el tiempo dirá si este esfuerzo es suficiente.

Translation of the Student Essay

Global warming brings with it severe risks to the well being of the planet. The rhythm at which both the world population as well as the industrial expansion has grown have endangered the natural defenses of the planet. As a result, on Earth there is an increased tendency of detrimental events such as natural disasters, food shortages, sickness outbreaks and a decrease of the vital resources necessary for survival. As a result, our lives have changed as well.

I would say that the most drastic changes have been evident in our daily lives. The prices of gas, food and transportation have gone up tremendously recently. For that reason, our daily economic life is even more difficult. Many people have suffered since their salaries don't go as far as before and it is difficult for their budget to pay for all of their needs. And given that recently there has been an increase in consciousness towards preserving the planet, we are seeing programs for recycling, saving energy, ride sharing, using local resources, discovering alternative energy sources, and even saving animals that are in danger of becoming extinct, particularly in the Antarctic zones. Our quality of life has also gone down as a result of global warming. For example, in many underdeveloped countries, the number of deaths caused by global warming has grown. Sicknesses like malaria will have more victims than ever because global warming allows insects to thrive and to survive more easily. The melting of Antarctic ice will bring more floods and with that more cases of cholera and other sicknesses. I myself have observed an increase in allergies and cardio-respiratory problems among my own family members. And just as the experts predicted, these problems are becoming evident now. If we had paid attention to the expert's warnings years ago, perhaps we wouldn't have found ourselves in this sad situation.

Finally, global warming has changed our way of thinking. New ways of planning the future have been formed. Experts are educating the public to change its way of thinking and its perception of the world. The individual has realized that one can indeed make a difference by preserving the planet and consuming more wisely. People are taking the necessary steps to save the environment. Each day we see more programs to help preserve the planet's natural, mineral, and human resources. We only hope that it is not too late.

In summary, it is known that the planet itself is the key to our existence and survival. Global warming, a phenomenon created by man, has come to point where the world has finally recognized its importance, and as a result, has modified its way of thinking and acting. However, the damage is extensive and requires that governments also support all the necessary options in order to save the planet. Only time will tell if this effort is enough.

Evaluation

This essay expresses ideas clearly and in an organized manner. It has a good flow and transitions, and it displays excellent grammatical control and breadth of vocabulary. At the end of the introduction, there should be some reference to the topics of the following paragraphs to ease transitions. Another improvement would be to tie the articles in a little bit more, as it referenced them in mostly general terms. Some specifics from the articles could have strengthened the essay. The writer didn't specifically identify the sources mentioned. Perhaps a few lines where he could have said "According to Source #1…" However, given the strong style, grammar, and organization, this essay would have still scored extremely well.

This essay has some very good grammatical points that you should try to use in your essay: Use of good transitions: *Por ello, en resumen, Finalmente, Tal como*. Advanced vocabulary: *ya que, consigo, se reconoce que*. Good use of subjunctive: *Esperamos que, Requiere que, para que*. Good use of verbs: *surgir, rendir, predecir, manifestarse, proliferar, sobrevivir, modificar*. Advanced/Native structures: *tanto…como; les es difícil*.

A good way to make a winning essay is to find vocabulary and expressions that you can use or modify to fit most essays. Choose a few expressions in each of the above categories from essays and readings and try to start inserting them in your essays each time you write in class. For example, "Por ello" is a more sophisticated way to say "por eso," and this is exactly the type of thing the readers are looking for in the essays. Keep a checklist and always try to incorporate some of them into your essay. It will definitely make a good impression with the readers. In addition, try to use a variety of tenses: The above essay used present tense, present progressive, present subjunctive, future, preterit, and conditional. Readers especially like to see the advanced tenses and past subjunctive as well. Don't be afraid to go over the minimum word requirement either; generally you do better by writing more as opposed to less.

SECTION II: PART B

SIMULATED CONVERSATION (PAGE 125)

Sample Script of Student Response with Translation

Narrador: Has solicitado una posición de aprendiz en una empresa multinacional latinoamericana. Imagina que recibes una llamada telefónica del director del Departamento de Recursos Humanos para hablar sobre la posición que has solicitado.

You have applied for an internship in a Latin American multinational company. Imagine that you receive a phone message from the director of Human Resources to speak about the position that you have applied for.

Ahora tienes un minuto para leer el esquema de la conversación.

Now you have one minute to read the conversation outline.

Ahora imagina que recibas una llamada del señor Rivero para realizar una entrevista.

Now imagine that you receive a phone call from Mr. Rivero to speak about the position.

MA: Buenos días, le habla el señor Luis Rivero director de Recursos Humanos de la Empresa Mundiales. Me gustaría hacerle algunas preguntas por teléfono sobre su solicitud. Primero, cuénteme por favor. ¿qué le motivó a solicitar una posición de aprendiz en nuestra compañía?

Good morning, this is Mr. Luis Rivero from the Human Resources Department of the Mundiales Company. I would like to ask you a few questions by phone about your application. First, please tell me, what prompted you to apply for a position in our company?

Tú: Pues, como su compañía cuenta entre los líderes de su industria, me pareció buena idea solicitar una posición con ustedes para poder aprender más sobre la industria.

Well, since your company is among the leaders of its industry, it seemed like a good idea to me to apply for a position to learn more about the industry.

MA: Muy bien. ¿Qué destrezas y habilidades podrá aportar a nuestro lugar de trabajo?

What skills and abilities could you contribute to our workplace?

Tú: Hablo tres idiomas: el español, el inglés y el francés. Además, domino varios programas de computadora y soy muy bueno resolviendo problemas.

I speak three languages: Spanish, English, and French. In addition, I am proficient in many computer programs and I am very good at resolving problems.

MA: ¿Qué dirían sus patrones o jefes anteriores sobre personalidad y calidad de trabajo?

What might your previous employers say about your personality and quality of your work?

Tú: Dirían que soy puntual, leal, y que trabajo bien en grupos. En cuanto a mi calidad de trabajo, dirían que soy trabajador, organizado, y diligente.

They would say I am punctual, loyal and that I work well in group situations. In terms of my work quality, they would say I am hard working, organized, and diligent.

MA: Quisiera saber, ¿cuándo está disponible para trabajar y cuándo podrá empezar?

I would like to know when you are available to work and when you could start.

Tú: Como las clases terminan a finales de junio, puedo trabajar los meses de julio y agosto. Puedo comenzar el 5 de julio.

As school finishes the end of June, I can work in July and August. I can start July 5th.

MA: Me gustaría que pasara por nuestra oficina para que conociera a algunos de mis compañeros de trabajo. ¿Podrá pasar por la oficina mañana a las 10 de la mañana?

I would like for you to pass by our office in order to meet some of my work colleagues. Could you stop by tomorrow at 10?

Tú: Desafortunadamente, asisto a la escuela hasta las tres de la tarde. Sería posible que le visitara a las 4?

Unfortunately, I have school until 3 pm. Would it be possible for me to visit at 4pm?

MA: No hay ningún inconveniente. Nos vemos entonces en esa fecha y hora.

No problem. We'll see you then at that date and time.

Tú: Espero con ganas poderle conocer mañana. Que pase buen día. Adiós.

I look forward to seeing you tomorrow, have a nice day. Goodbye.

Evaluation

The answers were clear, appropriate, and had some complex structures like conditional and past subjunctive (*sería posible que le visitara*), and subjunctive (*que pase buen día*). The rest of the responses advanced the conversation and more than fulfilled the requirements. It would receive at least a 4 due to the quality of its grammar and topic development.

ORAL PRESENTATION (PAGE 127)

Translation of the Question

It is known that languages enrich us. Explain in what way languages have influenced the society in which you live and in another Spanish-speaking country that you have observed, studied or visited.

Compare your observations about the communities in which you have been with those of a region of the Spanish-speaking world that you have studied. You can refer to what you have studied, experienced, observed, heard, etc.

Sample Student Response

Los idiomas no sólo facilitan la comunicación entre otros, sino que también aporta la oportunidad de que las culturas se asimilen. En los Estados Unidos vemos cada día más que estamos desarrollando una sociedad bilingüe. Hay más de 40 millones de hispanos viviendo en los Estados Unidos. Este grupo reserva poder económico, social, y político, e influencian los acontecimientos en muchas de las comunidades donde viven. Pero al nivel humano, como cualquier inmigrante, el hispanohablante trae consigo una larga y rica cultura también. Como resultado de este tremendo oleaje de inmigrantes, la música, comida, vocabulario, y lenguaje de la sociedad reflejan una mayor influencia hispana. En mi comunidad, hay letreros bilingües, servicios bilingües, y mayores oportunidades de empleo para los bilingües. Casi cada solicitud de empleo hoy en día busca candidatos bilingües.

Paraguay es un país que disfruta una rica cultura gracias a los idiomas. Cuando los españoles asentaron el país, no erradicaron la cultura indígena. Es más, los pioneros españoles aprendieron el idioma de los indígenas—el guaraní. A la vez, los guaranís aprendieron el español. Ambos idiomas son lenguas oficiales de Paraguay, y casi todos los paraguayos dominan los dos. El guaraní es el idioma del amor, de la música, la poesía, y de la vida cotidiana, mientras que el español se usa en los periódicos, la televisión, y los negocios. Cada uno ocupa un lugar en la sociedad, y el país como resultado, ha beneficiado.

Hoy en día en muchos lugares del mundo hay movimientos que están a favor de adoptar un solo idioma oficial. Pero realmente vemos que la sociedad beneficia y hasta se vuelve más tolerante al tener varios idiomas presentes en la sociedad.

Translation

Languages not only facilitate our communication with others, but they also allow cultures to assimilate with each other. In the United States we see each day more and more that were are developing a bilingual society. There are more than 40 million Hispanics living in the United States. This group holds economic, political and social power and influences the events in many of the communities in which they live. But at the same time, like any immigrant, the Hispanics bring with them a rich and long cultural tradition. As a result of this tremendous wave of immigration, the music, food, vocabulary, and language of society reflects a growing Hispanic influence. In my community there are bilingual signs, services and greater opportunities for bilinguals. Almost every job application today seeks bilingual candidates.

Paraguay is a country that enjoys a rich culture thanks to its languages. When the Spanish settled in the country, they did not eradicate the native culture. They actually learned the language of the natives—Guarani. The Guarani in turn learned Spanish. Both languages are official languages of Paraguay, and almost all Paraguayans speak both fluently. Guaraní is the language of love, music, poetry and daily life, while Spanish is used in newspapers, television and business. Each one occupies a place in society, and the country, as a result, has benefitted.

Nowadays in many parts of the world there are movements to adopt one official language. However, we truly see that society benefits from multiple languages and even becomes more tolerant when different languages are present in daily life.

Evaluation

The response got better as it went along. The question really wanted to hear more about the personal experience of the writer, which to some extent was absent in the first paragraph. The second paragraph was much stronger because it demonstrated a familiarity with another culture, and most importantly, specific facts. This is what you will need to make the grade on this section. You could have chosen other options: Puerto Rico, Andean languages, Panamá. Notice how you will need to know information on the various regions of the Spanish-speaking world. This response fulfilled the requirements, was well composed and showed knowledge of the culture. It would have scored 4 on the AP exam.

8

PRACTICE TEST 2

Note to Reader

Following are the audio track numbers for Practice Test 2.

- Track 15: Interpretive Communication, Selección Uno

- Track 16: Interpretive Communication, Selección Dos

- Track 17: Interpretive Communication, Selección Tres

- Track 18: Interpretive Communication, Selección Cuatro

- Track 19: Presentational Writing (Fuente No. 3)

- Track 20: Interpersonal Speaking

Good luck!

AP® Spanish Language and Culture

SECTION I: Multiple-Choice Questions

DO NOT OPEN THIS BOOKLET UNTIL YOU ARE TOLD TO DO SO.

At a Glance

Total Time
1 hour and 35 minutes
Number of Questions
65
Percent of Total Grade
50%
Writing Instrument
Pencil required

Instructions

Section I of this examination contains 65 multiple-choice questions. Fill in only the ovals for numbers 1 through 65 on your answer sheet.

Indicate all of your answers to the multiple-choice questions on the answer sheet. No credit will be given for anything written in this exam booklet, but you may use the booklet for notes or scratch work. After you have decided which of the suggested answers is best, completely fill in the corresponding oval on the answer sheet. Give 6 one answer to each question. If you change an answer, be sure that the previous mark is erased completely. Here is a sample question and answer.

Sample Question   Sample Answer

Chicago is a   Ⓐ ● Ⓒ Ⓓ Ⓔ
(A) state
(B) city
(C) country
(D) continent
(E) village

Use your time effectively, working as quickly as you can without losing accuracy. Do not spend too much time on any one question. Go on to other questions and come back to the ones you have not answered if you have time. It is not expected that everyone will know the answers to all the multiple-choice questions.

About Guessing

Many candidates wonder whether or not to guess the answers to questions about which they are not certain. Multiple choice scores are based on the number of questions answered correctly. Points are not deducted for incorrect answers, and no points are awarded for unanswered questions. Because points are not deducted for incorrect answer, you are encouraged to answer all multiple-choice questions. On any questions you do not know the answer to, you should eliminate as many choices as you can, and then select the best answer among the remaining choices.

This page intentionally left blank.

Part A

INTERPRETIVE COMMUNICATION: PRINT TEXTS

Approximate Time—40 minutes

Directions: Read the following selections carefully for comprehension. Each selection is followed by a series of questions. Choose the BEST answer based on the passage and fill in the corresponding oval the answer sheet. There is no sample for this part.

Instrucciones: Lee con cuidado cada una de las selecciones siguientes. Cada selección va seguida de una serie de preguntas. Elige la MEJOR respuesta según la selección y rellena el óvalo correspondiente en la hoja de respuestas. No hay ejemplo en esta parte.

SECCIÓN UNO

Mamá, Ana y la chiquitina fueron a visitar al abuelo, pero el pobre papá no pudo ir porque tuvo que quedarse en casa para trabajar.

Línea
5 —¿Qué haré yo sin ti?—dijo él.

—Te escribiré cartas, tres cartas,—contestó Ana—. Te diré lo que estemos haciendo aquí sin ti.

—¿Sabes escribir una carta?—pregunto papá.

—¡Oh sí, lo puedo escribir!—dijo Ana—. Ya tengo siete años. Verás que puedo escribir una carta.

10 Ana se divirtió mucho. Un día dijo:

—Abuelita, ¿puedo tomar una pluma? Quiero escribir a Papá.

—Sí—dijo su abuela—, en el escritorio hay plumas. Ana corrió al escritorio de su abuelo.

15 —¡Oh, Abuelita! aquí hay una pluma muy rara.

—Ésta es una pluma de ave—dijo la abuela—. Tu abuelo la cortó para mí. Es una pluma de ganso; en tiempos pasados todo el mundo escribía con plumas de ave.

20 —Me parece muy bonita—dijo Ana—. No creo que pueda escribir con ella.

Tomó otra pluma y se fue. Al poco tiempo, volvió al escritorio. Y allí vio que la chiquitina había tomado la pluma de ave y había escrito con ella a su papá. ¡Y

25 qué carta había escrito! Ana se dio cuenta de que había derramado la tinta sobre el escritorio.

—¡Oh, chiquitina, chiquitina! ¿por qué has hecho esto?

Mamá envió la carta de la chiquitina a su papá y él dijo que se alegraba de recibir las dos cartas.

30 CARTA DE ANA A SU PADRE.

Aracataca, 12 de julio de 1917.

Mi querido Papá:

Nos estamos divirtiendo mucho. Mi abuelito tiene un gran caballo oscuro. Algunas veces me monta en el caballo. ¡Es tan

35 *divertido! Juego mucho en el prado. Mi abuelito me deja pasear sobre los montones de hierba y recojo moras para mi abuelita. Nos dan queso con el café. Quisiera que estuvieses aquí con nosotros. La chiquitina te ha escrito una carta. Tomó la pluma*

de ave de nuestra abuela, y derramó la tinta. *¿Puedes leer su*
40 *carta? Dice que ha escrito: "¿Cómo estás, papá? Te quiero mucho".*

Tu hijita,
Ana

1. ¿Cómo se puede entender de qué se trata la carta de la chiquitina?

   (A) Según la carta misma

   (B) Según la carta de Ana

   (C) Según lo que dice la abuela al padre

   (D) Según el narrador

2. ¿Quién duda que Ana pueda escribir la carta?

   (A) La abuela

   (B) El padre

   (C) El abuelo

   (D) La chiquitina

3. Según la selección ¿por qué escribe Ana "¿Puedes leer su carta?" a su padre?

   (A) Porque sabe que su padre tiene la vista débil.

   (B) Porque sabe que la carta ha llegado.

   (C) Porque cree que no puede leer la carta de la chiquitina.

   (D) Porque sabe que en tiempos pasados todo el mundo escribía con plumas de ave.

GO ON TO THE NEXT PAGE.

4. La siguiente oración se puede añadir al texto: "Captada por la novedad, la manoseaba por un rato, luego la retornó a su recinto". ¿Dónde serviría mejor la oración?

   (A) Posición A (línea 14)

   (B) Posición B (línea 19)

   (C) Posición C (línea 29)

   (D) Posición D (línea 38)

5. ¿Quién es la "ella" (24) con que la chiquitina escribió la carta?

   (A) La abuela

   (B) La pluma

   (C) Ana

   (D) La madre

6. ¿Por qué busca una pluma Ana?

   (A) Porque quiere escribir tres cartas.

   (B) Porque quiere escribir un libro.

   (C) Porque quiere derramar la tinta.

   (D) Porque necesita a su padre.

7. ¿Quién manda la carta a Papá?

   (A) La abuela

   (B) Ana

   (C) La chiquitina

   (D) La madre

SECCIÓN DOS

¡Cuidado! Cebras Trabajando En La Calle

No son personajes de Disney o mascotas que promocionan una marca o producto. Las "cebras" que circulan por las calles de La Paz, tienen un trabajo muy
Línea especial: son educadores urbanos que enseñan a la
5   gente a caminar con seguridad por toda la ciudad. Día a día, cubren su cuerpo con un disfraz y una máscara: se mueven, saltan, gritan y agitan banderines para llamar la atención de los peatones. Según datos de la organización municipal "Cultura Ciudadana" alrededor de 240 jóvenes
10   trabajan en dos turnos, cuatro horas por día y veinte horas a la semana.

El tráfico vehicular y peatonal es cada vez mayor en la ciudad sede del gobierno boliviano. Los automóviles no respetan los semáforos y la gente cruza las calles por
15   cualquier lugar. El caos es total. La vida de la gente, especialmente de los niños, está en permanente peligro. Por eso, la autoridad municipal decidió tomar medidas concretas. Así nacieron las "cebras".

En el año 2001, la alcaldía creó un proyecto a
20   través de la entidad "Cultura Ciudadana" con el fin de descongestionar el tráfico vehicular. "Las cebras emergieron con el objetivo de indicar el paso peatonal a los ciudadanos de a pie", aclara Kathia Salazar, coordinadora del "Proyecto Cebras". Este movimiento de
25   cultura ciudadana se inició en Colombia. Ahí se trabajaba con mimos educadores. En las calles, grupos de niños y estudiantes hacían juegos para demostrar cómo debía cruzarse un paso peatonal.

La representante municipal afirma que este proyecto
30   posee dos pilares fundamentales: educativo y social. La mayoría de los muchachos que trabaja como cebras tiene entre 16 y 22 años y está autorizada por la municipalidad para descongestionar el tráfico vehicular y facilitar el tránsito de los peatones.
35   "Los requisitos para trabajar como cebra son la voluntad, el emprendimiento, la creatividad y los deseos de salir adelante. Desde la alcaldía nos comprometemos a acompañar un proyecto de vida", devela Salazar.

Todos los días, las cebras se cubren el cuerpo con
40   trajes de algodón y tela blanca adornada con líneas de color negro. Mientras los peatones desesperados avanzan a la orden del semáforo, ellas bailan, juegan, bromean y gesticulan sin cesar. Cuando se van, los niños y ancianos las extrañan y el caos retorna a las calles. El
45   sueldo mensual que perciben asciende a 450 bolivianos (unos US$ 65). Las líderes o guías pueden llegar a ganar hasta Bs.1000 (cerca de US$ 144) por su exclusividad al Proyecto Cebras.

GO ON TO THE NEXT PAGE.

Cultura ciudadana

50   Julia Andrea Marca (21 años) trabaja como cebra desde
hace un año y nueve meses. Para ejercer el cargo de
educadora urbana tuvo que asistir a varios talleres de
enseñanza y aprendizaje impartidos por Kathia Salazar.
"Los niños me abrazan y agarran con mucho cariño.
55   Con esto, buscamos educar y enseñar a los infantes",
señala. Julia estudia además todas las mañanas en la
Universidad Mayor de San Andrés y cursa el primer año
de Bioquímica. "La única experiencia negativa que tuve
durante este tiempo fue que un auto me atropelló, pero no
60   fue un accidente muy grave. En un principio, la gente no
conocía el paso peatonal. Pero ahora, gracias a nosotros,
los ciudadanos respetan las señales de tránsito", agrega.
      Amanda Pinos (29 años), lleva ocho años en esta
iniciativa municipal. Brinca por las calles en cuanto la
65   luz del semáforo cambia a roja. Día a día, se ubica muy
cerca de la Plaza del Estudiante y de esta forma, evita
que los conductores se pasen por alto el semáforo y
provoquen incidentes y más congestionamiento vial. Su
función principal radica en transmitir valores de Cultura
70   Ciudadana a toda la gente. "He visto accidentes muy
terribles, es algo realmente muy triste", indica. "La tarea
principal de los educadores urbanos es generar reflexión
en cada uno de los ciudadanos de La Paz y generar
concienciación de la forma más cariñosa y respetuosa".
75   Pinos, quien se desempeña como guía del proyecto, relata
que las "cebras son jóvenes interesados en participar de
esta familia y los educadores urbanos van aconsejando
con la prevención". Añade que algunas frases que dicen
a los peatones son: "Señor cuídese mucho"; "tenga
80   cuidado, por favor"; "no cruce las calles; ¡alto por favor!".
      Para nuestras entrevistadas trabajar como cebra es
más un oficio que una profesión. Para varias de ellas,
el trabajo de educadora urbana significa una forma de
apoyar, querer, amar y cambiar la ciudad. Así de sencillo.

85   *¿La Paz?*

      El Censo Nacional de 2001, reportó una población de
1.552.156 habitantes en toda el área metropolitana de
La Paz, incluyendo la ciudad de El Alto. La población
estimada al año 2010 es de cerca de 2 millones de
90   habitantes, sin incluir a El Alto, de casi 1,2 millones
de personas. En su conjunto forman la aglomeración
urbana más grande del país. Según Datos del Instituto
Nacional de Estadística de Bolivia, el parque automotor
en La Paz, llegó a cerca de 220.000 vehículos en 2009. Si
95   bien existen leyes y multas que regulan el tráfico en La
Paz, la mayoría de los choferes no respetan la luz roja
del semáforo. Mucho menos el derecho de los peatones,
ni las líneas de cruce. Es por ese motivo, que las cebras
se encuentran en casi todas las esquinas de la ciudad,
100 ayudando a la gente a cruzar la calle, y disciplinando a
los conductores, desde las primeras horas de la mañana
hasta caer la noche.

Used by permission of VeinteMundos.com

8. ¿Cuál es el propósito de este artículo?

   (A) Presentar una forma graciosa de lidiar con un problema urbano

   (B) Narrar las experiencias de jóvenes que se unen a una causa

   (C) Demostrar que los empleos pueden ser tanto satisfactorios como educativos

   (D) Ilustrar cómo una ciudad respondió a una necesidad urgente con creatividad

9. ¿Cuál de las siguientes afirmaciones mejor resume el artículo?

   (A) Es casi imposible cambiar la forma de pensar de la gente.

   (B) En América del Sur, por no contar con fondos para obras públicas como los países del Primer Mundo, hay que buscar alternativas para resolver problemas.

   (C) Una ciudanía educada y respetuosa puede mejorar la vida y bienestar de todos.

   (D) Tantos los choferes como los peatones juegan un papel en la seguridad de todos.

10. ¿Qué podemos inferir de las cifras sobre el Censo Nacional en 2001 y 2009?

   (A) Por la crisis económica, más personas están convirtiéndose en peatones.

   (B) Por la explosión demográfica, la autoridad municipal simplemente no puede acomodar tantos peatones en las calles.

   (C) Los números de automóviles no han aumentado al ritmo del crecimiento de la población.

   (D) Con el aumento del número de residentes en La Paz y las afueras en años recientes, ahora hay mayores riesgos para el peatón.

11. Si fueras a realizar una investigación más profundizada sobre el mismo tema del artículo, ¿a cuál de la siguientes fuentes te acudirías?

   (A) El censo boliviano de 2013

   (B) Planificación Urbana de La Paz

   (C) El ministerio de Transporte y Carreteras

   (D) El Registro Civil

GO ON TO THE NEXT PAGE.

12. ¿Cuál es un punto negativo del programa?

   (A) Los choferes no necesariamente respetarían a un joven vestido de cebra de la misma manera que respetarían a un policía o miembro del ejército.

   (B) Las cebras siempre tendrán el riesgo de ser arrollados por vehículos.

   (C) El pago y las horas que reciben los trabajadores apenas alcanza para mantenerse uno.

   (D) los fondos atados al programa podrían ser revocados en cualquier momento.

13. ¿Cuál es el problema que trata este proyecto?

   (A) La mayor incidencia de accidentes

   (B) Los peatones no saben dónde cruzar las calles por falta de indicaciones

   (C) Los choferes básicamente ignoran las leyes de transito

   (D) Los conflictos entre peatón y chofer son cada día más comunes.

SECCIÓN TRES

El Guarani en Paraguay

Fue perseguido y prohibido por varias décadas en Paraguay. Nunca pudo ser enseñado formalmente. Pero sirvió como mecanismo de defensa en las guerras y hoy es hablado por casi nueve millones de personas en diferentes países de Sudamérica. A partir de 1992 es idioma oficial junto con el español en todo Paraguay. El guaraní ha sorteado grandes desafíos a lo largo de los años y aún pretende hacerlo, en pleno siglo XXI.

Según el censo poblacional de 2002, la población indígena de Paraguay llega casi a los 100.000 habitantes y reúne a más de 17 etnias. Pese a que la cifra no es significativa dentro del total nacional (el país cuenta con casi 7 millones de habitantes), el 87% de los paraguayos habla guaraní. Por lo tanto, esta nación latinoamericana es bilingüe.

¿Y por qué tanta gente habla esta lengua originaria? Según María Antonia Rojas, del instituto cultural "Ateneo Guaraní", el dialecto pertenece a los primeros habitantes de esta zona de Sudamérica y ha sido defendido como idioma por los propios paraguayos. "Es así como hoy en día, constituye un elemento transcendental en la cultura cotidiana", afirma la licenciada.

Comenzando por el nombre Paraguay, que significa "río que sale al mar", este idioma ha formado parte de la cultura del país. Es más, una gran cantidad de nombres de plantas, animales, canciones, comidas y actitudes puede ser señalada únicamente en esta lengua.

Pese a la fuerte defensa hecha por los paraguayos, durante mucho tiempo el idioma guaraní fue prohibido, incluso a través de persecución política, incluyendo castigos a todos los niños y jóvenes que lo hablasen en las escuelas y colegios. Esa realidad cambió cuando la dictadura de Alfredo Stroessner (1954-1989) cayó y se creó una nueva constitución. De esta forma, le otorgó el rango de oficial junto al español en 1992. A partir de ese momento y con el nuevo sistema educativo, el guaraní fue enseñado obligatoriamente en todas las escuelas del país. Además, recientemente fue aprobada una ley que protege a 20 idiomas de todo el territorio y que crea las condiciones para proteger la cultura que hay detrás de estas lenguas. La nueva normativa permitirá que la ortografía y gramática guaraní sean oficiales; además, se contará con un diccionario unificado de esta lengua.

Lengua moderna

Este idioma, además de ser oficial en Paraguay, lo es también en Bolivia (junto al quechua y aymara), en la provincia argentina de Corrientes y en el municipio brasileño de Takuru. A partir de 2005 es el tercer idioma

GO ON TO THE NEXT PAGE.

del Mercado Común del Sur (MERCOSUR), luego del
50 castellano y el portugués. En los centros de compras
paraguayos como mercados, restaurantes y galerías se
usa el guaraní; los comerciantes atraen a sus clientes con
esta lengua. Algunos programas de TV lo utilizan y los
locutores de radio emplean el idioma para comunicarse.
55 En diferentes tipos de celebraciones festivas, tanto la
música como los discursos son en guaraní. "El guaraní no
es un lengua primitiva, sino que es un idioma moderno,
vivo e interesante como cualquier otro utilizado hoy"
señala David Galeano Olivera, director del "Ateneo de
60 Lengua y Cultura Guaraní". El catedrático agrega que "a
pesar de los problemas que tuvo durante toda su historia,
es una lengua del tercer milenio, que es hablada por casi
9 millones de personas en toda Sudamérica".

Su importancia no solo radica en el uso cotidiano, sino
65 también en la investigación y estudio que hay al respecto.
Es enseñado no solamente en universidades paraguayas,
argentinas y brasileñas, sino también en prestigiosos
centros de estudios de EE.UU. y Europa. Universidades
como La Sorbona (Francia), Mainz (Alemania), Autónoma
70 de Madrid (España), Zurich (Suiza) y Bari (Italia) tienen
cátedras de esta lengua y cursos de postgrado. Las clases
son dictadas tanto por académicos paraguayos como
por investigadores europeos, muchos de ellos con una
importante permanencia en Paraguay. Algunos eran
75 diplomáticos, mientras que otros simplemente fueron
seducidos por esta lengua.

Es así como también en Internet, el guaraní ha tenido
gran auge, y hoy se encuentra presente en miles de sitios.
Es más, en la Web se le conoce a esta lengua nativa como
80 ta'anga veve, que significa "imágenes que vuelan". "Las
lenguas que tienen poca o ninguna presencia en Internet
son aquéllas que están condenadas a la muerte o la
desaparición", reflexiona Olivera. Y es así como tanto
Google como Wikipedia tienen su versión del avañe'e
("idioma del hombre"). En la red podemos encontrar
85 desde traductores en línea hasta poemas en este idioma.
Sin embargo, el mercado digital aún resulta complicado
para el guaraní. Como idioma casi oral, poca gente lee
o escribe en esta lengua. Por eso, la demanda es aún
reducida por parte de la gente común, no así por curiosos
90 y académicos. Esto constituye un nuevo desafío para el
guaraní, y probablemente no sea el único que le queda
a esta lengua que ha sabido sobrevivir a lo largo de los
años.

Used by permission of VeinteMundos.com

14. El guaraní sufrió subyugación en Paraguay por
motivos

(A) lingüísticos

(B) nacionalistas

(C) políticos

(D) económicos

15. ¿Qué podemos inferir del gobierno de Alfredo
Stroessner?

(A) Fue un gran defensor del idioma.

(B) Creía que un solo idioma debe ser el idioma
oficial.

(C) Alentó el uso de guaraní en guerras como
defensa.

(D) Le otorgó el rango de idioma oficial al guaraní.

16. El idioma ha podido superar los varios intentos de
eliminarlo ya que

(A) hay presencia en los países vecinos

(B) los paraguayos lo perciben como parte integral
de su cultura y nación

(C) es diferente de otros idiomas indígenas ya que
tiene una parte escrita

(D) la constitución garantizó su sobrevivencia

17. Un reto para la sobrevivencia de guaraní en la época
tecnológica es que

(A) hay poca demanda para su traducción

(B) hasta ahora la demanda para aprender el
guaraní solo existe en los centros académicos

(C) la mayoría de los hablantes no dominan ni la
lectura ni la escritura en la lengua

(D) tiene poca presencia en el Internet

18. La situación de Paraguay es única comparada con
otros países sudamericanos ya que

(A) es el único país que tiene dos idiomas oficiales

(B) una población no indígena habla un idioma
indígena

(C) ha protegido a todas sus idiomas indígenas por
legislación

(D) el renacimiento del idioma ha traído consigo
muchos retos no percibos antes

GO ON TO THE NEXT PAGE.

19. El interés en el exterior hacia el guaraní tiene su ímpetu a causa de

   (A) el comercio con otros países

   (B) el hecho que es el tercer idioma más utilizado en el Cono Sur

   (C) los académicos que lo estudiaron y lo enseñaron por interés en la cultura paraguaya

   (D) su nueva presencia en la Red

20. ¿Cuál de las siguientes afirmaciones mejor resume el artículo?

   (A) Sin el guaraní, Paraguay deja de ser Paraguay.

   (B) El guaraní tiene una posición delicada en el mundo de los idiomas.

   (C) La sobrevivencia del guaraní sólo lo pueden garantizar los paraguayos.

   (D) El guaraní merita el mismo respeto que recibe el español.

SECCIÓN CUATRO

El Lado B de la Fiestas Patrias

Este año, los chilenos celebraron "el doble" de tiempo sus fiestas nacionales. La razón se debe a que junto a los tradicionales días libres del 18 y 19 de septiembre, se
Línea agregaron otros dos más: 17 y 20. Bueno, se trataba de
5 las festividades del Bicentenario de la Independencia y había que celebrarlo como corresponde. Resultado: las jornadas festivas fueron viernes, sábado, domingo y lunes… ¡uf! Un fin de semana largo completo, que incluye casi unas mini vacaciones para toda la población,
10 tiene sus consecuencias. El aumento de peso producto del alto número de calorías de las carnes asadas y bebidas alcohólicas, junto con las deudas acumuladas, terminan siendo protagonistas.

En las tradicionales fondas y ramadas chilenas, recintos
15 especialmente construidos de ramas para las Fiestas Patrias, hasta el propio Presidente de la República debe bailar la cueca. Más aún, sobre todo cuando los medios de comunicación siempre están presentes en esta celebración nacional.
20 Los precios de comidas y bebidas típicas son altos en estos lugares: una empanada de pino cuesta alrededor de 800 pesos (US$ 1,5), un choripán mil pesos (US$ 2) y una cerveza de 350 cc dos mil pesos (US$ 4). Si se tiene en cuenta que un asado promedio para cuatro personas (más
25 la correspondiente cantidad de bebida, vino y pisco) tiene un costo de 27 mil pesos (US$ 55), no es un misterio que se necesita tener "sólidos ingresos".

Dado que muchos chilenos no cuentan con los suficientes recursos para ello, es común que en esta época
30 pidan créditos de consumo que los distintos bancos ofrecen para aumentar su presupuesto. Laura Soto, jefa División Créditos de Consumo del Banco CrediChile sucursal Viña del Mar, afirma que "septiembre es un mes en el que generalmente hay más demanda de
35 créditos. Si bien a fin de año se entregan más préstamos de dinero, por las fiestas de Navidad y Año Nuevo, además de las vacaciones, este mes de septiembre ha sido comparativamente mejor que en el pasado. Tal vez por las celebraciones del Bicentenario".
40 Soto señala que los créditos van de los 150 mil (US$ 300) hasta los ¡11 millones de pesos! (US$ 24.000). "Es exagerado, pues para financiar viajes o la compra de un auto se justificaría, pero no en esta fecha". Sin embargo, aclara, el porcentaje de deudores es bajo, ya que en
45 general la gente logra pagar los préstamos. Según sostienen expertos, las principales causas para no pagar la deuda son la pérdida del trabajo o compromisos con otro organismo financiero.

GO ON TO THE NEXT PAGE.

Más dinero para celebrar

50　En Chile un 60% de las empresas privadas entrega aguinaldos, una cantidad de dinero extra, a sus trabajadores en Fiestas Patrias. El rango varía entre los 22 y los 325 mil pesos (US$ 45 y US$ 750), y junto a Perú son los únicos países de Latinoamérica que incluyen
55　estas gratificaciones en su estructura del sueldo. No sólo las compañías privadas dan aguinaldos; los organismos públicos también lo hacen. Los montos se dan de acuerdo a cuánto reciba el empleado: a quienes reciben alrededor de 500 mil pesos (US$ 1.000) mensuales o una cantidad
60　menor les corresponde aproximadamente 50 mil pesos (US$ 100).

　　　Para Ricardo Iglesias, Licenciado en Historia y Máster en América Latina Contemporánea, "lo más probable es que el entusiasmo se deba a que el 18 y 19 de septiembre
65　son las únicas fiestas nacionales. En el resto del continente están los carnavales, los cuales tienen un significado religioso: celebran la cuaresma, los 40 días restantes para Semana Santa, como ocurre en Brasil y Uruguay". A juicio de Iglesias, otro aspecto positivo de los carnavales
70　es que "la gente se disfraza y no es posible determinar su condición social. Además, la fiesta se desarrolla en un solo lugar. En el caso chileno, ocurre que hay bastantes ramadas y fondas, teniendo como resultado que cada persona escoge de acuerdo a su gusto y conveniencia,
75　situación que trae consigo falta de unión entre los compatriotas". El profesor está convencido que en Chile falta una "cultura de festejos", por lo que los excesos con el alcohol podrían encontrar ahí su causa. "En Chile a la gente le gusta beber alcohol, porque simplemente le
80　gusta. Creo que no se relaciona con las crisis económicas que nos han afectado o con penas puntuales. Cualquier excusa sirve para comprar abundante cantidad de alcohol, siendo el 18 de septiembre una fecha ideal".

Riesgo de sobrepeso

85　Otro tema que suele complicar en las Fiestas Patrias es el exceso de calorías consumidas. "Una persona puede subir entre uno y cinco kilogramos, según las calorías que acumule, pensando que son cuatro días feriados", afirma Janet Cossio, directora de la carrera de
90　Nutrición y Dietética de la Universidad Andrés Bello. En el caso que la persona termine pagando altas sumas de dinero mensuales y si además engordó los tradicionales kilogramos extra, en Chile se usa una frase muy conocida como consuelo: A final de cuentas, lo comido y lo bailado
95　no me lo quita nadie.

　　　　　　　Used by permission of VeinteMundos.com

21. ¿Qué papel desarrolla el alcohol en Chile durante estas celebraciones?

(A) El consumo del alcohol aumenta durante la crisis económica.

(B) El consumo de alcohol es parte de cualquier costumbre cultural en Chile.

(C) Las penalidades de la borrachería son severas y limitan el consumo.

(D) El alto consumo del alcohol influencia la mayor tasa de obesidad en Chile.

22. ¿Cómo se diferencia el ambiente social durante las celebraciones en Chile y sus países vecinos?

(A) Durante estas celebraciones las clases sociales en Chile se mezclan más de lo normal.

(B) En los otros países, tal vez por la anonimidad, hay más probabilidad de que las clases sociales se mezclen.

(C) Las celebraciones chilenas tienden a ser más cortas.

(D) El gobierno hace que los patrones de los empleados les provean un dinero extra durante la época de las fiestas patrias.

23. ¿Qué opina Soto en cuanto a los préstamos realizados durante la época de las Fiestas Patrias?

(A) Que muchos chilenos no cumplen con su deuda

(B) Que no tiene sentido asumir un préstamo gigantesco para una sencilla celebración

(C) Que los préstamos otorgados durante septiembre sobrepasan los de las épocas navideñas.

(D) Que la proporción de préstamos se vincula directamente al estado de la economía

24. ¿Qué son ramadas?

(A) viviendas temporales

(B) quioscos

(C) un cobertizo hecho de árboles

(D) un escenario

GO ON TO THE NEXT PAGE.

25. ¿Por qué se prolongó la celebración este año?

    (A) Cayó un fin de semana.

    (B) Para poder estimular la economía chilena.

    (C) Coincidieron con la celebración de 200 años de independencia del país.

    (D) Lo mandó el presidente chileno para honrar la cueca.

26. Al final del artículo, ¿a qué se refiere la frase, "Al final de cuentas, lo comido y lo bailado no me lo quita nadie"?

    (A) La diversión que experimenta uno valió la pena.

    (B) Durante una celebración uno no cuida la dieta.

    (C) La comida y el baile son selecciones individuales y dependen del gusto del uno.

    (D) No hay remedio para una decisión que ya se tomó.

SECCIÓN CINCO

La Marinera

Una expresión de nacionalismo, una vista histórica, y un homenaje a las influencias del país. Son éstas las descripciones más populares de La Marinera, baile
Línea nacional del Perú. Los expertos no concuerdan en los
5 orígenes exactos del baile, pero al escuchar la música del baile, se sienten tonos españoles, andinas, gitanas, y moros. Aunque un baile del estilo Marinera ya existía por siglos en el Perú, ganó el nombre Marinera en homenaje a la marina peruana que luchó valientemente defendiendo
10 su patria durante la Guerra del Pacífico contra Chile en 1879. Algunos recuerdan que el baile, que representa el cortejo entre un gallo y una gallina, y cuyo contacto principal se maneja a través de pañuelos blandidos por los bailadores, era una extensión de la cueca, baile
15 nacional chilena, y que llegó a las orillas peruanas con los invasores chilenos que entremezclaban con la señoritas peruanas. Sin embargo, la teoría que más sentido tiene, y que explica las varias influencias nacionales, afirma que los incas, hacía más de 600 años, bailaban algo muy
20 parecido a la Marinera, y que simplemente tras los siglos el baile ha sido evolucionándose e incorporando las varias influencias históricamente predominantes en el área nacional. Indígena o importada, lo que sí se sabe es que La Marinera sigue siendo la expresión de orgullo
25 más visible y adorada entre la gente peruana. El baile hoy en día es más popular entre los jóvenes, que asisten a académicas especiales para perfeccionar sus habilidades, con el sueño de concursar entre los más destacados bailadores juveniles del país en las competencias
30 celebradas cada año en las grandes ciudades peruanas.

27. Según los expertos, ¿Cuál no es un origen posible de la Marinera?

    (A) La influencia del país vecino, Chile, durante la Guerra del Pacífico

    (B) Un intercambio entre las varias culturas del país

    (C) Un baile similar que existía con la gente indígena del Perú hace siglos

    (D) Una influencia rural campesina

GO ON TO THE NEXT PAGE.

28. ¿Cuál es un ejemplo de cómo La Marinera es una expresión del nacionalismo?

    (A) El nombre del baile

    (B) Los movimientos del baile

    (C) El pasado inca del baile

    (D) La popularidad entre los jóvenes

29. La influencia chilena en la danza peruana es un ejemplo de

    (A) la asimilación

    (B) la adaptación

    (C) el imperialismo

    (D) un intercambio cultural

30. ¿A qué se refiere la palabra "cortejo" en el artículo (línea 12)

    (A) un encuentro al azar

    (B) un reto

    (C) un romance

    (D) una pelea

GO ON TO THE NEXT PAGE.

Part B

INTERPRETIVE COMMUNICATION: PRINT AND AUDIO TEXTS (COMBINED)

Approximate Time—55 minutes

Directions: You will hear one or more audio selections. Some may be accompanied by reading selections. When a reading selection is included, you will be given a certain amount of time to read it. For each audio selection, you will first receive a certain amount of time to read a brief preview of the selection and the questions you will be asked. Each selection will be played twice. You may take notes as you listen. After listening to each selection the first time, you will have one minute to begin answering the questions. After listening to each question the second time, you will have 15 seconds per question to finish answering the questions. Choose the best answer based on the selections and mark it on your answer sheet.

Instrucciones: Escuchará una o varias grabaciones. Algunos vendrán acompañados de lecturas. Cuando se incluye una lectura, se le dará un tiempo específico para leerla. Para cada grabación, recibirá primero un tiempo determinado para leer una introducción y prever las preguntas. Puedes apuntar información pertinente si desea mientras escucha. Después de escuchar, cada selección por primera vez, dispondrá de 15 segundos por pregunta para terminar de contestarlas. Escoja la mejor respuesta según las fuentes y márquela en su hoja de respuestas.

SELECCIÓN UNO

Fuente No. 1

Tienes que dar una presentación en tu clase de español sobre el siguiente tema:

En abril de 2013, la junta legislativa del estado de Florida tuvo unas mesas redondas sobre la posibilidad de aumentar la edad mínima para sacar el permiso de aprendiz de conducir de 15 a 16 años, y la edad mínima para licencia completa de 17 a 18 años. El primer artículo es una presentación de parte de Lorena Pérez, abogada y presidente de la organización, Salvando la Juventud. La segunda selección es un informe de radio que presenta las ideas de varios jóvenes estadounidenses sobre esta propuesta. En una presentación oral compara y contrasta las opiniones de los jóvenes con las de la abogada.

Fuente: Discurso, Lorena Pérez, ante la Junta Legislativa Hispana, Tallahassee, Florida, presentado en mayo de 2013.

Los conductores adolescentes: No hay prisa

"Estimados compañeros: Pueden imaginar la angustia que abarca a un padre al recibir esa llamada telefónica informándole que ha fallecido su único hijo en un accidente automovilístico. Muchas veces es más que alguien se encuentre en el lugar equivocado en el momento inoportuno. Más bien, se trata de que a nuestros adolescentes les carecen la madurez y la experiencia como chóferes. Accidentarse hoy en día es demasiado fácil. No tienen por qué estar recorriendo las carreteras y calles a su temprana edad, y menos con otros amigos en el coche. Los riesgos a la vida sobrepasan cualquier beneficio otorgado por tener la licencia a muy temprana edad.

Según las cifras del gobierno, mueren más de 42.000 personas anualmente en accidentes automovilísticos. Esto sobrepasa las cifras de todas las guerras en las cuales ha luchado nuestra nación. Y de esas muertes, los chóferes adolescentes entre las edades de 16 y 19 comprenden más del 40% del total. Es de esperarse que mientras los chóferes vayan aumentando de edad, conseguirán más años de experiencia, más madurez, y como resultado, las cifras empezarán a bajar.

En muchos estados, la legislación reciente tiene como meta reducir esos números a través de programas de adiestramiento y estándares para licenciamiento por edad. Es mejor que repartamos los derechos de manejar gradualmente. De esa manera los chóferes jóvenes poseerían licencias restringidas, y poco a poco irían mejorando y adquiriendo entrenamiento obligatorio. Cada año recibiría mayores derechos siempre y cuando hayan cumplido con las horas de entrenamiento ya sean de cursos prácticos o de aprendizaje formal. Así aumentamos en etapas su nivel de experiencia.

GO ON TO THE NEXT PAGE.

No es una idea nueva; muchos estados están examinando la posibilidad de adoptar ese plan, y muchos que lo apoyan proponen que ese umbral sea de 18 años. Muchos países europeos ya tienen como edad mínima los dieciocho años para otorgar las licencias de manejar. Otros países han impuesto limitaciones en cuanto a los límites de velocidad, los horarios, el uso de las carreteras y hasta identificación expuesta en el vehículo para identificar chóferes juveniles.

Muchos adolescentes opinarán que con estas leyes pretendamos negarles su independencia o sus derechos. Al contrario, tenemos la obligación de proteger a nuestros ciudadanos más vulnerables. Algunos científicos mantienen que existen diferencias de madurez entre los 16 y los 18 años, y se sabe que en cuanto al desarrollo el ser humano no alcanza niveles de madurez en decisiones ejecutivos hasta el final de los años adolescentes o hasta que se llegue a los 20 años. Les exhorto que consideren esta importante oportunidad para salvarles la vida a nuestros jóvenes".

Fuente No. 2

Tienes 2 minutos para leer la introducción y prever la preguntas.

AUDIO CD: Track 15

Informe de radio

Fuente: Las opiniones de estos jóvenes aparecieron en un grupo focal sobre el tema de conductores adolescentes en Miami.

[A continuación escucharás las opiniones de varios jóvenes sobre la posibilidad de elevar las edades mínimas para manejar.]

31. Los jóvenes entrevistados mayormente opinan que

(A) económicamente es necesario que manejen

(B) que tendrán que depender más de los adultos si la edad mínima se reduce

(C) no hay necesidad de elevar la edad mínima para manejar ya que no logra nada

(D) socialmente es imprescindible que los jóvenes manejen

32. Lorena Pérez basa su teoría en la necesidad de elevar la edad mínima de manejar

(A) en experiencia propia

(B) en la inferencia que la edad trae madurez

(C) en pruebas científicas de otros países europeos

(D) en el hecho que los jóvenes no pueden diferenciar entre lo bien y lo mal

33. Diría Lorena Pérez que un factor que contribuye a los muertos elevados por accidentes automovilísticos es

(A) legislación leve

(B) la falta de suficiente horas de practica

(C) el número de compañeros en el carro

(D) falta de madurez o desarrollo

34. ¿Cuál sería un ejemplo de mayor adiestramiento?

(A) Evaluación de destrezas practicas después de cierto tiempo

(B) Intervención académica

(C) Entrevistas para determinar el nivel de madurez

(D) Experiencia práctica

GO ON TO THE NEXT PAGE.

35. ¿Cuáles de las afirmaciones mejor resume este artículo?

(A) Hay posibilidades de salvarles la vida a algunos jóvenes si se cambia la edad mínima para manejar a los 18 años.

(B) Aunque hay información que indica que el requisito de una mayor edad puede traer beneficios, los jóvenes tienen necesidad de manejar.

(C) Las bajas por accidentes automovilísticos son el ímpetu para cambiar la edad mínima para manejar.

(D) Se requiere más prueba científica para determinar con absoluta seguridad si la edad del chofer realmente influencia la tendencia de accidentarse.

36. ¿Cuál es el tono de la presentación de Lorena Pérez?

(A) Inconvincente

(B) Emocionante

(C) Práctica

(D) Lógica

37. Según la fuente auditiva, ¿cuál es el tono de John Grant?

(A) Negativo

(B) Arrogante

(C) Desconfiado

(D) Preocupado

38. ¿Cuál de los jóvenes opina lo opuesto de lo que argumenta Lorena Perez?

(A) Felicia Badillo

(B) Cielo Ramirez

(C) Andre Cruz

(D) Amanda Estevez

GO ON TO THE NEXT PAGE.

SELECCIÓN DOS

Tienes 2 minutos para leer la introducción y prever las preguntas.

AUDIO CD: Track 16

Introducción: Esta grabación se basa en una investigación realizada por la revista *Veinte Mundos* y trata de los pros y las contras de la cirugía estética.

39. ¿Cuál es el propósito del artículo?

   (A) Presentar cómo la cultura afecta la estética

   (B) Enseñar hasta dónde puede llegar una obsesión

   (C) Explicar por qué Colombia se ubica a la vanguardia de la cirugía estética

   (D) Comparar y contrastar la estética en Colombia y los EEUU

40. Según el artículo, ¿qué significa la frase "valor agregado"?

   (A) recuperar algo perdido

   (B) llegar a un acuerdo

   (C) postularse para un acenso en el trabajo

   (D) mejorar su posición ya sea social o económica

41. La cirugía plástica para muchos es conveniente ya que

   (A) la recuperación tiende a ser rápida

   (B) no hay que viajar al exterior

   (C) quita la necesidad de hacer régimen

   (D) mejora la autoestima inmediatamente

42. ¿Con qué propósito se menciona el éxito de las colombianas en los concursos de belleza?

   (A) Demostrar que la obsesión por la belleza es parte de la cultura

   (B) Demostrar que los cirujanos colombianos están entre los mejores del mundo

   (C) Demostrar que para concursar es necesario haberse sometido a una intervención estética

   (D) Demostrar que las colombianas de verdad tienen fama de ser lindas.

43. Según el artículo, El Doctor Edilson Machabajoy López advierte que

   (A) la cirugía no resuelve todos los problemas de uno

   (B) la cirugía puede ser hasta dañino al paciente

   (C) la cirugía estética es una decisión personal que trae diferentes resultados para cada persona

   (D) ninguna de estas respuestas es correcta

44. Según la fuente auditiva, ¿qué les motiva a las mujeres a someterse a la cirugía estética?

   (A) La avaricia

   (B) La obsesión por la belleza

   (C) El acceso económico

   (D) La presión que ejerce la sociedad para tener el cuerpo perfecto

45. En la fuente auditiva, ¿por qué algunas jóvenes logran tener la cirugía estética aunque los expertos no lo aconsejan?

   (A) Es una parte de la cultura.

   (B) Los padres se preocupan por su bienestar.

   (C) Hoy en día se necesita cualquier ventaja para superar a los demás.

   (D) Por qué la sociedad lo acepta y promueve.

GO ON TO THE NEXT PAGE.

46. ¿Cuál es la diferencia entre los servicios de cirugía estética en Colombia y en los Estados Unidos?

    (A) La calidad no es la misma en Colombia.

    (B) Los candidatos en Colombia pueden combinar servicios de salud con el turismo.

    (C) No hay edad mínima en Colombia para someterse a una intervención estética.

    (D) La tasa de crecimiento de en Colombia es mayor que la de los EEUU.

47. ¿Cómo puede beneficiar la sociedad colombiana de la cirugía estética?

    (A) Todo el mundo ya puede lucirse mejor

    (B) Impacta dramáticamente de manera favorable el autoestima de uno

    (C) Al atraer nuevos clientes del exterior, otras industrias florecen

    (D) El precio ha bajado dramáticamente en los últimos anos

48. ¿Cuál es un riesgo mayor al someterse a la cirugía estética?

    (A) Hacer una cirugía a muy temprana edad antes de que el cuerpo se haya desarrollado completamente

    (B) Uno no esté satisfecho con los resultados

    (C) Por tratar de economizarse, se someten a las cirugías encabezadas por personas no diestras

    (D) Convertirse en adicto de la cirugía por tratar de parecerse a una estrella

49. Según el artículo, ¿cuál puede ser una decepción que podrá resultar de la cirugía estética?

    (A) Las personas pueden convertirse en adictas de la cirugía y pierden el aspecto natural de su físico.

    (B) Los problemas de autoestima no desaparecen completamente.

    (C) Los resultados nunca quedan exactamente como uno piensa.

    (D) Muchas veces una sola cirugía no resuelve el problema; varias sesiones se vuelven necesarias.

50. El acceso popular a la cirugía estética es resultado de

    (A) las divisas de unas actividades ilícitas

    (B) la necesidad de poder competir en concursos de belleza

    (C) el bajo costo de los procedimientos

    (D) las altas expectativas de la sociedad en general

GO ON TO THE NEXT PAGE.

SELECCIÓN TRES

AUDIO CD: Track 17

51. ¿Cuántos años tenía "Beli" (Belisario Féliz Jiménez) cuando se hizo esta entrevista?

(A)   93

(B)   103

(C)   101

(D)   100

52. ¿Por qué el papa de Beli no lo dejaba tocar el acordeón?

(A)   Porque tenía un trauma de infancia.

(B)   Porque quería que Beli estudiara.

(C)   Porque no le gustaba el sonido del instrumento.

(D)   Porque no era un instrumental tradicional dominicano.

53. ¿Cómo aprendió Beli a tocar el acordeón?

(A)   Su papá le enseñó.

(B)   Fue a una academia de música.

(C)   Aprendió completamente solo.

(D)   Estudió con algunos de los más celebres músicos dominicanos.

54. Además de crear ritmos, a Beli le fascinan

(A)   bailar al ritmo del merengue

(B)   las mujeres que bailan al ritmo del acordeón

(C)   cantar canciones dominicanas

(D)   aprender a tocar nuevos instrumentos

55. Beli tenía muchas enamoradas. ¿Cuántos hijos tuvo que criar y mantener?

(A)   20

(B)   1

(C)   82

(D)   más de 20

56. ¿Qué es lo único que Beli le pide a Dios?

(A)   Más hijos

(B)   Morirse sin dolores

(C)   Salud y no morirse todavía

(D)   Reconocimiento de sus admiradores

57. ¿Qué es lo que más aprecia de la vida hoy en día?

(A)   La admiración de su familia, la salud, la larga vida y la música

(B)   La admiración de los presidentes, la salud, la larga vida y la música

(C)   El amor de su mujer, la salud, la larga vida y la música

(D)   La oportunidad de haber conocido a varios presidentes

GO ON TO THE NEXT PAGE.

58. Cuando Beli dice "Yo estaba asfixiado de mi acordeón" implica que

    (A) ya no soportaba más al instrumento

    (B) le consumía su vida por complete

    (C) el costo de mantenerlo era sumamente caro

    (D) fue la causa de mucho conflicto con su padre.

59. Cuando Beli dice, "Cada loco con su tema", significa que

    (A) la música de hoy no compara con la de ayer

    (B) los gustos personales varían de persona a persona

    (C) con una persona terca no se puede razonar

    (D) las prioridades en la vida las escogemos nosotros

60. ¿Cual nos enseña esta entrevista?

    (A) El esfuerzo de una persona puede mejorar la vida de los demás.

    (B) Con las ganas, todo es posible.

    (C) La pobreza no es un obstáculo al éxito.

    (D) La música es una lengua internacional que todos entendemos.

GO ON TO THE NEXT PAGE.

SELECCIÓN CUATRO

AUDIO CD: Track 18

61. El Perú es un país que

(A) sufre aislamiento por tener tantas zonas geográficas

(B) fue colonizado por europeos e indígenas

(C) disfruta de una diversidad la cual no posee todos los países del continente

(D) perdió mucho de su sabor indígena a causa de la influencia europea

62. Las tradiciones europeas abundan

(A) tanto en la costa como en la selva

(B) en la sierra mayormente

(C) en las tres zonas

(D) en la costa debido a la inmigración europea

63. ¿Quién sería el autor de este artículo?

(A) Un político peruano

(B) Un promovedor de turismo peruano

(C) Un antropólogo peruano

(D) Un sociólogo peruano

64. ¿Qué relación existe entre la geografía y la etnia en el Perú?

(A) Mayormente los indígenas son la población predominante en 2 de las 3 regiones principales.

(B) La decisión de las tribus de no asimilarse hace que la selva sea la parte más atrasada del Perú.

(C) La geografía es el factor determinante en la composición étnica y cultural del país.

(D) Por el aislamiento geográfico hay poco contacto entre los grupos étnicos en el Perú.

65. ¿Cuál es un ejemplo de la asimilación en el Perú?

(A) La preservación de la quechua

(B) La diversidad europea en la costa

(C) La siesta y el lonche

(D) La enseñanza del español en la selva

END OF SECTION I

IF YOU FINISH BEFORE TIME IS CALLED, YOU MAY CHECK YOUR WORK ON THIS SECTION.

GO ON TO THE NEXT PAGE.

SPANISH LANGUAGE AND CULTURE

SECTION II

Approximate Time—85 minutes

50% of total grade

Part A

INTERPERSONAL WRITING: EMAIL REPLY

Directions: You will write a reply to an email message. You will have 15 minutes to read the message and write your reply. Your reply should include a greeting, closing and responses to all the questions and requests in the message.

Instrucciones: Usted escribirá una respuesta a un mensaje electrónico. Tendrá 15 minutos para leer el mensaje y escribir su respuesta. Debe incluir un saludo, una despedida y respuestas a todas las preguntas y peticiones en el mensaje.

MANOS A LA OBRA
FUNDACION DE OBRAS BENEFICAS
LA CEIBA, HONDURAS
www.manosalaobra.com

Estimado Estudiante:

Gracias por su interés en trabajar como voluntario/a en Honduras. La siguiente carta es para informarle de una oportunidad para participar en un programa de reconstrucción de casas en Honduras este verano. El programa dura 4 semanas y usted vivirá con una familia hondureña en la ciudad La Ceiba que se encargara de su hospedaje, comidas, y necesidades personales. El programa nuestro se encargara de su vuelo a Honduras, transportación dentro del país, seguro médico, y entrenamiento de voluntario. Esa información le llegara pronto.

Como ya sabe, el año pasado varios huracanes devastaron la costa atlántica de Honduras y en su camino quedo destrozada la pequeña industria pesquera de la cual dependían los residentes para mantener a sus familias. Honduras carece de una infraestructura nacional para ayudar a los miles de personas necesitadas que residen en estas áreas costeñas.

Nuestra agencia se responsabiliza por colocar a los voluntarios en el área que mejor emprenda su experiencia y talento. Por ello, le ofrecemos la oportunidad de trabajar en diferentes áreas:

EDUCACION: En Honduras más de la mitad de la población vive en pobreza y más de 400,000 personas están desempleadas. Tiene una de las tasas de alfabetización más bajas de América Latina. Los voluntarios necesitan ser modelos para enseñar habilidades básicas, inglés, y español a jóvenes en los pueblos rurales.

SERVICIO DE SALUD: Aunque no es necesario tener experiencia médica, los voluntarios también pueden ayudar a los profesionales en orfelinatos y escuelas primarias especialmente en las zonas más retiradas.

DESARROLLO DE LA COMUNIDAD: Hay muchas áreas en que un voluntario puede ayudar a una comunidad a sostenerse. Puede trabajar con organizaciones que contribuyen a la tasa de empleo y crecimiento económico: estas se concentran mayormente en formar talleres de tejer, obras de construcción, reutilizar materiales recicladas como bicicletas, y más importante aun, arar la tierra.

GO ON TO THE NEXT PAGE.

CONSTRUCCION: Las viviendas muchas veces vienen siendo covachas con techo de paja o estaño. Muchas veces no tienen ni ventanas ni pisos. No resisten la destrucción de terremotos ni huracanes. Como voluntario de construcción, trabajara con arquitectos y carpinteros a mejorar la calidad de viviendas en solo un par de horas. Es una excelente oportunidad de mejorar la calidad de vida y el nivel de esperanza entre los residentes de un pueblo. El año pasado construimos 7000 casas de cemento y ladrillo en más de 45 pueblos hondureños.

Favor de incluir una respuesta en la cual indica:

- en qué área prefiere trabajar y por que
- que otras habilidades posee que puedan ser útiles durante su estadía
- alguna situación personal que debamos tener en cuenta para hacer su estadio lo más agradable posible
- algunas preguntas que tenga sobre el programa

Esperamos con muchas ganas su respuesta. Siempre a sus órdenes,

Delfin Carrasquillo
Coordinador, Manos a la Obra, La Ceiba Honduras

GO ON TO THE NEXT PAGE.

PRESENTATIONAL WRITING: PERSUASIVE ESSAY

Directions: The following question is based on the accompanying sources 1–3. The sources include both print and audio material. First, you will have 6 minutes to read the printed material. Afterward, you will hear the audio material twice; you should take notes while you listen. Then, you will have 40 minutes to write your essay. Your essay should be at least 200 words in length.

This question is designed to test your ability to interpret and synthesize different sources. Your essay should use the information from the sources to support your ideas. You should refer to ALL of the sources. As you refer to the sources, identify them appropriately. Avoid simply summarizing the sources individually.

Instrucciones: La pregunta siguiente se basa en las Fuentes 1-3. Las fuentes comprenden material tanto impreso como auditivo. Primero, dispondrás de 6 minutos para leer el material impreso. Después escucharás el material auditivo dos veces; debes tomar apuntes mientras escuches. Luego, tendrás 40 minutos para escribir tu ensayo. El ensayo debe tener una extensión mínima de 200 palabras.

El objetivo de esta pregunta es medir tu capacidad de interpretar y sintetizar varias fuentes. Tu ensayo debe utilizar información de TODAS las fuentes, citándolas apropiadamente. Evita un simple resumen de cada una de ellas.

¿Se debe cambiar la semana escolar de 5 a 4 días?

GO ON TO THE NEXT PAGE.

Fuente No. 1

Texto impreso

Compara y contrasta las diferentes opiniones sobre la opción de reducir la semana escolar de 5 a 4 días.

Fuente 1: El siguiente artículo se creó en la Junta Directiva de Educación del Distrito #242 de Los Ángeles sobre la posibilidad de ofrecerles a padres la opción de reducir la semana escolar de 5 a 4 días.

Tema: Cambiando la rutina: Reducir la semana escolar de 5 a 4 días

Estimados padres:

Entiendo cómo la inflación reciente y el aumento en el costo de la vida han afectado a ustedes y sus familias. Es un tiempo difícil para todos. Ya sufriendo del aumento en el costo de combustible para los buses, de calentar y enfriar los edificios, de alimentar a los estudiantes y de casi todos los materiales, los distritos escolares alrededor del país están considerando la idea de reducir la semana escolar de 5 a 4 días. Es una opción que debemos considerar seriamente.

Más de 150 escuelas a través del país ya han adoptado esta opción y por lo visto están contentos con los resultados. Un distrito en Topeka, Kansas ha adoptado un horario de martes a viernes y terminó ahorrando $248.000 de un presupuesto de $8,7 millones. Ese dinero se utilizó en reembolsos a los residentes del distrito. También reportaron mejoras de asistencia estudiantil y mejores resultados en los exámenes estandardizados.

Existen otros beneficios. Un fin de semana de tres días proveerá más tiempo familiar, algo que falta en la sociedad de hoy. Además, los estudiantes podrían dedicarles más tiempo a las asignaturas escolares sin la presión de una semana escolar de 5 días.

Los gastos asociados con el mantenimiento de nuestros edificios y la transportación de nuestros estudiantes son agobiantes. Como nos confronta un futuro inseguro de precios de combustible, tenemos que actuar ahora. Obviamente, la reducción de gastos es la respuesta, y agregar 1,5 horas al cada día escolar y así eliminar un día completo representa ahorros económicos significativos sin la necesidad de sacrificar trabajos, instrucción académica ni programas estudiantiles. Sin estos ahorros, los estudiantes que viven a menos de 2 millas de sus escuelas perderán el beneficio de la transportación gratuita proveída por el distrito.

Les invito a que asistan al foro público que se celebrará en la Escuela Fleetwood el 23 de julio de 2008 a las 7 de la noche. Ahí podemos dialogar más sobre este asunto.

Atentamente,
Luis Maldonado
Superintendente, Distrito 242

GO ON TO THE NEXT PAGE.

Fuente No. 2

5 – 1 = Éxito

Es un día escolar para la mayoría del país, pero no lo es para Erica Bongiardina, una estudiante del cuarto grado en la escuela Betsy Ross en Aspen, Colorado, los viernes los pasa en el pisto de esquí con su familia. "Me encanta. Tengo un fin de semana de 3 días,¡es super nítido!"

Su escuela estrenó la semana de cuatro día este año, principalmente para reducir costos en el presupuesto. Según los oficiales de la escuela, la escuela redujo en un 20% sus costos de transportación, servicios alimenticios, limpieza y combustible. En total estiman gozar de un ahorro de $200,000.

Varios estados han experimentado con una semana escolar de 4 semanas. Lo que no ha hecho la escuela Betsy Ross es reducir el currículo académico: las clases son más largas y se ha agregado un periodo adicional de estudio. La escuela empieza a las 8:30 a.m. y termina a las 4:15 p.m. para los estudiantes, "lo cual representa un día bastante largo", explica Sophie Zbeig directora de la escuela.

"Una semana comprimida significa que los estudiantes tienen que aplicarse aún más, aprenden la importancia de tener disciplina. Los estudiantes simplemente no tienen tiempo para meterse en problemas", explica Zbeig.

Los resultados hablan

Un estudio reciente en el estado de Colorado demuestra que no hay diferencia académico en los resultados en los exámenes estatales entre los estudiantes de escuelas de cuatro o cinco días semanales. "Hay menos ausencias. Las actividades como deportes se programan los viernes, así que los estudiantes no pierden horas de estudio durante la semana. Y los padres tienden a programar citas o asuntos familiares los viernes, y entonces ya no tienden a sacarlos de la escuela de lunes a jueves", ofrece Zbeig.

"Lo bonito también es que te da un dio completo para pasarlo bien con mis hijos. Y cuando tengan la edad, pueden trabajar un día más para conseguir las cosas que necesitan, que me ayuda económicamente", dice Carina Guichane, una madre de tres hijos de 6 a 14 años.

Otro beneficio potencial es con el día más largo, los estudiantes estarán llegando a casa a la misma hora que sus padres, lo cual elimina la necesidad de buscar ayuda para cuidar a los niños, otro beneficio económico. Sin embargo, los viernes presentan un problema para algunos que necesitan ahora buscar alguien que cuide a sus niños un día completo.

Los que niegan los beneficios de la semana reducida indica que los estudiantes estadounidenses, que por años han sido inferiores a los estudiantes europeos y asiáticos en las ciencias y matemáticas, estarán perdiendo la oportunidad de competir globalmente. Algunos temen que con un fin de semana más larga, los estudiantes no retendrán la misma cantidad de información.

GO ON TO THE NEXT PAGE.

Fuente No. 3

Reunion de padres, Junta Directiva Educativa, Fleetwood School

AUDIO CD: Track 19

GO ON TO THE NEXT PAGE.

SPANISH LANGUAGE AND CULTURE

SECTION II

Part B

INTERPERSONAL SPEAKING: CONVERSATION

AUDIO CD: Track 20

Directions: You will now participate in a simulated conversation. First, you will have 30 seconds to read the outline of the conversation. Then, you will listen to a message and have one minute to read the outline of the conversation again. Afterward, the conversation will begin, following the outline. Each time it is your turn, you will have 20 seconds to respond; a tone will indicate when you should begin and end speaking. You should participate in the conversation as fully and appropriately as possible.

Instrucciones: Ahora participarás en una conversación simulada. Primero, tendrás 30 segundos para leer el esquema de la conversación. Luego, escucharás un mensaje y tendrás un minuto para leer de nuevo el esquema de la conversación. Después, empezará la conversación, siguiendo el esquema. Siempre que te toque un turno, tendrás 20 segundos para responder; una señal te indicará cuando debes empezar y terminar de hablar. Debes participar en la conversación de la manera más completa y apropiada posible.

(A) Tu amiga Laura te llama para hablarte sobre una experiencia que tuviste el fin de semana pasada cuando fuiste a las montañas a divertirte.

(B) La conversación

[The shaded lines reflect what you will hear on the recording.
Las líneas en gris reflejan lo que escucharás en la grabación.]

GO ON TO THE NEXT PAGE.

Laura	Te saluda
Tú	Salúdala, Dile tu evaluación del viaje
Laura	Te hace una pregunta
Tú	Contesta la pregunta
Laura	Te hace una pregunta
Tú	Contesta la pregunta
Laura	Te hace una pregunta
Tú	Contesta que no es posible y ofrece una alternativa
Laura	Continua la conversación
Tú	Contesta la pregunta
Laura	Continua la conversación
Tú	Contesta la conversación
Laura	Se despide

GO ON TO THE NEXT PAGE.

PRESENTATIONAL SPEAKING: CULTURAL COMPARISON

Directions: You will deliver an oral presentation to your class on a given cultural topic. You will have 4 minutes to read the presentation topic and formulate your presentation. Then you will have 2 minutes to record your presentation.

In your presentation, you should compare the community in which you reside to an area of the Hispanic world that you have studied. You will need to demonstrate an understanding of the cultural aspects of the Hispanic world. Your presentation should also be organized appropriately.

Instrucciones: Usted dará una presentación oral a su clase sobre un tema cultural. Dispondrá de 4 minutos para leer el tema de la presentación y formular su repuesta.

En su presentación, debe comparar la comunidad en la cual vive con una del mundo hispánico que haya estudiado. Tendrá que demostrar tu comprensión de los aspectos culturales del mundo hispánico. Su presentación debe ser organizada de manera clara.

En nuestra sociedad vemos que las tradiciones de la cultura defina un pueblo. Sin embargo, lo que hace la vida interesante son las diferencias entre culturas. En su experiencia, compara y contrasta algunas tradiciones culturales que ha observado en su comunidad con las de otros países del mundo hispanohablante.

STOP

END OF EXAM

_____

9

PRACTICE TEST 2:
ANSWERS AND EXPLANATIONS

ANSWER KEY

Section I: Part A

1.	B	11.	C	21.	B
2.	B	12.	B	22.	B
3.	C	13.	C	23.	B
4.	B	14.	C	24.	C
5.	B	15.	B	25.	C
6.	A	16.	B	26.	A
7.	D	17.	C	27.	D
8.	A	18.	A	28.	A
9.	C	19.	C	29.	B
10.	D	20.	A	30.	C

Section I: Part B

31.	A	43.	B	55.	D
32.	B	44.	B	56.	C
33.	B	45.	B	57.	A
34.	D	46.	B	58.	B
35.	B	47.	C	59.	B
36.	D	48.	C	60.	B
37.	C	49.	A	61.	C
38.	D	50.	A	62.	D
39.	C	51.	C	63.	B
40.	D	52.	B	64.	A
41.	C	53.	C	65.	C
42.	A	54.	B		

Section II

See explanations beginning on page 224.

SECTION I: PART A

INTERPRETIVE COMMUNICATION: PRINT TEXTS (PAGE 168)

Sección Uno: Translated Passage and Questions, with Explanations

Mamá, Ana, and the baby went to visit Grandpa, but poor Papá could not go because he had to stay at home to work.

"What shall I do without you?" he asked.

"I will write you letters, three letters," Ana answered. "I will tell you what we are doing here without you."

"Do you know how to write a letter?" asked Papá.

"Oh, yes, I can write one," said Ana. "I am seven now. You will see that I can write a letter."

Ana had a very good time. One day she said, "Grandma, may I take a pen? I want to write to Papá."

"Yes," said Grandma, "there are pens on the desk."

Ana ran to Grandpa's desk. "Oh, Grandma! Here is such a strange pen!"

"That is a quill pen," said her Grandma. "Grandpa made it for me. It is a goose quill; in the old days everybody used to write with quill pens."

"I think it is very pretty," said Ana. "I don't think I can write with it."

She took another pen and went off. In a little while she went back to the desk. And there she saw that the baby had taken the quill pen and she had been writing to Papá with it. And what a letter she had written! Ana realized that she had spilled the ink over the desk.

"Oh, baby, baby! What did you do that for?"

Mamá sent baby's letter to Papá, and he said he was glad to get both letters.

ANA'S LETTER TO HER FATHER.

Aracataca, July 12, 1917.

Dear Papá:

We are having a very good time. Grandpa has a big bay horse. Sometimes he puts me on the horse's back. It is such fun! I play in the field a great deal. Grandpa lets me walk on the haycocks and I pick berries for Grandma. They give us cheese with our coffee. I wish you were here with us. Baby has written you a letter. She took Grandma's quill pen, and she spilled the ink. Can you read her letter? She says she wrote, "How are you, Papá? I love you a great deal."

Your little girl,
Ana

1. How can one understand what the baby's letter is about?

   (A) according to the letter itself

   (B) according to Ana's letter

   (C) according to what the grandmother says to the father

   (D) according to the narrator

Because the baby's "writing" consists of spilling ink all over the desk, her letter cannot be understood by itself (A), which is why Ana facetiously asks her father if he can read it and then offers a translation of what the baby was trying to say. She does this within her letter to her father, making (B) the correct answer. You could have eliminated (C) because the grandmother and the father do not have a conversation in this selection. The narrating voice does not offer any information about the contents of the letter, so (D) is also incorrect.

2. Who doubts that Ana can write the letter?

   (A) her grandmother

   (B) her father

   (C) her grandfather

   (D) the baby

This is a straightforward comprehension question. After Ana indicates that she will write letters, Ana's father introduces doubt by asking her if she knows how to write a letter in the first place, making (B) the correct answer.

3. According to the selection, why does Ana write, "Can you understand her letter?" in lines 39-40 to her father?

   (A) Because she knows he has poor vision.

   (B) Because she knows the letter has arrived.

   (C) Because she knows he cannot read the baby's letter.

   (D) Because she knows that in the old days everyone used to write with quill pens.

Ana asked her father if he could read the baby's letter, knowing that he could not because it was illegible. Answer choice (C) is correct. Answer choice (D) merely rehashes some of the text and choices (A) and (B) are entirely unrelated.

4. The following sentence can be added to the text. **"Fascinated by the novelty, she handled it for a moment, and then she returned it to its proper place."** Where would this sentence fit best?

   (A) Position A (line 14)

   (B) Position B (line 19)

   (C) Position C (line 29)

   (D) Position D (line 38)

This passage becomes confusing because the word "pluma" here is used to refer to both a feather pen and a regular pen. The reader may have difficulty in distinguishing between the two. As the feather pen is a source of fascination to the young girl, she would naturally pick it up and examine it. In line 14, she hasn't discovered the feather pen yet. Line 19, would be the best fit, as she remarks how beautiful it is and that she doesn't think she can write with the feather pen. Immediately afterwards, she takes a regular pen and leaves, implying she had put the feather pen back. Thus, (B) is the best answer.

5. Who is the "her" ("it") with whom the baby writes the letter (line 24)?

    (A) the grandmother

    (B) the pen

    (C) Ana

    (D) the mother

Since the mother is not mentioned in this scene, you can eliminate choice (D) right away. If you look closely at the line, the only possible answer is (B), as the "ella" ("it" in English) refers to "la pluma," which is a feminine noun and not a person. You know that no one wrote the letter with the baby because she was unsupervised.

6. Why does Ana look for a pen?

    (A) Because she wants to write a letter.

    (B) Because she wants to write a book.

    (C) Because she wants to spill the ink.

    (D) Because she needs her father.

This is an easy question, but notice how far into the question set you had to work to get here. Because the questions do not move in a clear order of difficulty, be sure not to trap yourself by spending too much time on a difficult question. Doing this would rob you of the easy points you could earn with questions like this. The entire plot of this passage is Ana writing a letter to her father: (A) is the correct answer.

7. Who sends the letter to Papá?

    (A) the grandmother

    (B) Ana

    (C) the baby

    (D) the mother

This question may seem strange, but it is actually the mother who *sends* the letter, not the baby (C), the grandmother (A), or Ana (B), who is the one who *writes* the letter. Therefore answer choice (D) is the correct answer.

Sección Dos: Translated Passage and Questions, with Explanations

Careful! Zebras Working on the Street

They aren't Disney characters or pets that are promoting a brand or a product. The zebras that circulate through the streets of La Paz have a very special job: they are urban educators that teach people to walk safely throughout the city. Each day, they cover their body with a costume and a mask: they move, jump, yell, and wave flags to call attention to the pedestrians. According to the municipal organization "City Culture" around 240 young people work in two shifts, four hours a day and 20 hours a week.

The vehicle and pedestrian traffic is getting worse each day in this city, which is the center of the Bolivian government. The automobiles don't respect the traffic lights and people cross the streets any place they can. It's total chaos. People's lives, especially those of the children are in constant danger. For that reason, the municipal authority decided to take concrete measures. Thus were born the "zebras."

In 2001, the mayor's office created a project through "City culture" with the goal of lessening vehicle traffic. "The zebras emerged with the objective of showing the pedestrians how to cross the street," explained Kathia Salazar, coordinator of the "Zebra Project".

The municipal representative explains that this project possesses two fundamental pillars: educational and social. The majority of young people who work as "zebras" are between 16 and 22 years old and are authorized by the municipality to decongest the vehicular traffic and to facilitate pedestrian transit. "The requirements to work as a zebra are strong will, effort, creativity, and the desire to get ahead. On the part of the mayor's office we are committed to staying with this project," revealed Salazar.

Every day the zebras cover their body with cotton suits and white fabric with black lines. When impatient pedestrians cross against the traffic lights they dance, play, joke, and gesture nonstop. When they leave, the children and old people miss them and chaos returns to the street. The monthly salary can be up to 450 Bolivianos; (about U.S. $65). The leaders or guide can earn up to Bs. 1000 (about 144 U.S. dollars) for their exclusivity to the Zebra Project.

City Culture

Julia Andrea Marca (21 years old) has been working as a zebra for 1 year and 9 months. To exercise the role of urban educators she had to attend various teaching and learning workshops taught by Kathia Salazar. "The children hug me and grab me with so much love. With this we try to educate and teach the young ones," she indicates. Julia also studies every morning in the University of San Andres, where she is in her first year of biochemistry. "The only negative experience I've had during this time was when I got hit by a car, but it wasn't a very serious accident," she says.

In turn, Amanda Pinos (29 years old) has been working for 8 years on this municipal initiative. She jumps through the streets as soon as the traffic light turns red. Each day she stands very close to the Student Plaza, she prevents drivers from going through red lights, causing accidents and more road congestion. Her principal function lies in transmitting the values of City Culture for everyone. "I have seen fairly terrible accidents, it is something truly sad," she indicates. " The principal job of the urban educators is to generate reflection on the part of each citizen of La Paz and generate awareness in the most loving and respectful way." Pinos, who currently works as a project leader, explains the "the zebras are young people who are interested in participating in this family and being urban educators who advise about prevention." She adds, "Some phrases that they say about pedestrians include: "Sir! Be careful!", "Be careful please!", "Don't cross the street!", "Stop please!"

For our interviewees, working as a zebra is more of a service than just a job. For many of them, the job of an urban educator is a form of supporting, loving and changing the city. It's that simple.

La Paz?

The 2001 Nation Census reported a population of 1,552,156 inhabitants in all of the metropolitan areas of La Paz, including the city of El Alto. The population estimate for the year 2010 was close to 2 million inhabitants without including El Alto, with its 1.2 million people. Together they form the largest urban area in the country. According to the data from the Nation Institute of Statistics the number of cars in LA Paz reached close to 220,000 cars in 2009. Although there are laws and fines that regulate the traffic in La Paz, the majority of drivers do not respect the red light, even less, the rights of the pedestrians or the crosswalk. It's for this reason that the zebras con be found on almost every corner in the city, helping people cross the street and training the drivers, from early morning till night fall.

8. What is the purpose of this article?

   (A) **Illustrate how a city responded creatively to an urgent need**

   (B) Tell the experiences of the young people who joined an important cause

   (C) Demonstrate how jobs can be both satisfying and educational

   (D) Present a comical way to deal with an urban problem

The best answer is (A). Choices (B) and (C) are true, but are not topics that prevail throughout the article. Choice (D) is somewhat true, but the zebras were not meant to be comical, they were based on previous models in other places, and were perhaps chosen more for their easily visibility.

9. Which of the following statements best summarizes the article?

   (A) It is almost impossible to change people's way of thinking.

   (B) In South America, because of the lack of funds for public works compared to First World countries, it's necessary to look for alternative solutions for problems.

   (C) An educated and respectful populace can improve the lives and well being of others.

   (D) Both drivers and pedestrians play a role in everyone's safety.

The correct answer is (C). Choice (B) is assuming information not in the article. Choice (A) is a judgment also not supported in the text. Choices (C) and (D) are both correct, but (C) is more true of the article as a whole, as the program aims to educate and teach respect among all parties on the street. The AP often goes for this type of questioning, where you must really split hairs to pick the better answer.

10. What can we infer from the 2001 and 2009 censuses?

    (A) Due to the economic crisis, more people are becoming pedestrians.

    (B) Due to the demographic explosion, the municipal authority cannot accommodate so many pedestrians in the street.

    (C) The number of cars has not increased at the same rhythm as the population.

    (D) With the increased number of residents in La Paz and the outskirts, there are more challenges for both pedestrians and motorists.

The population explosion does mean more pedestrians and probably more drivers, which means choice (D) is the best answer.

11. If you were to do a more in-depth investigation of the topic discussed in the article, which one of these sources might you use?

    (A) The Bolivian census of 2013

    (B) The Urban Planning Board of La Paz

    (C) The Ministry of Transportation and Highways

    (D) The Civil Registry

One would most likely want to know how the program is working, which would mean investigating the number of accidents and automotive-pedestrian incidents, making choice (C) the best answer.

12. What is the negative part of the program?

    (A) The drivers won't necessarily respect a young person dressed a zebra in the same way that they would respect a police officer or army officer.

    (B) The zebras will always have the risk of being hit by cars.

    (C) The pay and hours that the zebras work is barely enough to live on.

    (D) The funds for the program could be revoked at any time.

Choice (A) is somewhat correct, but (B) is the better answer as the accidents are mentioned in the article. Choices (C) and (D) are not referenced or inferred in the article.

13. What is the problem addressed by this project?

    (A) The high incidence of accidents

    (B) That pedestrians don't know where to cross the street

    (C) That drivers basically ignore the traffic laws

    (D) The conflict between driver and pedestrian are more common each day.

Choices (A) and (D) are not supported by any data. The project was more to help pedestrians stay safe and to keep drivers from going through red lights and ignoring the law, which is also mentioned in the census information. Thus (C) is the best answer.

Sección Tres: Translated Passage and Questions, with Explanations

Guarani in Paraguay

It was prosecuted and prohibited for many decades in Paraguay. It could never be taught formally. Put it served as a defense mechanism in wars and today is spoken by almost 9 million people in different South American countries. Since 1992 it is, along with Spanish, the official language in all of Paraguay. Guarani has overcome many great challenges throughout the years and still faces challenges, even in the 21st century.

According to the 2002 census, the indigenous population of Paraguay is almost 100,000 inhabitants and includes almost 17 ethnic groups. In spite of the fact that this total is not significant among the total population (the country has almost 7 million people), 87% of Paraguayans speak Guarani. Therefore, this Latin American nation is bilingual.

And why do so many people speak the country's original language? According to Maria Antonia Rojas of the cultural institute "Guarani Symposium," the dialect belongs to the first inhabitants of this zone of South America and has been defended by the Paraguayans themselves. "Nowadays it is like a transcendental element in the daily culture," she says.

Beginning with the name Paraguay, which means "river the flows into the sea," this language has formed part of the country's culture. In addition, many of the names of plants, animals, songs, foods and attitudes can be expressed only in this language.

In spite of the strong defense made by the Paraguayans, for many years the Guarani language was prohibited, including by political prosecution, including punishment for all the children and teenagers who spoke it at school. That changed when the dictatorship of Alfredo Stroessner (1954–1989) fell and a new constitution was created. As a result, it was given official status alongside Spanish in 1992. From this moment on, and with the new educational system, Guarani was required to be taught in all the schools in the country. Also, a law was recently approved that protects 20 languages throughout the country and creates the conditions to protect the cultures associated with those languages. The new laws will allow Guarani writing and grammar to now be considered official; in addition there will be a unified dictionary in the language.

Modern Language

This language, aside from being an official one in Paraguay, is also one in Bolivia (along with Quechua and Aymara) in the Argentinean province of Corrientes and in the Brazilian state of Takuru, Since 2005, it is the third language in MERCOSUR after Spanish and Portuguese. In Paraguayan shopping centers like in markets and restaurants and malls, Guarani is used; the sellers attract buyers with this language. Some TV shows use it and the radio announcers use it to communicate. In different types of festive celebrations, both the music and the speeches are in Guarani. "Guarani is not a primitive language, but rather a modern, alive and interesting one, like any other language used today," explains David Galeano Olivera, director of Guarani Language and Culture Foundation. The professor adds, "In spite of the problems that it has had throughout its history, it is a language of the third millennium, that is spoken by almost 9 million people in all of South America."

Its importance lies not only in its daily use, but also in the investigation and study of the language. It is taught, not only in Paraguayan, Argentinean and Brazilian universities, but also in prestigious learning centers in the U.S. and Europe. Universities in France, Germany, Spain, Switzerland, Italy have departments for this language and post graduate courses. The classes are given by Paraguayan academics as well as European researchers. Some were even diplomats, while others were just seduced by this language.

Guarani has also experienced a great resurgence on the Internet and today is found on thousands of sites. In addition, on the Web it is known as "ta'anga veve" which means "images that fly." "Languages that have little or no Internet presence are condemned to death or disappearance," reflects Olivera. And thus it is that Google as well as Wikipedia have their version of avañ'e (language of man). On the Web we can find online translations to poems in this language. However, the digital market has even made things complicated for Guarani. As with almost all oral languages, few people read or write in this language. For that reason, there is little interest on the part of the common people, but not on the part of those curious about the language, or on the part of academics. This constitutes a new challenge for Guarani, and probably will not be the only one this language that has learned to survive throughout the years will face.

14. Guarani suffered subjugation in Paraguay for _____ motives.

   (A) linguistic

   (B) nationalistic

   (C) political

   (D) economic

The correct answer is (C), which is evidenced by the article's mention of political prosecution.

15. What can we infer about the government of Alfredo Stoessner?

    (A) It was a great defender of the language.

    (B) It believed that only one language should be the official one.

    (C) It promoted the use of Guarani as a defense mechanism.

    (D) It granted Guarani the rank of official language.

The correct answer is choice (B). As one of the most notorious self-centered leaders of his time, Stoessner was not keen on preserving the Guarani culture. All the positive changes for the language, as the article mentions, were made after his downfall.

16. The language has been able to overcome various attempts to eliminate it, since

    (A) it is present in neighboring countries

    (B) Paraguayans perceive it as an integral part of their nation

    (C) it is different from other languages since it has a written component

    (D) the constitution guarantees its survival

The article discusses how Paraguayans defended the language and how it is now an integral part of the culture, making choice (B) the right answer.

17. A challenge to the survival of Guarani in the technological age is

    (A) There is not much demand for its translation.

    (B) Until now, the demand to learn Guarani has only existed in academic centers.

    (C) The majority of the inhabitants don't read or write the language well.

    (D) It has a small presence on the Internet.

Guarani is a mostly spoken language. Written elements are only recently becoming commonplace, due to legislation and technology. The issue is that most Paraguayans never had a need to write or read it; thus the correct answer is choice (C).

18. The situation in Paraguay is unique compared with other South American countries because

    (A) a non-indigenous population speaks an indigenous language

    (B) it is the only South American country with two official languages

    (C) it has protected all of its languages with legislation

    (D) the rebirth of the language has brought many unanticipated challenges

The article mentions that only 100,000 true indigenous people live there, but 87 percent of the population speaks Guarani. Thus, the answer is choice (A).

19. The overseas interest in Guarani is due to

(A) commerce between countries

(B) the fact that it is the third most utilized language in the Southern Cone

(C) the academic experts have studied and taught it because of their interest in culture

(D) the new presence it enjoys on the Web

Guarani is enjoying a thriving international resurgence due to academic study overseas and Paraguayans living abroad, so the answer is choice (C).

20. Which of the following statements best summarizes the article?

(A) Without Guarani, Paraguay would not be Paraguay.

(B) Guarani holds a delicate position in Paraguayan society.

(C) The survival of Guarani can only be guaranteed by the Paraguayans themselves.

(D) Guarani deserves the same respect as Spanish.

The article discusses how the language is so intertwined in the culture that without it, Paraguay would lose much of its identity and character. Thus the answer is choice (A).

Sección Cuatro: Translated Passage and Questions, with Explanations

El Lado B de las Fiestas Patrias

This year, Chileans celebrated "Double" time during their Independence Day celebrations. The reason is that in addition to the traditional days off, the 18th and 19th of September, two more were added, the 17th and the 20th. Well, it was due to the fact that the Bicentennial Independence festivities had to be celebrated correctly. The result, the holidays were, Friday, Saturday, Sunday and Monday… Uf! A complete long weekend that included practically a mini vacation for the whole population has its consequences. The increase in weight resulting from the high number of calories in barbecued meat and alcoholic beverages along with accumulated debt, wind up being the outcome. In the traditional Chilean outdoor huts, constructed especially for the independence celebrations, even the president of the Republic himself is supposed to dance the Cueca, especially when the media are always present at this national celebration. When one keeps in mind that the average barbeque for four people (along with the corresponding amount of drinks, wine and Pisco) costs twenty-seven thousand pesos (USD $55) it's not a mystery that one must have a "solid income."

Given that most Chileans don't have sufficient resources for this, it is common at this time to ask for loans that various banks offer in order to increase their budget. Laura Soto, head of the credit consumption division of the bank "CrediChile" Viña del Mar branch, affirms that "September is a month in which there is generally more demand for loans." Even if at the end of the year they are handing out more loans because of Christmas and New Year's in addition to vacations, this September has been comparatively better than in the past. Maybe it's because of the bicentennial celebrations."

Soto shows that the loans granted go from 150,000 (U.S. $300) up to 11 million pesos! (U.S. $24,000). "It's too much, using loans to buy a car or pay for a trip would be justifiable, but not just for this holiday." However, she clarifies that the percentage of indebted people is low given that in general, the people are able to pay off their loans. According to experts, the principal causes for not paying the debt are loss of jobs or commitments to another financial institution.

More Money for Celebration

In Chile, 60% of private companies hand out bonuses, an extra amount of money workers receive during the patriotic celebrations. The range varies between 22 and 325 thousand pesos (U.S. $45 and $750), and along with Peru, Chile is the only Latin America country that includes these bonuses in its salary structure. Not only do companies provide bonuses, public organizations also do. The amount varies according to what the employee receives; some receiving 500,000 pesos (U.S. $1,000) monthly and others receiving a lesser quantity that corresponds to 50,000 pesos (U.S. $100). For Ricardo Iglesias, a graduate in history with a master's degree in contemporary Latin American affairs, "The most probable that the enthusiasm is due to that the 18th and 19th of September are the only national celebrations. In the rest of the continent, there are carnivals which have a religious meaning; they celebrate Lent, the 40 remaining days until Holy Week, like in Brazil and Uruguay." According to Iglesias, another positive aspect of the carnivals is that "people wear costumes and it's not possible to determine their social class. In addition, the party takes place in just one place. In the case of Chile, the result is that there are many ramadas and refreshment stands, the result being that each person chooses according to their tastes and convenience, a situation that brings about a lack of unity among compatriots." The professor is convinced that in Chile there is a lack of celebratory culture because of such celebrations leading to the abuse of alcohol. "In Chile, people like to drink alcohol simply because they like it. I don't think it has anything to do with the economic crisis that has affected us or with prompt penalties. Any excuse is fine in order to buy a large amount of alcohol and the 18th of September is the perfect date."

Risk of Obesity

Another topic that tends to come up during the patriotic celebrations is the excessive consumption of calories. "A person can gain between 1–5 kilograms according to the number of calories they accumulate. Assuming that there are 4 days of celebrations", explains Janet Cossio, director of nutrition at the University Andres Bello. In the case that a person winds up paying high amounts of monthly payments and if they also gained the traditional kilograms, in Chile, a very well-known phrase is used as consolation: when all is said and done, no one can take away from me all the eating and dancing I've done.

21. What role does alcohol play during these celebrations in Chile?

(A) Consumption increases during the economic crisis.

(B) Consumption of alcohol is part of any cultural celebration in Chile.

(C) The penalties for drunkenness are severe and limit the consumption.

(D) They high consumption of alcohol influences the higher obesity rate in Chile.

The article discusses how, among Chileans, any celebration is an excuse to drink.

_____

22. How is the social environment in Chile different during these celebrations compared to its neighboring countries?

    (A) During these celebrations the social classes in Chile mix more than usual.

    (B) In other countries, maybe because of the anonymous factor, there is more probability that the social classes may mix.

    (C) Chilean celebrations tend to be shorter.

    (D) The government makes employers provide workers extra money during the patriotic celebrations.

The article discusses that *Carnaval* is a long celebration with masks and costumes, which may be a reason why people who do not know each other may be more inclined to socialize.

23. What does Laura Soto think about the loans made during the period of Patriotic Festivals?

    (A) That many Chileans do not honor their debt

    (B) That it doesn't make sense to assume a large loan for a simply patriotic celebration

    (C) That the loans granted during September surpass those given during Christmas time

    (D) That the proportion of loans is directly tied to the economy

Laura states that it is justifiable to take a loan for a car or a trip, but not simply for a celebration during the month of September.

24. What are ramadas?

    (A) Temporary housing

    (B) Stands

    (C) A shelter made from trees

    (D) A setting

The article discusses the word "rama," which means "branches."

25. Why was the celebration longer this year?

    (A) It fell on a weekend.

    (B) To stimulate the Chilean economy.

    (C) It coincided with the celebration of 200 years of Independence.

    (D) The Chilean president ordered it as homage to the Cueca.

The article discusses the bicentennial celebration, which is a 200-year celebration.

26. At the end of the article, what does the following phrase refer to?
"Al final de cuentas, lo comido y lo bailado no me lo quita nadie".

    (A) The fun that one experiences is worth it.

    (B) During a celebration one doesn't stick to a diet.

    (C) Food and dance are individual selections that depend on individual tastes.

    (D) There's no undoing of a decision you already made.

This phrase is used when one has paid a price for partying or drinking heavily.

Sección Cinco: Translated Passage and Questions, with Explanations

The Marinera

An expression of nationalism, a historical vision, a tribute to the country's influences. These are the most popular descriptions of the Marinera, the national dance of Peru. The experts do not agree on the exact origin of the dance, but when listening to the music from the dance, one hears Spanish, Andean, Gypsy, and Moorish tones. Although the Marinera style of dance has existed for centuries in Peru, it earned the name "Marinera" in homage to the Peruvian navy that fought valiantly defending its homeland during the War of the Pacific against Chile in 1879. Some may remember that the dance which represents a courtship between a rooster and a hen, and whose contact is mainly through handkerchiefs waved by the dancers, was an extension of the Cueca, the national dance of Chile, and arrived to Peruvian shores via the Chilean invaders who mixed with the young Peruvian ladies. However, the theory that makes the most sense, and that explains the various national influences, affirms that the Incas, more than 600 years ago, danced something very similar to the Marinera and simply through the centuries the dance has evolved and incorporated the various predominant historical influences within the country. Indigenous or imported, what we do know is that the Marinera continues to be the most visible and adored expression of national pride among the Peruvian people. The dance is most popular today among young people, who attend special learning centers to perfect their abilities, with the dream of competing amongst the most accomplished young dancers in the country in competitions held every year in the largest Peruvian cities.

27. According to the experts, which is NOT a possible origin of the Marinera?

    (A) The influence of a neighboring country, Chile, during the War of the Pacific

    (B) An exchange among the various cultures of the country

    (C) A similar dance that existed with the indigenous people of Peru centuries ago

    (D) A rural influence

The first three are mentioned in the article, although the only rural influence could be the rooster and the hen reference, the actually origin of the dance is traced to many cultural influences listed in choices (A) through (C).

28. Which is an example of how the Marinera is an expression of nationalism?

    (A) The name of the dance

    (B) The movements of the dance

    (C) The Incan past related to the dance

    (D) The popularity among the young people

The "Marinera" is named for the Peruvian navy.

29. The Chilean influence in the Peruvian dance is an example of

    (A) assimilation

    (B) adaptation

    (C) imperialism

    (D) cultural exchange

The dance, having its own name, could not be an assimilation from Chile, nor was it a result of an exchange between the two countries. Although the Chileans invaded Peru, it was not a imperialistic goal of Chile. The article classifies it as an "extensión" which is most closely defined here as an "adaption."

30. What does the Word "cortejo" refer to?

    (A) A random meeting

    (B) A challenge

    (C) A romance

    (D) A fight

"Cortejo" means courtship in Spanish, most closely related to choice (C), a romance.

SECTION I: PART B

INTERPRETIVE COMMUNICATION: PRINT AND AUDIO TEXTS (COMBINED) (PAGE 177)

Selección Uno: Audio Track 15

Informe de radio

Fuente: Las opiniones de estos jóvenes aparecieron en un grupo focal sobre el tema de conductores adolescentes en Miami.

[A continuación escucharás las opiniones de varios jóvenes sobre la posibilidad de elevar las edades mínimas para manejar.

Amanda Estévez, 18 años

"Yo veo el problema de otra forma. Si es importante recibir más entrenamiento, y mis padres están completamente a favor de que yo consiga cuanta experiencia pueda. Pero hay que tomar en cuenta que muchos estudiantes de 16 y 17 años necesitan transportación a actividades escolares, a la práctica de deportes, y para socializar o estudiar en la biblioteca. Si los jóvenes no pueden guiar hasta los 18 años, entonces sus padres lo tendrán que compensar".

Felicia Badillo, 16 años

"Tal vez sería mejor subir la edad mínima porque los adolescentes mayores son más maduros".

John Grant, 17 años

¿Cómo llegaré a mi trabajo? Trabajo después de la escuela y ambos padres trabajan. No hay recursos para tomar taxi todos los días, y no existen líneas de transportación pública confiables. Mi ingreso es una parte importante de los gastos familiares. Esto es otro ejemplo de una generación de adultos quienes temen y limitan a las oportunidades de los jóvenes. Primero limitaron los cigarrillos, censuraron las películas, y ahora se meten con la edad para manejar. No terminará con esto nomás, te lo aseguro".

Barri Marlowe, 16 años

"La economía también se afectaría si los jóvenes no pudieran manejar, similarmente como lo pasaría si los inmigrantes ilegales se deportaran. No habrá gente para ocupar esos trabajos vacantes. Es más, los jóvenes ganarían menos plata y por lo tanto habría menos consumo de su parte de productos y servicios, y la economía del país sufriría mucho. Aportamos mucho como consumidores a la economía nacional".

Alex Nestle, 16 años

"Se dice que más de un cuarto de jóvenes de 16 años trabajan fuera de la casa durante el año escolar, y más de un tercio durante el verano cuando no está en sesión la escuela. Los negocios sufrirían mucho si sus trabajadores no pudieran llegar a sus negocios".

Cielo Ramírez, 18 años

"Tal vez no es imprescindible que cambiemos la edad mínima. Si todos los estados fueran a tener como requisito clases obligatorias empezando a la edad de 15, estaríamos más diestros en el manejar, y contaríamos con esa experiencia adicional antes de embarcarnos en las carreteras".

Andre Cruz, 16 años

"No es la edad que cuenta sino la personalidad. Habrá jóvenes que pueden manejar responsablemente y otros, aunque tengan 35 años, nunca podrán respetar las reglas del tráfico ni usar el sentido común. La edad es simplemente un número, es la persona en sí que figura más en el manejar".]

31. The interviewed teens for the most part believe that

   (A) it is economically necessary for them to drive

   (B) that they would have to depend on adults if the minimum age is lowered

   (C) there is no need to raise the age to drive since it doesn't achieve anything

   (D) socially it is vital for teens to drive

The majority of the teens interviewed cited economic reasons for needing to drive.

32. Lorena Pérez bases her theory on the need to raise the minimum driving age on

   (A) personal experience

   (B) the inference that age brings more maturity

   (C) scientific studies from other European countries

   (D) the fact that youth can't tell the difference between right and wrong

Lorena Perez classifies maturity as a key factor in assuming the responsibility to drive.

33. Lorena Pérez would say that a contributing factor to the higher death toll by automobile accidents is

   (A) weak legislation

   (B) the lack of enough practice hours

   (C) the number of companions in the car

   (D) lack of maturity or development

Lorena Pérez is a proponent of gradually providing full driving privileges after courses and training.

34. What would be an example of further training?

   (A) An evaluation of skills after a certain period of time

   (B) Academic intervention

   (C) Interviews to determine the maturity level

   (D) Practical experience

All of the other options are ways of determining skill level, while choice (D) discusses practical experience, which is, in essence, training.

35. Which of these statements best summarizes the article?

    (A) There are possibilities to saving the lives of some of the youth if the minimum driving age is changed to 18 years old.

    (B) Although there is data that indicates that the requirement of a higher driving age can bring benefits, young people need to drive.

    (C) The deaths from auto accidents are the impulse to change the minimum driving age.

    (D) More scientific investigation is needed to determine with absolute certainty if the age of the driver truly influences the tendency to have accidents.

Be careful! This question refers to the article only; thus even though choice (B) is the best summary of both sources, the question refers to the article, which discusses saving lives by raising the age.

36. What is the tone of Lorena Perez's presentation?

    (A) Unconvincing

    (B) Emotional

    (C) Practical

    (D) Logical

Lorena Pérez discusses many sources and although she makes some emotional references to losing lives, overall she uses data and reasoning to prove her point. Thus the best answer is choice (D).

37. According to the auditory source, what is John Grant's tone?

    (A) Negative

    (B) Arrogant

    (C) Distrusting

    (D) Worried

John Grant thinks that this will only be the beginning of the limitation of young people's rights.

38. Which one of the young people thinks the opposite of what Lorena Perez is proposing?

    (A) Felicia Badillo

    (B) Cielo Ramirez

    (C) Andre Cruz

    (D) Amanda Estevez

The other three respondents are not in favor of reducing the driving age.

Selección Dos: Audio Track 16

El Boom de las Cirugías Estéticas

Desde que aparecieron las cirugías estéticas, muchas personas han tenido la oportunidad de mejorar su aspecto físico de manera fácil y rápida. Incluso a muchos, ni siquiera les importa los costos que implican dichas operaciones. Ya no es necesario acudir a largas horas de gimnasio y hacer estrictas dietas para tener un buen cuerpo. En Colombia ha tomado bastante fuerza este fenómeno en los últimos años. La obsesión por la belleza ha llevado a este país a posicionarse en los primeros lugares en cirugías plásticas a nivel mundial.

La Sociedad Colombiana de Cirugía Plástica (SCCP) afirma que cada año se hacen en este país más de diez mil intervenciones estéticas, una cifra que ha crecido en la última década un 70%. Además, los costos son más bajos en comparación con países como Estados Unidos. En Norteamérica, una cirugía de la nariz cuesta ocho mil dólares, mientras que en Colombia puede costar la mitad.

¿Y por qué ocurre este fenómeno? En los años 90, cuando los problemas de narcotráfico invadían el país, los "narco-dólares" permitieron que muchas mujeres tuvieran fácil acceso a las cirugías estéticas. La alta demanda de esta práctica generó una mejor calidad del servicio y los precios eran cada vez más bajos.

Esta obsesión por la perfección de los cuerpos pone hoy a Colombia en el "top" de la cirugía estética. Esta nación cuenta con una industria desarrollada, en la que trabajan más de setecientos cirujanos especializados. El culto a la estética se extiende a todos los géneros, razas y estratos sociales de este país. Cabe recordar que Colombia, concentra el mayor número de competencias de belleza y sus mujeres han llegado a las finales de Miss Universo en veintiuna ocasiones.

El Doctor Edilson Machabajoy López afirma que las motivaciones para someterse a una cirugía plástica se relacionan con lograr un valor agregado. "Muchas veces quieren recuperar una relación amorosa o conseguir un mejor trabajo. Sin embargo, son falsas ilusiones. Los resultados de la cirugía pueden traer problemas psicológicos y resultados poco satisfactorios por el paciente".

La misma cultura colombiana ha creado una especie de familiaridad y confianza para someterse a las cirugías estéticas. No solamente por la facilidad en los precios, sino por el culto al cuerpo ideal. Asimismo, los cosmetólogos han aumentado sus ventas en un 55% de acuerdo con el Departamento Nacional de Estadística Colombiano (DANE).

Cirugía y turismo

El valor de una operación en Colombia está entre 20% y 80% más barata que en otros países. Además, las agencias de turismo locales incluyen como extras: el billete de avión, alojamiento y excursiones guiadas por diversos lugares típicos del país. Es por esto que muchos personajes famosos como Maradona, viajan con más frecuencia a Colombia con el fin de realizarse una cirugía estética. Dicho fenómeno ha desarrollado el turismo nacional colombiano. Muchas agencias ofrecen una combinación única entre turismo, salud, estética y belleza. Esto permite a pacientes a nivel nacional e internacional, acceder a diferentes tratamientos quirúrgicos, estéticos y servicios médicos especializados, mientras disfrutan de una agradable estadía en Colombia. La mayoría proviene de Canadá, Estados Unidos, México y Reino Unido.

Pros y contras

En Colombia la cirugía estética también se ha puesto de moda entre las jóvenes que cumplen 15 años. Éstas piden a sus padres como regalo un arreglo en su cuerpo con una cirugía, en vez de un viaje o una gran fiesta. A pesar de que los especialistas no las aconsejan hasta que el cuerpo esté formado completamente, muchos padres terminan concediéndole este deseo a sus hijas.

Dagoberto Gómez (52 años), empleado público de Cali, cuenta que ha visto los sufrimientos de su hija de 16 años para bajar de peso. Está de acuerdo en colaborarle para que se practique una cirugía estética. "El problema se solucionaría rápido y ella estaría feliz". Aunque su esposa no está de acuerdo con esta decisión, ya que ha visto noticias donde jovencitas mueren al practicarse esta clase de operaciones.

"Tengo varias amigas que se han realizado cirugías para aumentar sus senos y me parece que han mejorado bastante", asegura Marínela Fernández (32 años), de Popayán. "Mejora su autoestima y por lo tanto se ven más seguras y lindas. Me parece que invertir dinero en tu cuerpo, es la mejor opción".

Fabián Martínez (29 años) abogado de Bogotá, plantea que está de acuerdo con las cirugías cuando son realmente necesarias. "Pero hay casos en que las mujeres abusan y terminan viéndose muy artificiales. Muchas recurren a las cirugías porque quieren parecerse a su estrella favorita y no para corregir algún defecto en su cuerpo".

Eso sí, si te vas a hacer una cirugía de este tipo, resulta muy importante tomar las precauciones necesarias. Por ejemplo, investigar que la clínica elegida sea legal y cuente con cirujanos certificados.

Las muertes producidas durante cirugías estéticas han llamado la atención de muchas personas. Por lo general, sus víctimas eran mujeres jóvenes y sanas que soñaban con tener una mejor figura, pues muchas personas al buscar costos demasiado económicos, caen en manos de médicos de dudosa capacidad.

Hombres en comparación a las mujeres

Las operaciones de estética más comunes que se practican en los quirófanos colombianos varían si las personas son hombres o mujeres. Los primeros optan mayoritariamente por implantes en el cuero cabelludo y liposucciones. Las mujeres, en cambio, prefieren eliminar grasa de los párpados, modificar el aspecto de su nariz y aumentar o reducir sus senos.

Used by permission of VeinteMundos.com

39. What is the purpose of this article?

   (A) Present how culture affects our view of aesthetics

   (B) Show to what point an obsession can grow

   (C) Explain why Colombia is at the vanguard of plastic surgery.

   (D) Compare and contrast aesthetics between Colombia and the U.S.

The article talks about Colombia's booming industry and the way surgery is a part of life there. The other choices are correct to a degree, but are not the overall theme of the article. Remember, you are looking for the best answer, and (C) is the most applicable to the article as a whole.

40. According to the article, what does "valor agregado" mean?

   (A) Recover something lost

   (B) Come to an agreement

   (C) Prime oneself for a promotion at work

   (D) Improve one's social or economic position

"Valor agregado" means an added value, and in the article it is talking about a competitive edge people seek with cosmetic surgery.

41. Plastic surgery is convenient for many because

    (A) recovery tends to be quick

    (B) one need not travel overseas

    (C) it eliminates the need for dieting and exercise

    (D) it immediately improves self esteem

The article discusses that the majority of surgery like liposuction, gives immediate results without the need for exercising or dieting.

42. ¿Why is the success of Colombian women in beauty pageants mentioned?

    (A) To show that the obsession with beauty is part of the culture

    (B) To show that the Colombian surgeons must be the best in the world

    (C) To show that in order to compete it is necessary to have cosmetic surgery

    (D) To show that Colombian women truly are known for their beauty

The fact that Colombians have done so well in the pageants not only shows that they are beautiful women, but more so that the desire for physical perfection is highly esteemed in the country, evidenced by the previous sentences which say that Colombia has a very high number of pageants.

43. According to the article, Doctor Edilson Machabajoy López warns that

    (A) surgery can't resolve all of your problems

    (B) surgery can be a negative for the patient

    (C) cosmetic surgery is a personal decision that brings different results to each person

    (D) none of these responses is correct

The doctor warns in the passage about surgery people have to look like someone else or regain a lost love, but which can instead bring depression and unsatisfactory results.

44. According to the passage, what is a key motivator for women to get cosmetic surgery?

    (A) Greed

    (B) Obsession with beauty

    (C) Easy economic access

    (D) The pressure by society to have the perfect body

Society places such a premium on looks in Colombia that women almost feel obligated to get it, and as we see with even the young people, it is a common decision.

45. In the listening piece, why do some young women wind up having cosmetic surgery even though experts advise against it?

(A) It's part of the culture.

(B) Parents worry about their well-being.

(C) Nowadays it is necessary to have any advantage to get ahead in life.

(D) Because society accepts and promotes it.

Parents in the article mentioned they did not want to see their children unhappy, so they acquiesced to their demands for surgery.

46. What is the difference between cosmetic surgery in Colombia and in the United States?

(A) The quality is not the same in Colombia.

(B) Potential patients in Colombia can combine health services and tourism.

(C) There is no minimum age in Colombia for having cosmetic surgery.

(D) The growth rate in Colombia is higher than in the USA.

Colombia attempts to attract European and American tourists with "surgery and tourism" tours.

47. How can Colombian society benefit from cosmetic surgery?

(A) Everyone can look better.

(B) It favorably and dramatically impacts one's self esteem.

(C) By bringing in clients from overseas, other industries can flourish.

(D) The price has decreased dramatically in recent years.

Colombia attempts to attract potential foreign patients by offering tourist packages and low prices, which means tourism and other industries grow as a result of the influx of customers.

48. What is a risk to having cosmetic surgery?

(A) Having surgery at an early age before the body has completely developed

(B) Not being happy with the results

(C) Trying to save money people by having surgery by untrained people

(D) Becoming addicted to surgery in order to look like a famous person

The article advises of the importance in finding licensed clinics with trained and experienced surgeons.

49. According to the Fabian Martinez, what might be a problem that could result from cosmetic surgery?

    (A) **People become addicted to the procedures and stop looking natural.**

    (B) Self-confidence issues do not go away completely.

    (C) The results don't turn out exactly as one planned.

    (D) Many times surgery doesn't resolve the problem and multiple sessions become necessary.

Fabian talks about women "abusing" plastic surgery and looking artificial.

_____

50. The initial popular access to cosmetic surgery is a result of

    (A) **profits from illegal activities**

    (B) the need to be able to compete in beauty pageants

    (C) the low cost of the procedures

    (D) society's high expectations

Colombia's drug export boom in the 1980s brought narco dollars into the country that gave more income to women who could afford these surgeries.

_____

Selección Tres: Audio Track 17

Belisario Féliz Jiménez, conocido por todos como "Beli", vino al mundo un 8 de marzo de 1909. Durante estos 101 años ha tenido una cómplice sin igual: la música, que según él, le mantiene fuerte y vivo. Y es que desde los ocho años de edad este anciano dominicano, se dejó seducir por la magia musical del sonido que hace el acordeón. Es sin dudas, un apasionado de este instrumento y continúa tocando, por lo que se le considera un verdadero hito del folklore dominicano.

¿Cuándo surge en usted el amor por el acordeón?
Yo era muy pequeño todavía cuando de inquieto me puse a embromar con el acordeón. Comenzó como un juego y 93 años después, sigo siendo un apasionado de este instrumento.

¿Se puede decir, entonces, que lo de usted y el acordeón fue "amor a primer tono"?
Sí, claro. Recuerdo que la primera vez que toqué un acordeón sentí por dentro deseos de no soltarlo nunca más. Recuerdo que me encerré en un armario, porque el acordeón era de mi papá y lo tomé a escondidas. Estuve horas haciendo ruido con él.

¿Y qué dijo después su papá?
Mi papá tenía el acordeón, porque en su juventud tocaba. Pero ya a él no le gustaba eso, entonces no quería que yo tocara. Según él, porque no quería que nada me distrajese la mente de los estudios y la escuela. Usted sabe cómo eran los viejos de antes, por lo que cada vez que llegaba del trabajo y me encontraba tocando, me pegaba y me ponía de castigo.

Entonces, ¿cómo aprendió a tocar?
Mi papá era muy terco, nunca me enseñó. Tampoco fui a ninguna escuela de música. Yo solito aprendí.

Escuchaba los sonidos que hacía el acordeón y después creaba melodías. Fui aprendiendo poco a poco. Cuando a usted le gusta algo, usted lo aprende.

¿Y a partir de entonces continuó tocando?
No. Siempre supe que tocar acordeón era mi vocación, pero hubo una parte de mi vida en la que fui débil y me dejé llevar por la presión de mi papá, quién quería que su hijo tuviese un trabajo estable. Cuando estaba en la adolescencia trabajé como agricultor, que era lo que se hacía en la época. En otro tiempo también trabajé como carbonero. Pero siempre continuaba tocando porque venía un amigo, algún vecino o un familiar que me buscaba para que tocara en una boda o en un cumpleaños. Y como a mí lo que de verdad me gustaba era el acordeón, entonces me iba y dejaba el trabajo.

¿Y no le preocupaba que lo despidiesen por dejar el trabajo incompleto?
No, porque en ese momento yo estaba asfixiado de mi acordeón. No quería soltarlo y era lo que más me importaba.

¿Y por qué le fascinaba tanto tocar acordeón?
Me gustaba crear ritmos, pero también una de las cosas que más disfrutaba era que tenía muchas enamoradas. Las mujeres de la época se volvían locas al oírme tocar y a mí me gustaba tocarles para ver cómo con mi ritmo se movían esos vestidos anchos y largos que usaban en esa época.

Llama la atención que a su edad tenga fuerza física y memoria para tocar. ¿Cuál es su secreto?
Bueno, a mí la memoria me falla cuando trato de recordar algunos nombres o fechas, pero nunca se me olvida una nota musical. La melodía no está en mi cerebro, sino en mi corazón, y mi corazón no envejece. Es verdad que a veces me canso, pero lo que hago es tocar sentado. Me paro un ratico y cuando me canso vuelvo y me siento.

¿Toca también otros instrumentos?
Sí, claro. Sé tocar el pandero y la güira; la mangulina, carabiné y merengue, que es lo que más se baila aquí en el sur, o por lo menos se bailaba antes. Usted sabe que ahora la juventud tiene otra música.

¿Y qué opina al respecto?
Hay cosas raras, pero también hay buenos músicos. Yo los dejo nomás, porque aquí tenemos un refrán que dice: "Cada loco con su tema".

En todo el sur de la República Dominicana la pobreza sobreabunda, ¿Tocar el acordeón fue, además de arte, una fuente de trabajo?
Claro que sí. A mí me pagaban por tocar y tocando mi acordeón mantuve y crié a mis 20 hijos declarados y también a unos cuantos cimarrones que tengo por ahí (sonríe). Por eso es que yo digo que en la música, además de amor por el arte, también encontré un medio para sobrevivir.

¿Y hoy continúa tocando y trabajando?
Me mantengo "acordeón en mano". Toco en fiestas y eventos políticos de por aquí.

Usted es un hombre de 101 años; debe tener muchas anécdotas...
Uf, tengo muchísimas. Le voy a contar una del presidente Trujillo, que fue un dictador. Pues bien, en uno de los controles del régimen caí preso. Venía de tocar en una fiesta y uno de los oficiales que trabajaba para Trujillo me encarceló así por no más, sin yo hacer nada. No tenía abogado ni nada porque eso era para gente rica. Entonces, como yo era músico, me puse a tocar para entretenerme. Tú sabes que los dominicanos desde que escuchamos música comenzamos a mover los pies y hubo un momento en que el oficial no se resistió a mi ritmo, me sacó de la celda y terminamos bailando todos en la cárcel. Hicimos tremenda fiesta.

Entonces gracias a su acordeón usted se codeó con un presidente dominicano.
No sólo con uno. También conocí al profesor Juan Bosch, que ese si fue un buen presidente. Una vez él hizo un concurso con todos los músicos del país y yo fui quien ganó.

¿Hay algo que usted piense que le falte lograr?
Bueno, yo a Dios lo único que le pido es salud y que todavía no me lleve. Yo sé que estoy un "chin" pasado de edad, pero todavía quiero seguir viviendo.

Hoy que es un hombre mayor, ¿qué es lo que más aprecia de la vida ahora?
La admiración de mi familia, sobretodo de mis 82 nietos. Mi salud, mi larga vida y la música, eso es lo más grande que yo tengo.

Reconocimiento.

Mucha gente considera a Beli un verdadero bastión del folklore dominicano y, además, es un personaje muy querido en su provincia natal, Barahona. De hecho, en julio de este año, el músico obtuvo un reconocimiento. El grupo empresarial Centro Cuesta Nacional (CCN) lo premió en el marco de la segunda edición del proyecto "Orgullo de mi tierra", que anualmente se realiza para resaltar los valores nacionales y culturales. "He trabajado mucho por la música de aquí y veo que mi trabajo se reconoce", afirma Beli.

Used by permission of VeinteMundos.com

51. How old was "Beli" (Belisario Féliz Jiménez) when this interview was conducted?

(A) 93

(B) 103

(C) 101

(D) 100

This is mentioned in the introduction to the interview.

52. Why **didn't** his father let him play the accordion?

(A) Because he had a trauma from childhood

(B) Because he wanted Beli to study

(C) Because his didn't like the sound of the instrument

(D) Because it was not a traditional Dominican instrument

Beli mentions that his father didn't want anything to distract Beli from his studies.

53. How did Beli learn how to play the accordion?

(A) His father taught him.

(B) He went to a music academy.

(C) He learned completely by himself.

(D) He had lessons with some of the most famous Dominican musicians.

Beli discusses how he picked up the instrument and started playing it.

54. In addition to creating rhythms, Beli loves to
    (A) dance to the rhythm of the merengue
    (B) have women dance to the rhythm of the accordion
    (C) sing Dominican songs
    (D) learn how to play new instruments

Beli mentions that he liked to see how the women's dresses would move as they moved to the rhythm.

55. Beli had many girlfriends. How many children did he have to raise and support?
    (A) 20
    (B) 1
    (C) 82
    (D) more than 20

Beli mentions that he had 20 (plus a couple more) "Cimarones," which refers to the escaped slaves during colonial times who would hide in the countryside. He refers to them possibly as some other children he had with other women.

56. What is the only thing Beli asks God for?
    (A) More children
    (B) To die without pain
    (C) Health and to not die yet
    (D) Recognition from his admirers

Beli mentions that he asks God only for health and to not take him yet.

57. What does he most value in life nowadays?
    (A) The admiration of his family, health, a long life, and music
    (B) The admiration of the presidents, family, health, a long life and music
    (C) The love of his wife, health, long life, and music
    (D) The opportunity to meet various presidents

Beli mentions this toward the end of the interview.

58. When Beli says "Yo estaba asfixiado de mi acordeón," that implies that
    (A) he couldn't put up with the instrument anymore
    (B) it consumed his life completely
    (C) the cost of maintaining it was very expensive
    (D) it was the cause of much conflict with his father

Normally *asfixiado* means asphyxiated, but in this case Beli is referring to his attachment to his accordion.

59. When Beli says, "Cada loco con su tema," he means that

(A) music today can't compare with the music of yesterday

(B) people's tastes vary from person to person

(C) you can't reason with a thick headed person

(D) we choose our own priorities in life

As Beli compares the music of today with yesterday, he says he isn't a big fan but that "each crazy man has his thing," meaning that everyone's tastes are different.

60. What does this interview show us?

(A) The effort of one person can make a difference in the life of others.

(B) If you want something and go for it, everything is possible.

(C) Poverty is not an obstacle to success.

(D) Music is an international language that we all understand.

Beli always knew he wanted to make music and never gave up on it; eventually making a living from it, providing for his family, and becoming famous.

Selección Cuatro: Audio Track 18

El Perú cuenta con una historia rica en tradición, folklore nativo y también las tradiciones europeas que le fueron importadas hace muchos siglos. Y como resultado de esa rica mezcla, el Perú disfruta de una de las culturas más diversas de todo el continente sudamericano. En realidad, El Perú viene siendo tres países en uno, ya que las diferentes zonas geográficas- la costa, la sierra, y la selva- son tan distintas geográfica e históricamente que cada uno ha desarrollado su propia cultura y estilo de vida. Por ejemplo, la costa peruana se conoce por su influencia europea: muchas familias datan sus raíces a Italia, España, Alemania, Francia e Inglaterra. Y es de esperar, que en las grandes ciudades de la costa encontramos la arquitectura europea impresionante, los toques coloniales en las iglesias y plazas, y además la tradición europea de "la siesta", un descanso a la hora de almuerzo en que los negocios cierran sus puertas por unas horas alrededor de mediodía. Hasta la tradición inglesa de tomar té por la tarde sigue en vigor con el "lonche" que es una merienda con café o té a las cuatro de la tarde. En la sierra, los majestuosos picos de los Andes dominan el paisaje y preservan la cultura incaica- es aquí donde late el corazón indígena del país. Aunque el verdadero inca ya no existe, sus descendientes todavía hablan quechua, idioma de los incas, y trabajan la tierra de la misma forma, cosechando las papas y criando llamas y alpacas para su lana. Y finalmente en la selva, las numerosas tribus que radican ahí, por su aislamiento geográfico, todavía huyen del contacto con el mundo exterior, y viven primitivamente cazando en la selva y viviendo de los numerosos recursos naturales que abundan en la Amazona. En Perú hay algo que satisface todo los gustos, y experimentarlo de primera mano es la única forma de captar el espíritu único que es el Perú.

61. Peru is a country that
    (A) suffers isolation as a result of having so many geographical zones
    (B) was colonized by Europeans and indigenous peoples
    (C) **enjoys a diversity that not all of the countries of the continent have**
    (D) lost much of its native flavor due to European influence.

The selection speaks in the beginning of Peru being one of the most diverse countries on the continent.

62. European traditions are strongest
    (A) in both the coast and the jungle
    (B) mostly in the sierra
    (C) in all three zones
    (D) **on the coast due to European immigration**

The European descendants on the coast have influenced many facets of society.

63. Who probably is the author of this article?
    (A) A Peruvian politician
    (B) **A promoter of Peruvian tourism**
    (C) A Peruvian anthropologist
    (D) A Peruvian sociologist

The article invites a visitor claiming that there is something for everyone in Peru and it is best experienced first-hand.

64. What relationship exists between geography and ethnicity in Peru?
    (A) **Indigenous groups predominate in 2 of 3 main regions.**
    (B) The decision of tribes to not assimilate makes the jungle the most backwards part of Peru.
    (C) Geography is the determining factor in the cultural and ethnic composition of the country.
    (D) Due to geographic isolation there is little contact between Peru's ethnic groups.

The Quechua-speaking peoples and the indigenous peoples of the jungle are both majorities in their regions, making choice (A) correct.

65. What is an example of assimilation in Peru?
    (A) The preservation of Quechua
    (B) The European diversity on the coast
    (C) **La siesta y el lonche**
    (D) The teaching of Spanish in the jungle

Both lonche and siesta are part of Peruvian culture thanks to the British and Spanish traditions brought by settlers. These are examples of other customs assimilating into mainstream culture.

SECTION II: PART A

INTERPERSONAL WRITING: EMAIL REPLY (PAGE 185)

Sample Student Response with Translation

Estimado Señor Carrasquillo:

Le agradezco su carta y su invitación para participar en el programa. La idea de ayudar a una comunidad tan necesitada como la de Honduras es algo que me motiva mucho. Sé que con la cooperación de muchos es posible hacer tener un gran impacto en las vidas de la gente que necesita ayuda.

He repasado las varias opciones de su programa, y creo que la que mejor me conviene es la construcción. El año pasado ayudé a mi familia a construir un garaje para mi casa y además he trabajado en los veranos en una compañía que instala techos en residencias, así que, el martillo y los clavos son amigos muy íntimos míos. La idea de mejorar las residencias para las personas me tiene un gran impacto ya que la felicidad empieza en el hogar, y si la gente tiene un bonito lugar donde vivir, su perspectiva hacia el futuro indudablemente mejora.

Tengo algunas habilidades que pueden beneficiar el programa. Soy músico, y toco la guitarra y los tambores, así que me encantaría tener la oportunidad de colaborar a ensenarles a los niños a tocar instrumentos y a cantar canciones en español. También he trabajado como socorrista por 2 años en mi comunidad, así que tengo entrenamiento en proveer los primeros auxilios a la gente.

Soy flexible y tranquilo—entonces lo único que necesito es buena comida y una cama donde dormir. Quisiera saber si es necesario tener algunas vacunas antes de llegar a Honduras, y si tendremos algunas oportunidades de visitar las playas, ya que me encanta correr tabla de vela!

Estoy muy emocionado de tener la oportunidad de trabajar con ustedes.

Atentamente,
Matthew Driscoll

Dear Mr. Carrasquillo:

Thank you for your letter and invitation to participate in the program. The idea of helping a community in need such as that of Honduras is a great motivation to me. I know that with the cooperation among many, it is possible to have a large impact on the lives people who need help.

I have reviewed the various options in your program, and I think that the best option for me is construction. Last year, I helped my family build a garage for my home and I have also worked summers in a company that installs roofs in houses, so, a hammer and nails are my best friends. The idea of improving residences for people has a great meaning for me, because as we know, happiness begins at home and if people have a nice place to live, their perspective towards life will undoubtedly improve.

I have several talents that can benefit the program. I am a musician, and I play the guitar and drums, so I would love to have the chance to collaborate and teach children how to play instruments and sing songs in Spanish. I also have worked as a paramedic for 2 years in my community, so I do have training in providing first aid to people.

I am flexible and calm—so the only thing I really need is good food and a place to live. I would like to know if it is necessary to have any vaccinations before arriving to Honduras, and if we will have the chance to visit the beach, since I love to wind surf!

I am very excited to have the opportunity to work with you.

Sincerely,
Matthew Driscoll

Evaluation

This response fulfilled the requirements and did so in a concise and organized manner. He even asked additional questions, which is always good to get a higher score. He would have scored higher had there been higher-level grammar and tenses. There weren't a lot of past subjunctive or advanced transitional words either. The approach was safe and would net a 4. To get a 5, it would need more detail, sophistication and depth of grammar. Try to always show this in your writing, by perhaps keeping a mental checklist of good transitional words, verb tenses, and vocabulary that you can incorporate into your responses.

PRESENTATIONAL WRITING: PERSUASIVE ESSAY (PAGE 188)

Translation for Source 1

The following document was created by the Board of Supervisors for Educational District #242, Los Angeles on the possibility of offering parents the option of reducing the school week from five days to four.

June 15, 2008

Re. Changing the routine: Reducing the school week from 5 days to 4

Dear Parents:

I understand how recent inflation and the rising cost of living have affected you and your families. This is a difficult time for all. Already affected by the rising costs of fuel for buses, for heating and cooling buildings, feeding students and of almost all materials, school districts across the country are considering the idea of reducing the school week from five days to four. It's an option we should seriously consider.

More than 150 schools across the country have already adopted this option and seem to be happy with the results. A district in Topeka, Kansas has adopted a Tuesday to Friday schedule and has saved $248,000 of its $8.7 million budget. This money was used for refunds to district residents. They also reported improved student attendance and better results on standardized tests.

There are other benefits. A three-day weekend would provide more family time, something lacking in today's society. In addition, students could spend more time on school assignments without the pressure of a 5-day school week.

The costs associated with the maintenance of our buildings and the transportation of our students are staggering. As we are faced with future uncertainty in fuel costs, we have to act now. Obviously, reducing costs is the answer, and cutting 1.5 hours from each school day, thus eliminating a full day represents economic savings without the necessity of sacrificing jobs, academic instruction or student programs. Without these savings, students living less than 2 miles from their schools will lose the free transportation provided by the district, and various jobs and programs will be affected.

I invite you to attend a public forum at Fleetwood July 23, 2008 at 7PM. There we can discuss this issue further.

Sincerely,

Luis Maldonado

Superintendant, District 242

Translation for Source 2

5 – 1 = Success

It's a school day for most of the country, but not for Erica Bongiardina, a student in the fourth grade of the Betsy Ross School in Aspen, Colorado. Fridays are spent on the ski slopes with her family. "I love it. I have a long weekend of three days. It's awesome!"

Her school debuted the 4-day week this year, mainly to reduce budget costs. According to school officials, the school reduced by 20% their transportation, food services, cleaning and fuel costs In all they estimate to enjoy a savings of $200,000.

Various states have experimented with the 4-day school week. What Betsy Ross has not done is reduce the academic curriculum: classes are longer, and an additional period of study has been added to the curriculum. The school begins at 8:30 a.m. and ends at 4:15 p.m. for the students, "which represents a rather long day," explains Sophie Zbeig, director of the school.

"A reduced week means that the students have to apply themselves even more. They learn the importance of having discipline. They simply don't have time to get into trouble," explains Zbeig.

Results talk
A recent study in Colorado shows that there is no academic difference in the state exam results among students from four day and five day schools. "There are fewer absences, The activities like sports are scheduled for Fridays, so students don't lose study time during the week. And parents tend to schedule appointments or family events on Fridays, and then they tend not to take them out of school from Monday to Thursday," offers Zbeig.

"The great thing is that it gives me a full day to spend with my kids. And when they are old enough, they can work a day more to get the things that they want, which helps me economically", says Carina Guichane, mother of three sons from 6 to 14 years old.

Another potential benefit with the longer day is that students will be arriving at home at the same time as their parents, which eliminates the need to look for child care help, another economic benefit. However, Friday represents a problem for some who must find someone to care for their children for a whole day.

Those who deny the benefit of the reduced school week indicate that the American students, who for years have been inferior to European and Asian students in science and math, are losing the chance to compete globally. Some fear that with a longer weekend, the students will not be able to retain the same amount of information.

Translation and Script for Audio Source 3

Meeting of parents, School Management Board, July 23, 2008, Fleetwood School

The following residents of Los Angeles expressed their opinions on the proposal to change the school week from five to four days.

Myrta Morales: "No estoy segura que no exista un límite sobre lo que un estudiante pueda aprender durante un día escolar. Y me preocupo especialmente por los niños del primer grado y del jardín infantil, con la posibilidad de que tengan que sentarse 90 minutos más. Se trata de calidad, no cantidad".

I'm not sure that there isn't a limit to what students can learn in a school day. And, I'm especially worried for children in the first grade and kindergarten possibly having to sit for an additional 90 minutes. It's about quality, not quantity.

Rene López: "Esto no ahorraría dinero, es más, los costos subirían. Para los que creen que se trata de ahorros de combustible, se equivocan. Muchos edificios grandes tienen que mantener un nivel especifico de temperatura por varios motivos, pero desde el punto de vista económico es más eficiente mantener un edificio a 65 grados por 3 días en vez de apagar la calefacción y tratar de calentar el edificio los lunes por la mañana. Además, no ahorraríamos dinero en sueldos, ya que los profesores estarían trabajando la misma cantidad de horas. Además, la ayuda fiscal estatal depende de horas de contacto diarias, que tiene que llegar a 180 días de asistencia. Si bajamos el numero de asistencia, corremos el riesgo de perder la ayuda fiscal estatal, y pagaríamos más impuestos".

This would not save money. What's more, costs would rise. For those who think this is about saving fuel, they are mistaken. Many large buildings have to maintain a specific level of temperature for various reasons: From the economic perspective, it's more efficient keep a building at 65 degrees for 3 days instead of turning off the heat and trying to heat up the building on Monday morning. In addition, we wouldn't save any money on salaries, as the teachers are still working the same number of hours. What's more, state financial aid is linked to the length of the school day, which has to equal 180 days of attendance. If we lower the attendance figures, we run the risk of losing state financial aid—and we would pay more taxes.

Roberto Méndez "Nuestros hijos necesitan más tiempo en la escuela en vez de menos tiempo. La educación es la base de nuestra sociedad. Tal vez esto se podría hacer con los estudiantes del colegio pero no se podría en la escuela primaria. Algunos niños tendrán problemas en acostumbrase a la escuela después de un fin de semana, ¡tres días libres serían un desastre! Como país necesitamos buscar fuentes alternativas para reducir el costo de energía. Reducir el tiempo que los niños pasan en la escuela, nos detendrá como nación. Necesitamos educarlos y abrirles la mente…. ¡son nuestro futuro!"

Our children need more time in school, rather than less. Education is the basis of our society. Perhaps this would work with high school students but not with grade school students. Some children will have problems getting used to school after the weekend. Three days off would be a disaster! As a country we need to find alternative ways to reduce energy costs. Reducing the time children spend in school will hold us back as a nation. We need to educate them and open their minds…they're our future!

Irene Ramos "Ya tenemos estudiantes que pasan más de una hora en el bus para llegar a la escuela. Agregar más horas a eso es simplemente demasiado para ellos".

We already have students who spend more than an hour on the bus to get to school. Adding more hours to this is simply too much for them.

Sample Student Response with Translation

Con los precios altos de energía, nos vemos comprometidos a encontrar nuevas maneras de ahorrar dinero y recursos. Ya no se puede dar por sentado todo lo que tenemos hoy, ya que puede que mañana no lo haya. Para tratar de ahorrar dinero, y controlar los gastos ascendientes, algunos distritos están considerando la opción de sólo operar 4 días por semana y extender cada día unos 90 minutos.

El superintendente explica que esto ahorraría dinero, mejoraría asistencia, y mejoraría rendimiento estudiantil en términos académicos. Sin embargo, la comunidad, demuestra que les importa más el éxito de sus niños que el ahorrar dinero. Además, señalan que es posible que no ahorren dinero. Cerrar las escuelas sin calefacción ni aire acondicionado podrá resultar más caro que simplemente mantenerlas a una temperatura estable. También, cuestionan la utilidad de extender el horario escolar. Sin embargo, un estudiante explica que el tiempo libre le permitiría dedicarle más tiempo a sus estudios, de acuerdo a lo que explica el Superintendente Maldonado.

Según la Fuente 2, los padres insisten en que sus hijos pasen más tiempo en la escuela, no menos. Y la ayuda financiera del estado exige 180 días, no menos. La conservación durante el día escolar podrá ser una manera de ahorrar energía: no hace falta tener luces todo el tiempo, y tal vez otras tecnologías pudieran ayudar a ahorrar energía. En realidad no hay una solución al problema; hay que considerar las dos caras de la moneda. Tal vez si todos los miembros de la comunidad se sentaran a conversar, y así considerar las opiniones de muchos, podrían llegar a un acuerdo y ver como resolver el problema.

Pero hemos visto segun la fuente 3, que economicamente las escuelas ahorran dinero y tienen los mismos resultados. Las familias benefician pues pasan más tiempo juntas. Y lo que me convence que esta política si tiene sentido es que el comportamiento y la asistencia de los estudiantes mejoran en un horario de cuatro días. Siendo estudiante, puedo decir que esos dos factores son vinculados al éxito escolar.

With the high prices of energy we are obliged to find new ways of saving money and resources. We can no longer take for granted what we have today, because it may not be here tomorrow. In order to try to save money and control rising costs, some districts are considering the option of operating only 4 days a week and extending each school day by 90 minutes.

The superintendent explains that this would save money, improve attendance, and improve student academic performance. However, the community demonstrates that they are more interested in the success of their children than saving money. In addition, they show that it is possible that money would not be saved. Closing the schools without heat or air conditioning could be more expensive than simply maintaining them at a stable temperature. And they question the usefulness of extending the school schedule. However, one student explains that the free time would allow him to dedicate more time to his studies, in accordance with what Superintendent Maldonado explained.

According to Source 2, parents want their children to spend more, not less, time in school. And the financial aid from the state requires 180 days, nothing less. Conservation during the school year could be a way to save money; it's not necessary to have lights on all the time and perhaps other technologies could help save energy. In reality, there isn't a solution to the problem; we have to consider both sides of the coin. Maybe if all of the members of the community sat down to speak and thus consider the many existing opinions, then they could come to an agreement and solve the issue.

But we see according to Source 3 that economically schools save money and have the same results. Families benefit because they spend more time together. And what convinces me that this policy does make sense is that student behavior and attendance improve in a four-day school week. Being a student, I can say that these two factors are extremely important to school success.

Evaluation

This response was adequate in addressing the three areas of topic development, task completion, and language usage. It was somewhat short and did summarize, although there is evidence of comparing and contrasting. Be sure to insert your opinion as well in these essays. There was a little too much summarizing and less inferencing and hypothesizing on this essay. This well-written but somewhat predictable and basic essay would merit a 3 on the exam.

SECTION II: PART B

INTERPERSONAL SPEAKING: CONVERSATION (PAGE 191)

Translation and Script for a Sample Student Response

Laura: *Hola, ¿Qué tal? Oye, Cuéntame cómo lo pasaste en tu excursión a las montañas?*

Hello, How are you? Tell me, how was your trip to the montains?

MA: *Hola Laura siempre me es muy grato hablarte. Claro está, me divertí mucho en la excursión, fue una experiencia inolvidable. Ojala estuvieras ahí.*

Hi Laura, it is always a pleasure to talk to you. Of course, I had a lot of fun on the trip, it was an unforgettable experience. I wish you had been there.

Laura: *¿Ah sí? Dime, ¿qué hiciste? ¿En qué actividades participaste?*

Oh, really? Tell me, what did you do? What activities did you participate in?

MA: *Pues, hicimos montañismo, esquiamos en la pista de esquí, exploramos la naturaleza y naturalmente hasta sacamos fotos de todos los animales y el lindo paisaje que vimos allá.*

Well, we went hiking, we skied, we explored nature and naturally we took pictures of the wildlife and the beautiful landscape that we saw there.

Laura: *Siempre me ha llamado la atención hacer una excursión a las montañas, pero tengo miedo. ¿Es peligroso, no?*

I have always wanted to take a trip to the mountains, but I'm afraid. It's dangerous, right?

MA: *De ninguna manera. No tengas miedo, es una experiencia muy placentera. Es muy seguro y bonito. No es necesario que uno vaya a la cima de las montañas, pues hay los áreas muy seguras para hacer campamento. Y fuimos un grupo grande de jóvenes.*

Not at all. Don't be afraid, it is a very pleasurable trip. It is beautiful and safe. It's not necessary to go to the top of the mountains since there are safe areas to go camping. And we were a big group of people.

Laura: *Tienes razón, debería ir…pero me encantaría que me acompañaras. ¿Te gustaría ir el próximo viernes?*

You're right, I should go…but I would love for you to go with me. Would you like to go next Friday?

MA: *No, lamentablemente no puedo; tengo un compromiso el viernes. ¿Por qué no vamos el mes que viene?*

No, unfortunately I can't, I have an engagement on Friday. Why don't we go next month?

Laura: *Me parece una excelente idea. Pero en realidad no sé qué llevarme, ni como alistarlo todo. ¿Alguna recomendación?*

That sounds like an excellent idea. But I really don't know what to take with me, or how to get it all ready. Do you have any recommendations?

MA: *Por supuesto. Yo diría que necesitas llevar ropa abrigadora, una cámara para sacar fotos, botas, y un saco de dormir si quieres hacer camping afuera, una linterna, comida, y por supuesto, una mente abierta.*

Of course. I would say you need to take warm clothes, a camera to take pictures, boots, a sleeping bag if you want to camp outside, food, and of course, an open mind.

Laura: *Ah perfecto, Ya tengo una idea. Mil gracias por tu ayuda. Entonces como lo haremos? ¿Dónde te encuentro? ¿Cómo vamos para allá?*

Oh, perfect, now I have an idea. Thanks for you help. So, how should we do this? Where should I meet you? How will we get there?

MA: *No te preocupes tanto. Puedo ir a tu casa a recogerte, metemos todo a mi auto y de allí manejamos a las montañas.*

Don't worry so much. I can pick you up at your house, we will put everything in my car, and from there we can drive to the mountains.

Laura: *Genial, Listo. Nos vemos entonces. Cuidate, ¡Chau!*

Perfect. Done. I'll see you then. Take care, bye!

Evaluation

Notice how the student filled up the entire time allotted with meaningful conversation. He also made sure to use proper agreement and upper-level grammar (subjunctive, conditional, good transitional words, and commands). It would probably get a 5 due to its well-presented responses.

PRESENTATIONAL SPEAKING: CULTURAL COMPARISON (PAGE 193)

Sample Student Response with Translation

Las diferencias entre la cultura hispana e la estadounidense penetran cada nivel de la vida. Hay diferencias en las celebraciones y las costumbres asociadas con dichas celebraciones.

En los Estados Unidos muchas celebraciones tienen un valor recreativo y hasta económico, mientras que en América Latina, tiene un tono religioso. El día de los muertos, en México, las familias van al camposanto a honrar a sus seres queridos, y hay misas para recordar a la gente muerta. En los Estados Unidos, El día de los muertos es un día de disfraces y fiestas, y los niños van de casa en casa pidiendo dulces. Se dice que la gente gasta mil-

lones de dólares en fiestas y disfraces. En América Latina, la Navidad es una fiesta religiosa, y no se intercambian muchos regalos. Eso se hace el 6 de enero, el día de los Reyes Magos. En los Estados Unidos, la gente decora árboles, intercambian regalos, y aprovechan las tremendas rebajas en las tiendas. Los hispanos no hacen tantas compras para Navidad.

En Chile, el día de los Inocentes es el 28 de diciembre y todo el mundo gasta bromas. Hasta los periódicos publican información escandalosa y falsa para asustar a la gente. Pero en realidad la celebración conmemora un hecho de la Biblia, cuando Herodes ordeno la matanza de los niños inocentes de Belén. En los Estados Unidos tenemos algo similar, el primero de abril, pero en realidad no es un día importante ni tiene una base religiosa.

Es evidente que la religión en el mundo hispano hablante influencia profundamente las celebraciones y las actitudes de la gente. En los Estados Unidos, tal vez por la diversidad de religiones y grupos, las celebraciones tienen otro sabor.

Question: In our society, we see that cultural traditions define a people. However, what makes life interesting are the differences between cultures. In your experience, compare and contrast some cultural traditions that you have observed in your community with those of other countries in the Spanish-speaking world.

Student Response: The differences between Hispanic and U.S. culture penetrate every level of life. There are differences in the celebrations and customs associated with these celebrations.

In the U.S., many celebrations have a recreational value and even an economic one, while in Latin America, they have a religious tone. On the Day of the Dead, in Mexico, families go to the cemetery to honor their dearly departed, and there are masses to remember them. In the U.S., the Day of the Dead is a day of costumes and parties, and children go door to door asking for candy. It is said that the people spend millions of dollars on parties and costumes. In Latin America, Christmas is a religious celebration, and presents are not overly exchanged. That is done on the 6th of January, Three Kings Day. In the U.S., people decorate trees, exchange gifts and take advantage of the tremendous sales in the stores. Hispanics do not do as much shopping for Christmas.

In Chile, the day of the Innocents is the 28th of December and everyone plays jokes. Even newspapers publish scandalous and fake information in order to scare people. But in reality, the celebration commemorates a fact from the Bible, when Herod ordered the killing of the innocent children of Bethlehem. In the U.S., we have something similar, April 1st, but in reality it is not an important day nor does it have a religious base.

It is evident that religion in the Spanish-speaking world profoundly influences celebrations and the attitudes of the people. In the U.S., perhaps for being so diverse in terms of groups and religions, the celebrations have another flavor.

Evaluation

With only 4 minutes to prepare your presentation, it will be impossible to write it all out. So you will need to outline quickly. Get a clear introductory paragraph, a main point, and then details to illustrate that point. Notice how the student here touched upon several holidays and incorporated several countries into the presentation. It is obvious that they knew specifics about the target culture: religion and celebrations. The comparing and contrasting was strong because there were definite differences between the two cultures. This is the part of the exam where you will need to be able to speak without reading, which means you need to keep careful control of your grammar. This student played it a little safe by keeping the sentences simple, but under pressure, this is to be expected. It was a clean, well-thought-out sample, which showed command of the language and the topic and would score a 4 on the exam.

ABOUT THE AUTHOR

Mary Leech has been teaching AP Spanish at Rye Country Day since 1989. She lives with her husband in Bedford, New York.

Michael Giammarino has been teaching AP Spanish for the past 10 years and has taught as an adjunct professor in various New York colleges. He has authored numerous college textbooks and ancillary materials for various publishing companies.

1. YOUR NAME:
(Print)
Last   First   M.I.

SIGNATURE: _____ DATE: ___/___/___

HOME ADDRESS:
(Print)
Number and Street

City   State   Zip Code

PHONE NO. :
(Print)

IMPORTANT: Please fill in these boxes exactly as shown on the back cover of your test book.

2. TEST FORM

3. TEST CODE

4. REGISTRATION NUMBER

5. YOUR NAME

First 4 letters of last name					FIRST INIT	MID INIT

6. DATE OF BIRTH

Month	Day	Year
JAN		
FEB		
MAR	0 0	0 0
APR	1 1	1 1
MAY	2 2	2 2
JUN	3 3	3 3
JUL	4 4	4 4
AUG	5 5	5 5
SEP	6 6	6 6
OCT	7 7	7 7
NOV	8 8	8 8
DEC	9 9	9 9

7. SEX
MALE
FEMALE

The Princeton Review

© TPR Education IP Holdings, LLC
FORM NO. 00001-PR

Section 1

Start with number 1 for each new section.
If a section has fewer questions than answer spaces, leave the extra answer spaces blank.

1. A B C D
2. A B C D
3. A B C D
4. A B C D
5. A B C D
6. A B C D
7. A B C D
8. A B C D
9. A B C D
10. A B C D
11. A B C D
12. A B C D
13. A B C D
14. A B C D
15. A B C D
16. A B C D
17. A B C D
18. A B C D
19. A B C D
20. A B C D
21. A B C D
22. A B C D
23. A B C D
24. A B C D
25. A B C D
26. A B C D
27. A B C D
28. A B C D
29. A B C D
30. A B C D

31. A B C D
32. A B C D
33. A B C D
34. A B C D
35. A B C D
36. A B C D
37. A B C D
38. A B C D
39. A B C D
40. A B C D
41. A B C D
42. A B C D
43. A B C D
44. A B C D
45. A B C D
46. A B C D
47. A B C D
48. A B C D
49. A B C D
50. A B C D
51. A B C D
52. A B C D
53. A B C D
54. A B C D
55. A B C D
56. A B C D
57. A B C D
58. A B C D
59. A B C D
60. A B C D

61. A B C D
62. A B C D
63. A B C D
64. A B C D
65. A B C D
66. A B C D
67. A B C D
68. A B C D
69. A B C D
70. A B C D
71. A B C D
72. A B C D
73. A B C D
74. A B C D
75. A B C D
76. A B C D
77. A B C D
78. A B C D
79. A B C D
80. A B C D
81. A B C D
82. A B C D
83. A B C D
84. A B C D
85. A B C D
86. A B C D
87. A B C D
88. A B C D
89. A B C D
90. A B C D

91. A B C D
92. A B C D
93. A B C D
94. A B C D
95. A B C D
96. A B C D
97. A B C D
98. A B C D
99. A B C D
100. A B C D
101. A B C D
102. A B C D
103. A B C D
104. A B C D
105. A B C D
106. A B C D
107. A B C D
108. A B C D
109. A B C D
110. A B C D
111. A B C D
112. A B C D
113. A B C D
114. A B C D
115. A B C D
116. A B C D
117. A B C D
118. A B C D
119. A B C D
120. A B C D

The Princeton Review

1. YOUR NAME:
(Print)
Last   First   M.I.

SIGNATURE: _____ DATE: ___ / ___ / ___

HOME ADDRESS: _____
(Print)
Number and Street

_____
City   State   Zip Code

PHONE NO. : _____
(Print)

IMPORTANT: Please fill in these boxes exactly as shown on the back cover of your test book.

2. TEST FORM

3. TEST CODE **4. REGISTRATION NUMBER**

6. DATE OF BIRTH

Month		Day	Year
○ JAN			
○ FEB			
○ MAR	⓪	⓪ ⓪	⓪ ⓪
○ APR	①	① ①	① ①
○ MAY	②	② ②	② ②
○ JUN	③	③ ③	③ ③
○ JUL		④ ④	④ ④
○ AUG		⑤ ⑤	⑤ ⑤
○ SEP		⑥ ⑥	⑥ ⑥
○ OCT		⑦ ⑦	⑦ ⑦
○ NOV		⑧ ⑧	⑧ ⑧
○ DEC		⑨ ⑨	⑨ ⑨

7. SEX
○ MALE
○ FEMALE

The Princeton Review
© TPR Education IP Holdings, LLC
FORM NO. 00001-PR

5. YOUR NAME

First 4 letters of last name				FIRST INIT	MID INIT

(Bubbles A–Z for each column)

Section 1

Start with number 1 for each new section.
If a section has fewer questions than answer spaces, leave the extra answer spaces blank.

1. Ⓐ Ⓑ Ⓒ Ⓓ
2. Ⓐ Ⓑ Ⓒ Ⓓ
3. Ⓐ Ⓑ Ⓒ Ⓓ
4. Ⓐ Ⓑ Ⓒ Ⓓ
5. Ⓐ Ⓑ Ⓒ Ⓓ
6. Ⓐ Ⓑ Ⓒ Ⓓ
7. Ⓐ Ⓑ Ⓒ Ⓓ
8. Ⓐ Ⓑ Ⓒ Ⓓ
9. Ⓐ Ⓑ Ⓒ Ⓓ
10. Ⓐ Ⓑ Ⓒ Ⓓ
11. Ⓐ Ⓑ Ⓒ Ⓓ
12. Ⓐ Ⓑ Ⓒ Ⓓ
13. Ⓐ Ⓑ Ⓒ Ⓓ
14. Ⓐ Ⓑ Ⓒ Ⓓ
15. Ⓐ Ⓑ Ⓒ Ⓓ
16. Ⓐ Ⓑ Ⓒ Ⓓ
17. Ⓐ Ⓑ Ⓒ Ⓓ
18. Ⓐ Ⓑ Ⓒ Ⓓ
19. Ⓐ Ⓑ Ⓒ Ⓓ
20. Ⓐ Ⓑ Ⓒ Ⓓ
21. Ⓐ Ⓑ Ⓒ Ⓓ
22. Ⓐ Ⓑ Ⓒ Ⓓ
23. Ⓐ Ⓑ Ⓒ Ⓓ
24. Ⓐ Ⓑ Ⓒ Ⓓ
25. Ⓐ Ⓑ Ⓒ Ⓓ
26. Ⓐ Ⓑ Ⓒ Ⓓ
27. Ⓐ Ⓑ Ⓒ Ⓓ
28. Ⓐ Ⓑ Ⓒ Ⓓ
29. Ⓐ Ⓑ Ⓒ Ⓓ
30. Ⓐ Ⓑ Ⓒ Ⓓ

31. Ⓐ Ⓑ Ⓒ Ⓓ
32. Ⓐ Ⓑ Ⓒ Ⓓ
33. Ⓐ Ⓑ Ⓒ Ⓓ
34. Ⓐ Ⓑ Ⓒ Ⓓ
35. Ⓐ Ⓑ Ⓒ Ⓓ
36. Ⓐ Ⓑ Ⓒ Ⓓ
37. Ⓐ Ⓑ Ⓒ Ⓓ
38. Ⓐ Ⓑ Ⓒ Ⓓ
39. Ⓐ Ⓑ Ⓒ Ⓓ
40. Ⓐ Ⓑ Ⓒ Ⓓ
41. Ⓐ Ⓑ Ⓒ Ⓓ
42. Ⓐ Ⓑ Ⓒ Ⓓ
43. Ⓐ Ⓑ Ⓒ Ⓓ
44. Ⓐ Ⓑ Ⓒ Ⓓ
45. Ⓐ Ⓑ Ⓒ Ⓓ
46. Ⓐ Ⓑ Ⓒ Ⓓ
47. Ⓐ Ⓑ Ⓒ Ⓓ
48. Ⓐ Ⓑ Ⓒ Ⓓ
49. Ⓐ Ⓑ Ⓒ Ⓓ
50. Ⓐ Ⓑ Ⓒ Ⓓ
51. Ⓐ Ⓑ Ⓒ Ⓓ
52. Ⓐ Ⓑ Ⓒ Ⓓ
53. Ⓐ Ⓑ Ⓒ Ⓓ
54. Ⓐ Ⓑ Ⓒ Ⓓ
55. Ⓐ Ⓑ Ⓒ Ⓓ
56. Ⓐ Ⓑ Ⓒ Ⓓ
57. Ⓐ Ⓑ Ⓒ Ⓓ
58. Ⓐ Ⓑ Ⓒ Ⓓ
59. Ⓐ Ⓑ Ⓒ Ⓓ
60. Ⓐ Ⓑ Ⓒ Ⓓ

61. Ⓐ Ⓑ Ⓒ Ⓓ
62. Ⓐ Ⓑ Ⓒ Ⓓ
63. Ⓐ Ⓑ Ⓒ Ⓓ
64. Ⓐ Ⓑ Ⓒ Ⓓ
65. Ⓐ Ⓑ Ⓒ Ⓓ
66. Ⓐ Ⓑ Ⓒ Ⓓ
67. Ⓐ Ⓑ Ⓒ Ⓓ
68. Ⓐ Ⓑ Ⓒ Ⓓ
69. Ⓐ Ⓑ Ⓒ Ⓓ
70. Ⓐ Ⓑ Ⓒ Ⓓ
71. Ⓐ Ⓑ Ⓒ Ⓓ
72. Ⓐ Ⓑ Ⓒ Ⓓ
73. Ⓐ Ⓑ Ⓒ Ⓓ
74. Ⓐ Ⓑ Ⓒ Ⓓ
75. Ⓐ Ⓑ Ⓒ Ⓓ
76. Ⓐ Ⓑ Ⓒ Ⓓ
77. Ⓐ Ⓑ Ⓒ Ⓓ
78. Ⓐ Ⓑ Ⓒ Ⓓ
79. Ⓐ Ⓑ Ⓒ Ⓓ
80. Ⓐ Ⓑ Ⓒ Ⓓ
81. Ⓐ Ⓑ Ⓒ Ⓓ
82. Ⓐ Ⓑ Ⓒ Ⓓ
83. Ⓐ Ⓑ Ⓒ Ⓓ
84. Ⓐ Ⓑ Ⓒ Ⓓ
85. Ⓐ Ⓑ Ⓒ Ⓓ
86. Ⓐ Ⓑ Ⓒ Ⓓ
87. Ⓐ Ⓑ Ⓒ Ⓓ
88. Ⓐ Ⓑ Ⓒ Ⓓ
89. Ⓐ Ⓑ Ⓒ Ⓓ
90. Ⓐ Ⓑ Ⓒ Ⓓ

91. Ⓐ Ⓑ Ⓒ Ⓓ
92. Ⓐ Ⓑ Ⓒ Ⓓ
93. Ⓐ Ⓑ Ⓒ Ⓓ
94. Ⓐ Ⓑ Ⓒ Ⓓ
95. Ⓐ Ⓑ Ⓒ Ⓓ
96. Ⓐ Ⓑ Ⓒ Ⓓ
97. Ⓐ Ⓑ Ⓒ Ⓓ
98. Ⓐ Ⓑ Ⓒ Ⓓ
99. Ⓐ Ⓑ Ⓒ Ⓓ
100. Ⓐ Ⓑ Ⓒ Ⓓ
101. Ⓐ Ⓑ Ⓒ Ⓓ
102. Ⓐ Ⓑ Ⓒ Ⓓ
103. Ⓐ Ⓑ Ⓒ Ⓓ
104. Ⓐ Ⓑ Ⓒ Ⓓ
105. Ⓐ Ⓑ Ⓒ Ⓓ
106. Ⓐ Ⓑ Ⓒ Ⓓ
107. Ⓐ Ⓑ Ⓒ Ⓓ
108. Ⓐ Ⓑ Ⓒ Ⓓ
109. Ⓐ Ⓑ Ⓒ Ⓓ
110. Ⓐ Ⓑ Ⓒ Ⓓ
111. Ⓐ Ⓑ Ⓒ Ⓓ
112. Ⓐ Ⓑ Ⓒ Ⓓ
113. Ⓐ Ⓑ Ⓒ Ⓓ
114. Ⓐ Ⓑ Ⓒ Ⓓ
115. Ⓐ Ⓑ Ⓒ Ⓓ
116. Ⓐ Ⓑ Ⓒ Ⓓ
117. Ⓐ Ⓑ Ⓒ Ⓓ
118. Ⓐ Ⓑ Ⓒ Ⓓ
119. Ⓐ Ⓑ Ⓒ Ⓓ
120. Ⓐ Ⓑ Ⓒ Ⓓ

NOTES

NOTES

NOTES

NOTES

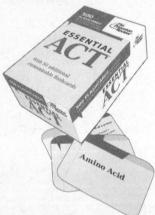

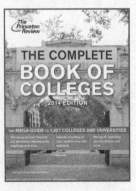

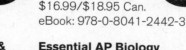